# CHASSON'S RUN

### THE PRISON BREAK THAT CAPTIVATED AMERICA AND THE LOVE STORY THAT FUELED IT

## DANIEL ZIMMERMAN

WildBluePress.com

*CHASSON'S RUN published by:*
*WILDBLUE PRESS*
*P.O. Box 102440*
*Denver, Colorado 80250*

*Publisher Disclaimer: Any opinions, statements of fact or fiction, descriptions, dialogue, and citations found in this book were provided by the author, and are solely those of the author. The publisher makes no claim as to their veracity or accuracy, and assumes no liability for the content.*

*Copyright 2025 by Daniel Zimmerman*

*All rights reserved. No part of this book may be reproduced in any form or by any means without the prior written consent of the Publisher, excepting brief quotes used in reviews.*

*WILDBLUE PRESS is registered at the U.S. Patent and Trademark Offices.*

*ISBN 978-1-964730-49-3 Hardcover*
*ISBN 978-1-964730-50-9 Trade Paperback*
*ISBN 978-1-964730-51-6 eBook*
*Cover design © 2025 WildBlue Press. All rights reserved.*

*Interior Formatting and Book Cover Design by Elijah Toten*
*www.totencreative.com*

# CHASSON'S RUN

*"The primary obligation of any prisoner is to escape,"*
—Emmanuel Goldstein, fictional
character in George Orwell's *1984*

For my beloved wife Mary,
loyal and supportive from the first to the last word.

**DISCLAIMER**: This book is based on accounts derived from an array of newspaper articles, police reports, court testimony, and discussions with actual witnesses. While the author has made every attempt to corroborate the information within, liability will not be accepted by the author or publisher for inaccuracies, errors, or omissions. At times, a degree of literary license was applied for added drama, particularly with dialogue, but in all instances, this portrayal is based on actual events. Some names have been changed.

**NOTE**: Source material is presented as-is (even if grammatically incorrect). Material may contain words or phrasing that some readers might find offensive and may not be suitable for all readers. Individual reader discretion is encouraged.

# CONTENTS

| | |
|---|---|
| One—Beer Run | 13 |
| Two—Chasson's Childhood | 22 |
| Three—Armed Robbery | 31 |
| Four—Freedom Awaits | 39 |
| Five—Brother's Death | 45 |
| Six—Hard Time | 53 |
| Seven—Pageant Field | 64 |
| Eight—Stabbing Victim | 72 |
| Nine—The Retreat | 77 |
| Ten—Hospital Trip | 82 |
| Eleven–Police Respond | 88 |
| Twelve—Chelsea Revisited | 98 |
| Thirteen—Somerville Detour | 107 |
| Fourteen—Somerville Siege | 115 |
| Fifteen—Police Interview | 123 |
| Sixteen—Boston Detour | 136 |
| Seventeen—Interviews Resume | 148 |
| Eighteen—Plain Sight | 155 |
| Nineteen—Milner Hotel | 163 |
| Twenty—Racette's Turn | 169 |
| Twenty-one—More Interviews | 180 |
| Twenty-two—Schottmiller Visit | 188 |
| Twenty-three—Leaving Boston | 194 |
| Twenty-four—Trooper Encounter | 199 |
| Twenty-five—Antique Shopping | 210 |
| Twenty-six—Chasson Captured | 222 |
| Twenty-seven—Bray Questioned | 232 |

| | |
|---|---|
| Twenty-eight—Chasson's Turn | 240 |
| Twenty-nine—Murder Trial | 253 |
| Thirty—In Waiting | 264 |
| Thirty-one—Prisoner Bloodshed | 270 |
| Thirty-two—Ambulance Response | 281 |
| Thirty-three—Chasson Transport | 292 |
| Thirty-four—Brazen Escape | 304 |
| Thirty-five—The Aftermath | 319 |
| Thirty-six—Chasson's Run | 329 |
| Thirty-seven—America's Most-Wanted | 344 |
| Thirty-eight—Fugitives Found | 353 |
| Thirty-nine—Kathleen's Friend | 358 |
| Epilogue | 367 |

# ONE-BEER RUN

As Bryan "Rocky" Fitzgerald sped along Warren Avenue in Chelsea, the headlamps of his little Fiat Spider sports car cut a swath on the roadway ahead. The asphalt beneath the wheels, damp from an earlier rainfall, glistened like scattered diamonds. He navigated a corridor of automobiles parked along the narrow residential street, the beams of light reflecting off side-view mirrors affixed to the waiting vehicles. Most of the homes lining the street were dark. It was mid-evening, nine o'clock, and many of the occupants had retired early in anticipation of the Wednesday morning commute and day of work.

The night air over Chelsea hung thick and damp with humidity. Among other scents common to this North Shore city, particularly during seasonal warmth, was the trace of burnt tinder, a smell akin to a freshly doused campfire. A number of years had passed since the Great Chelsea Fire, which in October 1973, consumed eighteen congested city blocks and more than three hundred structures, both homes and businesses. The intense conflagration, driven by high winds and a lack of sufficient water, took several days to fully extinguish and required fire apparatus and manpower numbering over a thousand from more than a hundred Massachusetts communities. Even after four years of rebuilding entire neighborhoods, a pungent, smoky stench lingered in many quarters of the gritty city.

Fitzgerald, however, wasn't thinking about smoke or fire or much of anything except how he was going to deal with the man seated to his right in the Fiat. With each passing moment, he grew more anxious. As he drove, a pit formed in the depths of his stomach and nausea gradually took hold. He should have skipped the last beer he downed before leaving the house party.

The tension in the car was palpable. Fitzgerald, twenty-four, was by no means the nervous type. At six-foot-six, he had little reason to fear anyone. To his family members, he was known as "the protector," and according to his sister Diane, he never hesitated to come to the aid of those in need. But growing up on the tough streets of Quincy in the seventies was challenging, and with the proliferation of drugs, overdoses, and crime, Fitzgerald developed a keen sense for danger. His passenger was clearly a dangerous man.

He hadn't known Leroy Chasson for long. In fact, his only previous encounter was a brief five-minute brush two weeks earlier. Fitzgerald had joined several friends at the Yellow Submarine, a popular Beacon Hill greasy spoon located alongside Boston's notorious Charles Street Jail. Fitzgerald was wolfing down a sandwich when he noticed a handful of acquaintances entering the establishment. They were accompanied by a man he did not recognize. Greetings soon commenced and before long, Fitzgerald was introduced to Chasson, who seemed entirely disinterested in meeting him.

During the Chelsea house party, he encountered Chasson a second time, again briefly. Fitzgerald spotted him in the spacious kitchen, knocking down a beer and chatting with a pair of attractive women. He seemed ordinary. Visually, there was nothing exceptional about the man. Handsome, certainly, with high cheekbones and chiseled features, but close-set, empty eyes and a Fu Manchu-style mustache diminished his good looks. In earlier days, he was described in a prison classification document as a "tall, blonde, baby-faced man."

Chasson came up in conversation with friends and Fitzgerald learned that he was far from your everyday chick magnet; rather, Chasson was an ex-convict with an extensive criminal history, including armed robbery. He had done time in more than a half-dozen Massachusetts jails and prisons, including the renowned Massachusetts Correctional Institution-Walpole, better known to the locals as MCI-Cedar Junction.

"I heard he was recently released from Concord," said one partygoer, referring to the expansive brick-walled correctional facility situated on Route 2 in the historic community of Concord, where a number of decisive Revolutionary War battles took place centuries ago.

First established in 1878, MCI-Concord was converted in 1972 from a reformatory for petty criminals and wayward boys to a medium-security facility for those offenders who treaded the middle ground of criminal misdeeds. One such noteworthy inmate during this era was Malcolm X, the prominent civil rights activist, who was jailed in the fifties for the crime of breaking and entering to commit larceny. In 1978, a major riot broke out in Concord that was put down by seventy-five Massachusetts State Troopers. Among the squad were four sharpshooters armed with sniper rifles. No shots were fired, however. Fourteen inmates escaped briefly but all were recaptured. Order was soon restored and no lives were lost.

In early 2024, it was decided that the aging MCI-Concord would follow MCI-Walpole and meet with a demolition wrecking ball. Prison overcrowding, which had plagued Massachusetts correctional facilities for decades, was no longer a problem. Inmate populations across the state had declined in recent years through a reduction in crime and alternative programs for offenders. And, of course, there was the value of the land to consider which, in Concord, was in great demand.

The bottom line, according to the Chelsea party chatter, was that Leroy Chasson was not the kind of guy you'd want anywhere near your loved ones, your valuables—or riding in your car.

As he urged the Fiat into a slight bend and accelerated, Fitzgerald noticed as Chasson instinctively leaned forward to grip the dash, bracing himself against the turn. A cigarette dangled from his thin lips, outlined by a gaunt jawline. The convertible top down, the wind in his sandy hair, he was thoroughly enjoying the quick jaunt in the powerful sports car; he was grinning like a child on a carnival thrill ride.

"Which packie we going to?" Chasson asked, raising his voice against the din of the laboring engine and the draft of humid air streaming into the car.

"Martignetti's."

He nodded and said, "You drove, so I'll buy."

Fitzgerald simply shrugged his broad shoulders. In hindsight, he wished he had made the beer run on his own before Chasson had asked to join him. It was obvious there was something behind the request. Something ominous, like storm clouds gathering on a windswept Midwest horizon. All sorts of possibilities raced through his mind. *Shit, what if he's planning to hold up the liquor store?* Fitzgerald thought. *I'll be fingered as his wheelman. I'll be an accessory to a fucking robbery, for Crissake. I should've just grabbed Jeanne, skipped out of the party, and got the hell out of Chelsea.* It no longer mattered to him that the house party was in Jeanne's honor to celebrate her departure for a Texas college, which was supposed to take place the next morning. Explaining to friends why they bailed out of the party was the least of his problems.

Sweating profusely despite the steady breeze, Fitzgerald guided the Fiat to Revere Beach Parkway and jabbed at the pedal beneath his foot, taking advantage of a channel of glowing green traffic lights. It was clear sailing to Martignetti's.

As they turned off the Parkway, Chasson muttered, "Nice wheels you got here." There were few cars in the lot, not surprising for a Tuesday night. Package stores like this saw more business on weekends and holidays. Fitzgerald angled into a prime spot adjacent to the front entrance.

"Thanks," Fitzgerald said, sticking to one-word replies. "Girlfriend's."

He killed the engine with a twist of the key and leaned back in the bucket seat. Gripping the steering wheel with both hands, he twisted his head from side to side, trying to ease the growing tension in his neck.

Chasson climbed out of the car, stood, and arched his back in a stretch. He hiked up his blue jeans and smoothed his shirt, which was a dark-blue button-down. Leroy discarded his cigarette with a flick, turned to Fitzgerald, and said, "Hey, Rocky, after I grab the beer and a pack of smokes, I need you to give me a lift to Quincy, okay?" While it was framed as a question, it sounded more like a demand. Leroy Chasson didn't wait for an answer as he turned and made his way toward the automatic doors and into the brightly lit store beyond.

Fitzgerald's mind was suddenly reeling. *Shit*, he thought. *Quincy? What the fuck? Why does he want to go to* Quincy? *I knew taking him along for the ride to the packie was a mistake.*

His first instinct was to get the hell out of there. Easy enough—just start the Fiat and go—that's what he should do. He could hurry back to Walnut Street, pick up Jeanne, and put some distance between himself and Chelsea. He would be long gone before Chasson could find the means to get back to the house party. Even a taxi would take time. But did he really want to provoke a guy like this—a guy with Chasson's history? While he did not know the man well, he had learned enough to understand it was not a good idea to antagonize him. Certainly, he would be pissed off. Who knew what he would do if they ever crossed paths again. No, he couldn't just leave Chasson standing on the curb. Far too perilous.

Fitzgerald sought an excuse to break away. What could he say that would discourage his passenger from making a trip to Quincy? He glanced at the fuel gauge, which, to his chagrin, indicated the Fiat's tank was full. He then remembered he and Jeanne had topped it off before heading out for the evening. Not that an empty tank would change anything. His unwelcome rider seemed to have plenty of cash and would likely offer gas money.

Oddly enough, Fitzgerald's eventual destination was also Quincy. He was a lifelong resident of the historic coastal city, located a stone's throw south of Boston. He lived with his family in a modest home at 267 Wilson Avenue. But he certainly didn't want to be driving there with the likes of Chasson. *What was behind his request for a ride?* Fitzgerald wasn't certain, but he believed his companion lived in Cambridge or Somerville or Everett or some other community north of Boston. He had heard it mentioned by someone at the house party. Quincy was south—the wrong direction. *What—or who—was in Quincy that interested Chasson?*

Fitzgerald could tell Chasson that he had to get his girlfriend Jeanne home. It was nine o'clock and she was heading off to Texas in the morning to start school at Sam Houston College. He was certain she did not want to be out too late, especially while her boyfriend ran a fool's errand. In her car, no less! And obviously, with the two-seater, he didn't have room for another passenger. While there was truth in that explanation, Fitzgerald sensed that very few people ever denied this guy.

Before long, Chasson emerged from the store, juggling a variety of six-packs. *At least he wasn't being chased by store security—a good sign*, Fitzgerald thought.

His ride-along managed to free his hand to open the car door. "I got Schlitz, Miller, and Michelob," he said, wedging the six-packs of beer on the floor and climbing into the car. "And a pack of Light."

Fitzgerald nodded and cut to the chase. "So, Leroy…"

"Don't call me Leroy," Chasson spat. His face suddenly clouded as he cast a menacing glare. "Tightly wound" did not begin to describe this guy.

For several alarming seconds, Fitzgerald saw an individual who clearly was not in his right state of mind. Despite the warmth of the night air, a chill ran up his spine and his heart began to race. Uncomfortable, he shifted his tall frame in the bucket seat. While he loved driving the Fiat, he and Jeanne agreed it was far too small for a man of his size. But this was a different discomfort, namely because of his unwelcome guest.

Hesitantly, he uttered, "Uh, okay…"

"Sorry, man—I don't like to be called that name," said Chasson, who, in later years, had a tattoo of a dagger superimposed over a drunken mistake reading "LEROY" on his right forearm. His left arm featured a likeness of the Devil with the phrase reading "BORN TO RAISE HELL."

Fitzgerald mumbled, "Sorry."

Chasson raised his hand, a stop sign indicating no harm, and said, "Reminds me too much of colored people. I'd rather you call me Lee, okay?"

*Jesus, this guy is crazy,* Fitzgerald surmised. *If looks could kill, I'd be dead right now. And over a fucking name!* "Sure, sure," Fitzgerald acquiesced. "Lee. Got it. So, Quincy?" Changing the subject seemed to be the safest tactic.

"Yeah, not a problem, I hope." Chasson settled into the passenger seat and lit a fresh smoke.

*Of course it's a fucking problem,* an infuriated Fitzgerald thought as he replied, "No, not at all."

"Whadda you say we take a spin around the city and check out a few of the hot spots?" his unwanted guest suggested. "I was thinking the Beachcomber for starters. We can grab a bite. On me!"

*Yeah, that's exactly what I want to do. Spend a night cruising around Quincy with a guy I barely know. This character is so tightly wound, who knows what could happen?* But with no other safe recourse available to him, Fitzgerald guided the Fiat back onto Revere Beach Parkway and made for Interstate 93. It occurred to him, as he nosed the car toward the southbound off-ramp that the purpose of the beer run was for the Chelsea partygoers. Obviously, the alcohol would not be delivered, at least not right away.

Traffic was light due to the late hour and the nearly fourteen-mile drive south to Quincy was less than twenty minutes. Thankfully, Chasson wasn't much of a conversationalist; the two men drove in relative silence.

Fitzgerald settled into the high-speed lane but did not stray far above the posted 55-mph limit. The high-profile orange Fiat was a magnet for state troopers, who were known to establish speed traps along the nine-mile strip of highway between Dorchester and Braintree. He didn't need to get pulled over by the cops to further complicate matters.

To his left, Fitzgerald glimpsed the landmark Boston Gas natural gas tank, which was built six years earlier on the shores of Dorchester Bay. Locals often shared an urban myth about the tank and the possibility of a rupture, substantial gas escape, and a fireball which could potentially wipe out a large segment of heavily populated Dorchester. Farfetched, according to officials and LNG (liquefied natural gas) analysts, but in early 1977, the Federal Energy Regulatory Commission released a report that claimed an explosion at the site could claim three thousand or more lives.

When he was certain it was safe, Fitzgerald risked a quick glance at his unwelcome companion. *Good-looking guy; medium height, a bit under six feet, and slim, but muscular and powerful. Sandy-brown hair, trimmed just below the ears. Piercing hazel eyes. Rebellious. Tough guy. A real ladies' man.*

He certainly had no way of knowing at the time, but as Bryan "Rocky" Fitzgerald made his way toward Quincy on the Southeast Expressway, the man occupying the passenger seat of his girlfriend's sports convertible, smoking a cigarette and relishing the wind coursing through his hair, would soon be a hunted killer.

# TWO — CHASSON'S CHILDHOOD

While many of his young friends were making their memories in the dense green forest surrounding Black Mountain or the churning rapids of the swift Androscoggin River, Leroy Joseph Chasson found himself in trouble with the law for breaking and entering a neighbor's home. He was an eight-year-old when he first felt the bite of cold steel handcuffs binding his wrists.

Born in Rumford, a small paper mill town in rural Western Maine, Leroy was the youngest son of Phillip, a native Canadian, and Jessie MacPherson Chasson, who was born and raised in Maine. The couple reared thirteen children, including two sets of twins. When Leroy joined the family on August 6, 1949, his eldest sibling, Kenneth, had already reached the age of eighteen. Twenty-three years separated the oldest from the youngest in the Chasson clan.

Growing up in a mill town, Chasson had several pursuits to occupy his time, but he chose to follow a path of wrongdoing and misdeeds. His father, a disciplinarian who ruled over a crowded, strict Catholic household, would have little to do with the boy. Reigning over such a large brood, there were few opportunities to spend time with any one child, particularly a capricious son. In Leroy's case, punishment seemed to fail—it only served to make matters worse, which would be a harbinger of things to come. Each time the elder Chasson chastised his son, the boy would grow bitter and his antisocial behavior escalated, partly in retaliation. Leroy grew more rebellious as he reached his preteen years.

His mother Jessie, while described as a hardy Down-Easter, was a warm and loving mother to the core. But she hardly had the time to cope with the boy's "acting out," as his delinquent conduct was characterized by schoolteachers and the Rumford authorities. It was the opinion of many that the incorrigible child would never mend his ways and was destined for a life of crime and punishment.

In the mid-fifties, the Chasson family relocated south to Massachusetts, seeking a change of surroundings and a fresh start. Except for the distant cities, Maine offered little for the ambitious Phillip Chasson. Other than a dead-end job in the paper mills, Rumford and the surrounding communities had few opportunities in the way of rewarding work. He sought the better prospects Massachusetts offered and, obviously, more income to feed his family. They settled in the bustling city of Cambridge, which was separated from neighboring Boston by the murky waters of the historic Charles River. The flatwater Charles snakes between the two cities, eventually emptying into the Atlantic Ocean.

Phillip Chasson soon found work as a house painter while his wife turned to a career as a nursing assistant, which was suitable after caring for such a large collection of children. The move from country to city, however, did little to change Leroy's predilection for wrongdoing. In fact, it wasn't long before his fledgling criminal career began in earnest. In addition to burglary, the youth had a taste for setting fires.

While attending the Abraham Lincoln Elementary School on Brattle Street in Cambridge, Leroy was often unruly and wild in the classroom. He was arrested for torching a random automobile. It was "just for kicks," as he later described it to the police. Other arson charges subsequently followed, including burning a small garage to the ground in 1958.

Some years later, when Massachusetts Department of Correction authorities were seeking to alleviate severe overcrowding in the state's prison system, a well-meaning social worker tasked with inmate placement proposed that the Plymouth Forestry Camp might offer suitable rehabilitation for young Leroy.

The minimum-security facility, established in the depths of the expansive Myles Standish State Forest in the mid-fifties, was an alternative corrections option allowing inmates to tend to the needs of the twelve-thousand-acre timberland, which straddled the historic towns of Plymouth and Carver, Massachusetts.

"Those who were aware of the prison camp typically held it in high regard because the men who stayed there, usually prisoners nearing the end of their sentence, were frequently dispatched to clear forest trails, work on municipal buildings or clean up town properties," wrote *Patriot Ledger* reporter Neal Simpson in an article describing the unique detention compound.

But Leroy Chasson? The social worker who suggested that the forestry camp might be a good fit for their rebellious prisoner was soundly rebuked by her well-informed colleagues. With a touch of sarcastic humor, she was reminded that a repeat arsonist armed with a book of matches did not mix well with a forest thick with dry tinder.

Early on, the Youth Service Board was merciful, granting Leroy probation for his assorted infractions, including the arson spree. He later added seven truancies, public drunkenness, and an arrest for disturbing the peace to his criminal dossier; but despite it all, Chasson was allowed to remain free, placed in the custody of his family.

On May 1, 1962, Chasson's probation was revoked on a more serious charge. As a twelve-year-old, Leroy was arrested for breaking and entering in the daytime with intent to commit larceny. Trouble, it seemed, always found the bungling young burglar. He was apprehended as he climbed out of a first-floor window of an apartment, a pillowcase filled with loot firmly in hand. Carted away by a pair of grinning Cambridge police officers, the repeat offender stewed in a foul-smelling jail cell for several days pending a hearing in juvenile court. Based on statutes in the early sixties, Leroy was deemed old enough to be classified as a juvenile delinquent. Age was not really a consideration in his instance—one glance at his multi-paged list of priors sealed the boy's fate. The judge granted no leniency. Before long, the troubled preadolescent was on his way to the Lyman School for Boys.

Established in 1886, Lyman was a notorious reformatory built in the bucolic Central Massachusetts community of Westborough, ten miles east of Worcester. Situated on a thousand-acre tract of rolling green meadow, the reform school was the first of its kind in the United States and one of seven built across the Bay State. Most of the children warehoused in these drab, decrepit buildings were between the ages of eight and seventeen. They were deemed too young by the judicial system to warrant incarceration in adult prisons, regardless of their crimes. Most of the inmates—"students," as they were known by their keepers—were placed in custody on drug-related offenses, breaking and entering, and a range of minor transgressions, such as petty larceny, truancy, and vagrancy.

The Lyman School, at capacity, housed as many as four hundred students segregated into seven individual cottages scattered across the sprawling campus. Placement of the young offenders was based on the magnitude of the crimes committed, as well as the individual's ability to heed a strict set of rules and regulations. Each cottage was managed by a live-in superintendent, typically a political patronage job and often part of a rigid husband-wife combination. These stern couples held sway over the frequently rebellious children under the threat of physical punishment or some form of solitary confinement.

"My first day there, I talked in the dining room and got fifty bucks—that's fifty blows with a stick on your open palm," shared former Walpole State Prison inmate Jon Connearney during a 1971 interview with *Boston Globe* reporter F.B. Taylor, who was tasked with writing a comprehensive four-part account of reform schools in Massachusetts. "Makes your hand swell up good."

Other interview subjects shared harrowing tales of beatings at the hands of the cottage masters and terms spent in solitary, particularly the dreaded Cottage Nine "tombs," located at the nearby Shirley Industrial School.

"The coffin-like rooms were aptly named," wrote Jerome G. Miller, former commissioner of the Massachusetts Department of Youth Services, who often paid unannounced visits to determine the extent of the abuse. "I asked to look inside one. The master unlocked the steel mesh door, and there, on the floor, nude in the darkness of his own tomb, sat a sixteen-year-old. He was being punished for having caused a scene in the cottage a few days earlier."

Miller, who wrote *Last One Over the Wall* (a detailed account of his relentless crusade to shut down the Massachusetts reform schools in the early seventies, which to a great extent was successful), maintained that the mistreatment of the young inmates was the result of a rather high rate of escape. The commissioner, conducting a tour of the Bridgewater reform facility with the wife of former governor Francis Sargent at his side, was a firsthand witness to an actual escape attempt.

"No one made it over the wall, but a couple of youngsters came close," he wrote. "They were dragged down, thrown to the ground, handcuffed, and beaten. Out of the din came a steady torrent of cursing, and the would-be escapees were carried off to isolation."

At fifteen, Chasson joined a lengthy list of Lyman escapees, making a break for it on a cool, crisp mid-September morning in 1964. The Westborough Police picked him up the very next day and returned him to the dreaded reformatory. A number of kindhearted police officers, wishing to remain unnamed, admitted to having misgivings about bringing kids back because of the punishments they understood awaited the petrified children.

Chasson was moved to the Shirley School in rural Shirley, Massachusetts, which was thought to be more secure. He proved otherwise, breaking out just before Thanksgiving 1965. Once again, he was back in state custody within twenty-four hours, explaining to his police escorts that he just wanted to be home with his family for the holiday. The third stop on his reform school tour was Bridgewater, which demonstrated proficiency at retaining prisoners.

Despite his frequent transgressions and escapes, officials held out hope that Chasson could be rehabilitated.

"Leroy seemed to adjust extremely well at Shirley School," a corrections social worker wrote in a classification report for Chasson (Inmate No. C40819). "He is described as patient, obedient, polite, and related well with his peers. Even when moved to Bridgewater, while occasionally sneaky and outspoken, his work habits were fair, and he performed his assigned tasks in the kitchen well. He was amiable and cooperative."

Upon release from Bridgewater, the eager youngster began to show promise and was allowed to rejoin his family. It seemed, at first, as if the Massachusetts Department of Correction had set Chasson on a trajectory to responsible adulthood.

Resolute, he returned to the classroom, finishing the sixth grade at Cambridge's M.E. Fitzgerald School, which was located at 70 Ringe Avenue. Later, he entered the high school ranks, attending Cambridge Rindge in the mid-sixties. Despite an avid interest in the carpentry trade, training that was offered by the school, Chasson was forced to drop out in the ninth grade after he was returned to the Lyman on a minor parole violation. This was at least one notable instance when the judicial system worked against the boy: Leroy was on a path to rehabilitation but instead of a potential career as a tradesman, he was driven back into the system that had failed him and many others.

Chasson rallied, once again, after he was set free in his late teens. First, he took a $47.30 weekly job as a line cook at a diner within walking distance of his home. Later, he gained employment with Charles Blevins Painting, a Cambridge-based house painting firm, earning a weekly wage of eighty-five dollars. His father, a foreman with the small company, vouched for his wayward son in hopes that the boy could overcome eighteen reckless years. His dad mistakenly believed that by holding down a steady job and earning an honest wage, Leroy would clean up his act. Instead, the young Chasson used his earnings to purchase alcohol and fuel a growing heroin addiction.

On February 28, 1968, several months before reaching his nineteenth birthday, Leroy Chasson graduated to the criminal big leagues when he was arrested by the Somerville Police on firearms charges.

According to responding Officers James Reardon and David Emery, who arrived at the scene just after eight o'clock in the evening, Chasson had fired a handgun from a second-floor window, striking a teenage girl on the street below. One of the officers remained with the victim, awaiting an ambulance, while his colleague entered the three-story structure and climbed the stairs to the second landing, gun drawn. Two additional police officers joined him. They were met by the assailant at his apartment door, which was ajar. He knew the police were coming and opened the door in advance of their arrival. They entered the sparse living room and surrounded the wrongdoer. In the apartment, there was a telltale odor of spent gunpowder. Chasson's face was pale and drawn. His eyes were bloodshot and half-closed. He was skittish and clearly inebriated. When asked if anyone had been shooting a gun from a rear window, the perpetrator lowered his gaze and remained silent.

"Someone fired a gun from the window," Officer Reardon declared harshly, his service revolver in his hand, lowered at his side but at the ready. "A young girl was shot in the face."

"I didn't mean to hurt anyone," the shooter blurted after a brief pause, confessing to the misdeed. Visibly distraught, he was slowly shaking his head back-and-forth. "Is the girl all right?"

Without delay, the officers turned the culprit, pinning him against the wall. They brought his arms together at his lower back and handcuffed his wrists as they read his rights.

"What's your name?" Reardon asked.

"Lee," was the response. "Lee Chasson."

"Anyone else in the apartment?"

"No, I'm alone."

"Where's the gun?"

Chasson, who reeked of alcohol, told the officers they'd find it in the bathroom, hidden in the gap beneath the claw-foot bathtub. Police retrieved a German-made .22-caliber Valor revolver. It was obvious the gun had recently been fired. In the adjacent bedroom, they retrieved forty-five rounds, including four spent shells.

As the Somerville contingent guided the shooting suspect to a waiting cruiser, he admitted to firing the weapon but claimed that he was only horsing around. Chasson explained that he had yelled out to a group of youths gathered beneath his apartment window. He urged them to come up and join him for a "fun time." As eighteen-year-old Leroy tried to justify his reckless actions, he said, "I just wanted to hang out with them—there were cute girls with them."

The teens began hurling insults back at him, coupled with laughter. They weren't the least bit interested in his invitation. Provoked, he grabbed his firearm and started randomly shooting. He told the police that when he fired the gun, it was only meant to "tease" the kids. He wasn't aiming at anyone in particular.

The injured party, a sixteen-year-old girl, sustained non-life-threatening wounds to her face, although it was likely she would struggle with permanent scarring. Chasson admitted that earlier, he and friends were seeking to get high by sniffing cleaning fluid. He claimed he was still wasted when he fired the gun.

Later, during indictment at the Middlesex Superior Court, it was revealed by prosecutors that Leroy Chasson had used the same firearm in the commission of three separate armed robberies over a ten-day span in early February 1968, prior to the Somerville shooting. The three holdups yielded thirty-three dollars, eleven dollars, and, subsequently, nothing.

Leroy Chasson was sentenced to a term of five years to be served at the Massachusetts Correctional Institute-Concord. He had been in and out of assorted police lockups and jails for half his life but Concord marked the first time the repeat offender faced incarceration in a prison setting.

# THREE—ARMED ROBBERY

On a warm, humid evening on Monday, July 12, 1971, twenty-one-year-old Leroy Chasson crossed the tenuous barrier from petty crime to flagrant offense when he committed an armed robbery of a Cambridge, Massachusetts pharmacy.

Prior to the brazen robbery, Chasson had served less than two years at the MCI-Concord Reformatory for a number of gun-related offenses, including randomly firing a weapon that wounded a teenage girl. After several parole board denials, he was released on March 18, 1970. While his permanent docket revealed an unblemished period of confinement, there were several minor infractions. On December 6, 1968, for instance, Chasson was belligerent to a corrections officer, refusing to report to his work assignment in the facility kitchen where he toiled as a cook. His denial led to a one-time charge of insolence that resulted in forty-eight hours in isolation and suspended privileges. However, the young inmate kept his cool, did as he was told, and earned points toward early parole. In fact, Chasson was a regular in the prison clinic, donating blood a half-dozen times in just over a one-year span, from July 1968 to September 1969. He had been drug free long enough to make his blood viable for recipients. This measure, on the part of the inmate, was not really a good deed but rather a strategy to earn sentence deductions toward parole.

A free man and back on the streets in early 1970, Chasson squandered the opportunity to go straight and try to make something of his life. His parents, Jessie and Phillip, were supportive and did all they could to provide guidance for their rebellious son. But before long, Leroy returned to frequent heroin use, an expensive pursuit.

Seeking the funds to feed his addiction, Chasson, his face masked, burst into Simpson's Drug Store on Cambridge Street. The thief and a pair of masked companions startled the two employees working at the counter—an elderly proprietor and his young apprentice. The subdued jingle of a signal bell affixed above the pharmacy entrance alerted the staff to the arrival of customers. But these were no ordinary customers.

"Give me the money!" Chasson commanded, pointing his .45-caliber automatic menacingly at the midsection of one of the two frightened workers. The elderly pharmacist raised his arms upward without being told to do so; it was a conditioned, instinctual reaction to the threat.

"C'mon, Pops, hand it over! Move it!"

The old-timer shuffled toward the register as ordered. But his gait was weak and he was moving far too slowly for Chasson. The crook stepped forward and without provocation, pistol-whipped the man, knocking him to the floor. His head impacted the worn tiles with a sickening thud. A thin trickle of blood streamed from the druggist's temple and down the side of his face. Some of it dripped to the lapel of his white laboratory coat, staining it red. He closed his eyes and groaned in pain.

The other store employee, a young man in his twenties, sensed that he might be next to meet with the wrath of the impatient thief. He rushed to the cash register. Trembling, he jabbed the release button to open the drawer and withdrew all of the money within, amounting to $225. As he handed the cash over to the robber, a Cambridge patrol car arrived, its tires screeching as it came to an abrupt stop in front of the store. The flashing lights on the vehicle's roof intermittently turned the interior of Simpson's pharmacy blue. It became obvious to Leroy Chasson that one of the two drug store employees had somehow managed to trigger a silent alarm and summon the police. If he had time, Chasson would most certainly dispense a beating for the deed.

"Fuck!" he hissed between tightly clenched teeth as additional patrol cars arrived one after another. A sizeable police force soon filled the street and readied to breach the little pharmacy.

Before Chasson could do anything to prevent it, his two accomplices bolted for the door and the outside, only to fall into the waiting clutches of the uniforms gathered on the sidewalk. They surrendered without resistance. Neither perpetrator was armed, which saved their skins. They were handcuffed and detained in separate cars while the cops turned their attention to the remaining culprit inside. A number of the police ran to their patrol cars and removed shotguns and other assault weapons. As he observed the activity through a large-paned window, it became apparent to Chasson that his accomplices had apprised the cops that he was armed.

"Fucking cowards," Chasson spat. He made a mental note to make the deserters pay if he ever crossed paths with them in the future.

Afforded precious extra seconds as law enforcement readied, the would-be armed robber frantically sought the means to evade capture. Unlike his cowardly partners, he wasn't about to give up without attempting an escape.

His head on a swivel, Chasson scanned the rectangular-shaped shop end to end and soon detected an open doorway just beyond the long waist-high coffee counter. With time slipping away, he made his way toward the door. He feared it might be a dead-end storage room but with the gathering storm of lawmen outside, a desperate Chasson had little choice. To his relief, he discovered the narrow passage led to a staircase and a basement below. Could he be so fortunate? Could there be an egress to the exterior?

As he crossed the threshold and made for the stairs, Chasson noticed it was lightless in the space ahead, like a pitch-black cavern. He didn't see a light switch nor did he have time to search for one. The telltale bell at the store entrance was jingling.

Stuffing the .45-caliber handgun in his waistband, Chasson grasped the metal railings fastened to the walls on both sides of the staircase. He descended two stairs at a time, risking a spill into the darkness below. His heart slamming heavily in his chest, Chasson soon reached the base of the rickety stairs. It was cool in the space, but he broke out in a sweat. As his eyes adjusted, Leroy craned his neck. To the left, he saw another doorway. Framed around the edges was a rectangular sliver of light. Based on where he stood in the basement, it was an exit that fed into an alley to the rear of the building, which was used to accept deliveries.

Heavy boots thudded on the floor above as the Cambridge Police made their way into the drug store, guns drawn. Some chambered rounds in shotguns and the terrifying "CHK-CHK" sound sent a chill racing up Chasson's spine. The cops above his head were obviously armed to the teeth.

Leroy heard one of the cops say to the elderly pharmacist, "Sir, are you all right?" If the man answered, he couldn't hear it from the basement. He wondered if he had knocked the old guy unconscious. Then a shout, "Get an ambulance started—he's bleeding!"

Chasson crossed the room quickly, blindly taking long strides. Fearful that he might stumble over an unseen object in his path, he reached forward, feeling around with his hands like a sightless man in an unfamiliar setting. His sweat-soaked jersey clinging to his skin like glue, Leroy reached for the door in the darkness and felt around for a knob or handle. Instead, he found a padlock. He had made himself a prisoner in this tomblike cellar. But what choice did he have?

"Shit!" he muttered under his breath. There seemed to be no way out of this self-made trap. Behind him, he heard the distinct THUMP-THUMP of heavy footsteps. One of the cops was slowly making his way down the stairs. Once the approaching man confirmed the prey was holed up in the storage basement, the entire Cambridge Police force would certainly follow. Chasson considered shooting the lock on the delivery door and bursting into the safety of the alley beyond. But in the pitch black of the basement, he couldn't be certain if his aim would be true enough to hit the target. He also realized such a drastic attempt could draw a hail of bullets from the advancing police. They might think he was shooting at them and return fire. Leroy wasn't about to die in this dingy basement.

Taking the tested route, Chasson darted back to the base of the staircase. He pressed his thin 165-pound frame tightly against the wooden structure. Concealed in the darkness, he waited. He tasted raw adrenaline and felt his pulse in his temples. The police officer, in no hurry to reach the basement, descended slowly, his flashlight trained on the creaky stairs beneath his feet. Chasson readied his gun. He had checked it before launching the robbery and knew there was a full magazine in the weapon. As the cop reached the landing, he turned to his left and swung the beam of his light in a wide arc. Calling upon his cat-like reflexes, Leroy lunged at the officer. He threw his arm around the man's thick, sweaty neck and tightened his grip in a deadly stranglehold. While Chasson pointed the .45 at the back of the man's neck, the stunned cop dropped both his gun and flashlight.

"Move and you're dead," the holdup man threatened, pressing the cold steel barrel of the handgun deeper into the man's flesh.

Chasson's captive mumbled something unintelligible. He spoke again, obviously terrified, "Don't shoot."

It was all too easy. Chasson found it shameful that a trained police officer would be so careless and walk headlong into a potentially deadly ambush. The police at the top of the staircase called out, "Mike, are you alright?"

"Don't come down here!" he cried to his rescuers in anguish. "He has a gun on me!"

"You heard him!" Chasson shouted. "Come down here and I'll shoot this guy."

All movement in the store above came to an abrupt stop. The police froze where they stood and nobody budged. The injured elderly pharmacist had already been removed to a waiting ambulance and his young associate was safely out of harm's way, sitting in the back of a patrol car.

Chasson had no idea what to do next. Seconds felt like minutes. It seemed as if time had slowed to a crawl, like a slow-motion special effect during a dramatic movie scene. Chasson had committed burglaries, robberies, and a myriad of crimes but had never taken a hostage. *And this was a police officer.* It was surreal. He was holding a gun to the neck of a cop, threatening to kill him. The terrifying realization came over Leroy realized that he likely would not be leaving the drug store basement alive. The heavily armed men above would never allow one of their own to be hurt or killed without violent retribution.

As if reading his mind, the petrified Cambridge police officer confirmed his beliefs. "Look, man, you gotta let me go," he pleaded. He gasped the words, partly from the terror of the moment and partly from the arm securely wrapped around his throat. "They'll kill you. You'll never get out of here alive."

"Shaddup!" Leroy snapped. "I'm thinking."

"Let me go and I promise that you won't get hurt," the captive begged breathlessly, his uniform now soaked in sweat. He was negotiating for his life. "You have my word."

Chasson considered the offer. He would certainly be going back to prison, and for a long stretch. While his near future was bleak, at least he would still be alive. The alternative awaiting him at the top of the staircase was in the form of hot lead raking his body from head to toe. He was by no means suicidal. He wasn't ready to die. He decided to surrender. He had no choice but to accept.

"All right," Leroy said at long last. "How do we do this?"

The police officer relaxed slightly, faltering as Leroy loosened the grip on his throat. "Let me tell my guys you're giving up, okay?"

"Yeah, yeah, go ahead."

The hostage yelled to the men above, who were preparing to storm the basement, "He's giving up! Don't shoot!"

Chasson lowered his weapon and allowed the officer to turn and face him. The flashlight on the floor illuminated the tense scene. The man's face was beet red and drenched in sweat. He was a young guy and Chasson figured he had a wife and kids. He considered how close he came to killing the man and the thought didn't sit well; he just needed cash and a fix. He didn't want to be anyone's executioner.

"All right, let me have your gun," the cop instructed. "Hand it over butt first."

Chasson relinquished the firearm. The policeman trained it on him, stooped to retrieve his own, and said, "Okay, raise your hands, and walk up the stairs, slowly. Don't make any sudden moves."

Several of the former hostage's brothers in blue greeted Leroy at the top of the staircase. He was cuffed, frisked for additional weapons, and escorted to a waiting cruiser.

Weeks later, after trial and sentencing, he was delivered to the notorious MCI-Walpole Prison to begin serving a seven-to-fifteen-year sentence for armed robbery, with concurrent sentences of five to ten years for assault and battery with a dangerous weapon, and three to five years for carrying a dangerous weapon. It was the beginning of a turbulent period of imprisonment for the habitual offender.

# FOUR—FREEDOM AWAITS

Quietly wiling away the morning in his six-by-nine accommodation at MCI-Concord in mid-July 1977, Leroy Chasson watched his small black-and-white television with rapt interest as New York City descended into utter chaos. A lightning strike had triggered a chain of electrical failures that plunged the entire city into a three-day power outage, resulting in widespread arson fires, rampant vandalism, looting, and rioting. More than a thousand buildings were reduced to ashes while the NYPD tried in vain to enforce law and order. Four thousand were arrested before power was finally restored. Four people were killed, including a looter armed with a crowbar who unwisely attacked a gun-wielding storeowner.

In the pitch darkness of night, citizens of this great city gone mad were understandably fearful—not only because of roving gangs of criminals but because of a serial killer who remained on the loose. David Berkowitz, better known as the Son of Sam, had killed six and wounded seven others over the last year, spanning back to July 29, 1976. He randomly targeted his victims with a .44-caliber Bulldog revolver, later claiming he killed in the name of a ritualistic Satanic cult. Berkowitz was arrested on August 10, 1977, and as of early 2025, at seventy-one years of age, is closing in on five decades behind bars.

Chasson couldn't fathom such a sentence. He had done five years so far, since first arriving at the gates of MCI-Walpole on June 12, 1972, for the armed robbery of Simpson's Drug Store in Cambridge. But fifty years? Who could, in their right mind, mentally survive such a bid? He'd do himself in before facing a life sentence without possibility of parole. Or, at the very least, attempt to escape.

He rose from the edge of his cot, crossed to the brushed metal sink/toilet combination bolted to the wall, splashed chilly water on his face, toweled off, and waited patiently for the door to his cell to open. When the corrections officer in the control room disengaged the locking mechanism, he exited and made his way down three flights to the main tier, where breakfast was underway in the mess hall. Grabbing a plastic tray from the tall multi-colored stack and a set of plastic utensils, he entered the crowded chow line. It was very uncommon for him to eat the food furnished by the prison. Normally, he would purchase canned goods at the canteen and eat in his cell. Chasson feared that the cooks, inmates themselves, were adding ingredients unknown. But on this morning, he was famished and decided to roll the dice. He loaded up on scrambled eggs, toast, and something that vaguely resembled bacon. Chasson added a carton of milk and an apple. The eggs, he noticed, were watery. In the past, he might have made a snide comment to the inmate tasked with dishing out the food in the line. But in recent weeks, he kept his mouth shut, avoiding confrontation. Leroy Chasson was rapidly closing in on release and he didn't want to do or say anything to jeopardize his approaching parole.

Taking his usual seat at a long steel table, he bade a good morning to the man seated opposite. "How's it going?"

"Going well," answered Mark Bray after a pause to finish chewing the food in his mouth. "Yourself?"

Chasson just grinned. Bray nodded, understanding the meaning behind the expression. His friend had originally bought a long stretch at the dreaded Walpole State Prison for armed robbery but by way of legal wrangling, over time, managed to have the sentence reduced. He was also moved to MCI-Concord, where he now resided.

"Have they given you a date?"

"No exact date yet but I've been told just a few weeks," Chasson replied. "Maybe early August."

Leroy was aware that his friend was considering an escape in the days ahead. It was nothing concrete but had been mentioned in passing. Bray, through good behavior at MCI-Concord, had earned the privilege of an off-site job, working as an attendant at the Fernald School in Waltham. He was preparing to decamp when the opportunity arose. The escape would not be anything elaborate or newsworthy—he would simply walk away from the Fernald. The two men refrained from discussing the plan. There were far too many inmates within earshot and none of them could be trusted. Some prisoners were known turncoats and, without hesitation, would reveal such intelligence in exchange for added privileges. These rats were often betrayed and frequently suffered the consequences.

Over the years, Chasson rode the undulating roller coaster of incarceration, including multiple reclassifications and related moves to alternative housing. From maximum security to minimum and back again, Leroy Chasson had endured the instability of the Massachusetts prison system.

While serving his bid, Chasson's inmate history and propensity for escape should have been sufficient grounds for the denial of furlough requests. He was only a couple of years removed from inciting a riot at MCI-Walpole, as well as assaulting and injuring several prison guards at Bridgewater, among other flagrant infractions. But he insisted he had turned the corner and was no longer a threat for violence or escape, and felt he had earned the privilege.

In the mid-seventies, Chasson began to submit applications for furloughs. In a letter attached to an August 1974 application, he expressed his desire to meet with the parents of his fiancée, Linell Travers. "I want to speak with them and to make arrangements for marriage to their daughter," he wrote.

The requests were denied. MCI-Walpole Commissioner Frank A. Hall cited the need for more documentation. "A decision on Mr. Chasson's furlough request is being deferred until I can receive a current classification and progress report," Hall wrote in explanation. "This in no way guarantees that Mr. Chasson will receive favorable action. However, it does provide me more recent information on which to make a sound judgment."

A year later, in July 1975, a social worker at MCI-Bridgewater gave Chasson hope that he would be approved, stating, "Leroy continues to exhibit an extremely mature attitude. Since his admission here he has gone from the laundry to the work detail in the Chapel and now in the Green House outside the walls. This worker believes that this resident has more than earned a furlough."

But Leroy was subsequently rejected, again by Commissioner Hall. "The application of Leroy Chasson is being denied. He has only been at Bridgewater five months which were preceded by serious disciplinary problems at Walpole. I feel more time is needed to evaluate his good intentions."

In the context of corrections, a furlough is defined as "the temporary release of a convict from prison." In Massachusetts, the legislative bill permitting such reprieves had been signed into law in 1972 by then Governor Francis Sargent. Sixteen years later, a presidential candidate capitalized on the furlough law to advance his campaign.

While there were far more salient issues facing the American people when they went to the polls to vote for a president in 1988, Vice President George H. W. Bush certainly touched a nerve with one theme. Bush discredited his opponent, Massachusetts Governor and Democratic presidential candidate Michael S. Dukakis, by running a gut-wrenching campaign advertisement featuring killer Willie Horton. There were stunning billboards posted along roadways depicting Dukakis and Horton and stating, "WEEKEND PRISON PASSES—DUKAKIS ON CRIME."

Horton, as many Massachusetts citizens might recall, was the poster child for those who were against the Dukakis prison furlough program, which the governor adopted from earlier administrations. The extended weekend passes were bestowed upon *deserving* inmates. But in some instances, these "GET OUT OF JAIL FREE" benefits were awarded to hardcore killers based on their record of cooperation and good behavior.

Horton, convicted in 1974 of stabbing a seventeen-year-old gas station attendant nineteen times and stuffing the teen's body in a trash can, was granted a furlough from MCI-Walpole in 1986. While at liberty, the vicious murderer traveled to Maryland, where he twice-raped a woman after pistol-whipping her fiancé.

Horton was convicted by the Maryland Justice Department, which refused to send him back to Massachusetts, fearing he would once again be set free on furlough. Officials from the Bay State wanted Horton back to serve the remainder of his sentence, with added time for the escape, but Maryland authorities had little faith that proper justice would be carried out and rejected the request to send him north. As of 2025, seventy-three-year-old William Horton remains incarcerated at the Jessup Correctional Institute in Jessup, Maryland, fifteen miles south of Baltimore.

The pivotal campaign ad, which many claim led to a Bush presidential victory, highlighted Horton and expressed the belief that the Massachusetts furlough program was misguided and exhibited unmistakable evidence that Dukakis was soft on crime.

The bill was never intended to be applied to convicted killers like Willie Horton. In fact, it was mandated that first-degree murderers would not be eligible for temporary release from prison, no matter the circumstances. It wasn't long, however, before the law was challenged by a number of crackpots, who believed that killers were entitled to the same privileges as the rest of the prison population. The Massachusetts Supreme Judicial Court agreed, setting in motion Horton's rampage.

Chasson was never granted permission for a furlough. All requests were delayed and denied. In recent years, the setback might have triggered a violent outburst, but he kept his cool and went with the flow. As 1977 rolled around, the wheels of justice began to turn in his favor and a pardon finally came into view. By mid-summer of that year, prison officials released Leroy Chasson back into society. The felon was "rehabilitated" and, according to a series of Massachusetts Department of Correction social workers, was no longer considered a threat.

# FIVE—BROTHER'S DEATH

In the early days of his imprisonment at MCI-Walpole, Leroy Chasson suffered a tragic loss. His father Phillip passed away in 1970, at the early age of fifty-nine, but Leroy was free at the time and able to join his mother and siblings in mourning the man's death. But it was in mid-1972, less than a year into his sentence for armed robbery, when misfortune once again struck the Chasson family. Leroy's older brother Daniel, the closest to him in age of the twelve siblings, was killed in a Cambridge bar.

Home to a pair of world-renowned higher-learning institutes, Harvard University and the Massachusetts Institute of Technology, Cambridge is thought by many to be a sophisticated, polished city. But it also has a dark side. In a thirty-year span, from 1959 to 1989, there were one hundred and twenty-one homicides committed within the city limits.

Of particular interest were the murders of four-year-old Richard Volpe, whose mother intentionally drowned the little boy in a bathtub; sixty-year-old Cosmo Reale, who was stabbed to death with an ice pick by a coworker during an argument; and bodyguards John Mills, forty-one, and Robert Donahue, thirty-two, both shot in the back of the head in an apparent Mob hit. In those killings, charges were eventually dropped against the alleged perpetrator, Robert

Gustin, when key prosecution witnesses vanished under questionable circumstances.

The year 1972 was a particularly violent time in this city of just over 100,000, featuring fifteen murders: nine shooting fatalities, two who were stabbed, two who fell victim to strangling, and a pair whose lives ended under unknown circumstances. Victim number ten in the grim catalog of 1972's Cambridge murders was a twenty-eight-year-old man who, on July 24, was an innocent bystander in a bar fight gone wrong.

Seeking the company of a cold beer after a long day's work under a scalding summer sun in downtown Cambridge, Daniel Chasson stepped into the shadows of Falcone's Café. This pub was a nondescript establishment situated at 2030 Massachusetts Avenue in the hectic Porter Square neighborhood. A decade later, Falcone's closed its doors and became the popular Andy's Diner.

Daniel Chasson, an Air Force veteran, was a road construction worker employed by Essex Bituminous Concrete Corporation, a firm out of Peabody, Massachusetts. The weary laborer, his clothing and boots cloaked in concrete dust, claimed a stool at the bar and wrapped his hands around the refreshing cold beer mug provided by the barkeep. Seated nearby, Edward J. Doyle, twenty-two, of Hazlett, New Jersey, soon became embroiled in a loud, expletive-filled argument with another patron. Chasson intervened, along with Michael Luongo, thirty-one, who hailed from nearby Arlington, and the bar's owner, James Falcone, twenty-nine, of Lexington.

According to Cambridge Police Sergeant Frank McCusker, Doyle grew irate over comments made. He stood to leave the bar but then, without warning, pulled out a .25-caliber pistol and began randomly firing. Doyle was later arrested in his apartment above the bar. The gun was in his possession when police entered the two-room flat; he did not resist.

Luongo was hit in the abdomen while Falcone sustained a flesh wound to his left wrist. When police arrived, they quickly quelled the disturbance and rushed the three wounded men by ambulance to nearby Cambridge City Hospital. Both Luongo and Falcone survived. Daniel Chasson, however, wasn't so fortunate. Shot in the head, he lingered in the hospital for several days before succumbing. Daniel left behind his wife, Joan; his mother, Jessie; and twelve siblings, including Leroy, who was five years his junior.

Word of the shooting soon reached Walpole State Prison. Local Boston news channels carried the story, as well as regional newspapers. Officials escorted Leroy down from Ten Block and delivered the dire news in a conference room typically utilized for parole hearings. It was a spacious room and the corrections officers chose it specifically for this tense notification, clearly expecting one of Leroy's sudden, violent outbursts. Extra chairs and other objects, which could become airborne missiles amid an altercation with the unpredictable inmate, were removed as part of safety protocols.

Understandably distraught, Leroy held it together. He didn't lash out. Instead, he buried his face in his hands and wept. He was thinking ahead and understood that if he failed to restrain himself and lost control over his emotions, the corrections officials would deny his forthcoming request to attend Daniel's funeral when he perished.

Leroy Chasson pressed his internal prison network for information, and to determine that it was, in fact, his brother, Daniel, who was shot during the bar fight. He asked one of the prison infirmary medics he had befriended to contact the hospital and find out the victim's identity and condition.

"Yes, Leroy, it is your brother," the medic confirmed. "And his condition is critical."

Chasson also paid a visit to the deputy's office, where a Mr. Butterworth allowed the inmate to place a phone call to his mother.

On the afternoon of Tuesday, July 25, a pair of corrections officers accompanied Leroy Chasson to Cambridge City Hospital, where he joined his mother and a number of siblings for a bedside vigil. Trussed up with waist chains and handcuffs, the inmate pleaded with corrections officials to spare him the humiliation. "It is my word of honor to act as a trusted man," Chasson said, "to save me much embarrassment in front of my relatives and friends."

Butterworth acquiesced and removed the shackles, closely watching the man known for his tendency to attempt escape. The officials also spoke at length with Jessie Chasson, Leroy's mother, explaining in detail the procedures she would have to follow in the event of a wake or funeral for her son.

Daniel Chasson died two days later on the morning of Thursday, July 27. His brother Leroy was returned to the deputy's office, where he learned of the death. He was also informed that he would be granted permission to attend the services, which was not typical.

"Usually, an inmate has his choice of seeing the relative prior to his death or at the wake or funeral after his death," wrote MCI-Walpole Acting Commissioner James F. Mahoney in his report. "In Chasson's case, he was allowed to have both."

It was a warm, windy Saturday morning when two corrections officers were dispatched to the "New Man" section to collect Leroy Chasson for the thirty-minute trip to the John E. MacEvoy Funeral Home in Arlington.

"Two transportation officers arrived and I got dressed," wrote Chasson in a letter describing the events of the day. He changed out of his prison-issued blue denim shirt and blue dungarees into a borrowed suit. "I was chained and cuffed (rather tightly), brought out of the Institution and into a State car and headed for the Funeral Home to pay respects to my brother and try to comfort my mother the best I could, under the circumstances."

Arriving at 12:55, Chasson realized that he was early. There had been little traffic on the roadways between Walpole and Arlington. His family members weren't expected until at least 1:30 that afternoon. The corrections officers stood nearby in silence as Leroy knelt in front of his brother's casket. When he raised his hands to clasp them together in prayer, the chains wrapped around his waist and attached to the handcuffs jingled. In the quiet of the empty room, the sound was pronounced. If anybody had been in the darkened, subdued room, they would certainly have noticed.

Remarkably, Chasson held his comments when his chaperone, Officer Robert Miller, reminded him that they would be leaving at a quarter after one, in less than fifteen minutes' time. The inmate knew that just wouldn't do. His family members, including his mother, were not due for at least thirty minutes.

"If we leave before they get here," said Miller, referring to the inmate's approaching family. "It will save you the embarrassment of being cuffed and chained."

Visibly incensed, Chasson then stood up and made his way across the viewing room to the visitor register book to sign his name. The book was resting on a chest-high podium. Again, it proved to be an exasperating task because of the irons. It was difficult to raise his hands high enough to add his name. He did his best to write neatly but his signature resembled a young child's scrawl.

Chasson turned to Miller and, almost pleading, said, "Could you please remove the handcuffs?"

"No, I won't do it," said the steadfast, inflexible Walpole guard, citing the institutional policy that requires inmates to always be handcuffed outside of the prison walls.

Chasson thought for a moment about Butterworth, who, two days earlier, was perfectly willing to bend the rules and temporarily free the prisoner out of respect. Of course, Chasson wasn't about to mention it to Miller. He didn't want Butterworth to face the music for a regulations transgression and he certainly didn't trust that Miller would keep it under his hat.

Suddenly, without further provocation, he lost control and verbally lashed out at his keeper. "You motherfucker, you're a piece of shit!" Chasson spat. "What hole did you crawl out of?"

"Listen, Leroy," Miller said calmly. "If you keep this up, we'll be leaving right now."

"I am not going to leave!" Chasson hollered, seething with anger. "You'll have to fucking drag me out of here."

"Suit yourself," said Miller. He left the inmate in the care of his partner, Officer R. Nobrega, and made his way to the funeral home foyer. He sought out an employee and asked to use a phone.

In the meantime, Chasson and Nobrega moved to the smoking room, where Leroy discovered his sister-in-law had arrived for her husband's wake.

"Hello, Joan," he said with a grasp of her arm and a light kiss on her cheek. Once again, his chains chimed as he moved. "I'm so sorry for your loss."

"Yours too," she replied tearfully.

He tried to embrace his brother Daniel's widow, but it was awkward at best, with the manacles binding his wrists.

At that moment, Miller returned. A pair of Arlington police officers trailed him into the room. The corrections officer had explained to the policemen, when he greeted them in the foyer, that he needed their assistance for added safety while returning the volatile inmate to their state transport car.

"Let's go, Chasson," he barked. "We're leaving now."

His sister-in-law Joan tried to come to Leroy's aid. "His mother is due here in just a few minutes," she implored. "Couldn't you let him wait?"

Miller just shook his head and said, "No, he's leaving right now."

Leroy said goodbye to Joan, then made his way back to his brother's coffin. Miller, Nobrega, and the two Arlington police officers followed. He asked Nobrega for a match and lit a memorial candle for Daniel. It was a struggle because the candles rested on a chest-high shelf and his bindings made it difficult to reach. He knelt for one last prayer, then stood, and without a word, made his way toward the foyer. His entourage followed closely behind.

Chasson did not resist as the Arlington Police guided him outside and deposited him in the rear seat of the state car. During the thirty-minute trip back to the prison, however, "Inmate Chasson was very loud and abusive," according to Miller.

In the aftermath of his brother's death and subsequent visits to the hospital and the funeral home, Leroy Chasson embarked on a letter-writing spree. It was likely that his assorted correspondences, most containing gripes about his treatment at the hands of certain guards, went largely ignored. The letters were entered into Chasson's permanent file, but the recipients turned a blind eye to the comments, obviously written by an angry, unstable man. One letter was three typewritten pages in length.

I, LEROY JOSEPH CHASSON (AN INMATE OF MCI-WALPOLE), WISH TO SUBMIT THE FOLLOWING STORY WHICH WILL LEAD TO MY COMPLAINT AGAINST AN OFFICER OF THIS INSTITUTION (MR. ROBERT MILLER) WHO I SINCERELY FEEL IS BY NO MEANS HUMANLY CAPABLE TO WORK WITH OR BE AROUND MEN SERVING TIME, HERE AT MCI-W.

IN MY OPINION, THIS WAS THE MOST EMBARRASSING AND DISRESPECTFUL INCIDENT THAT COULD EVER HAPPEN TO A HUMAN BEING (PRISONER OR NOT). THE OFFICER THAT

I ACCUSE IN MY COMPLAINT (MR. ROBERT MILLER) HAS ALSO HAD MUCH TROUBLE WITH OTHER INMATES OF THIS INSTITUTION AND THE ADMINISTRATION HAS THIS MAN NOW WORKING IN "CONTROLS" SO THAT HE DOES NOT COME INTO MUCH CONTACT WITH THE INMATES HERE BUT UNFORTUNATELY, MR. MILLER WAS ASSIGNED TO TRANSPORTATION ON THIS DAY, WHEN I WAS TO BE TAKEN TO MY BROTHER'S WAKE.

HOPEFULLY, THIS TYPE OF OFFICER WILL NOT BE ASSIGNED TO SUCH A JOB (THAT DEALS WITH HUMANS) AGAIN.

At Chasson's request, a face-to-face conference was later held with Commissioner Mahoney. He attempted to excuse his actions. "I had become unduly excited," the inmate claimed. "I was emotionally upset."

Leroy also repeated much of what he had written in his letters but discussion about Officer Miller was off the table. Mahoney reminded Chasson that he had been granted not one but two trips outside of the prison, which was highly uncommon. He also spoke briefly about the restraints. "Mr. Chasson, it is not a department rule that the officer removes the handcuffs from the prisoner," Mahoney explained, referring to notes that were submitted by the prison personnel who had accompanied the inmate. "The officer is well within his rights to leave the handcuffs on if he feels any danger is present."

Mahoney closed the investigation on September 8, 1972, filing a memorandum with Commissioner John G. Boone. Along with a detailed outline of the incident, Mahoney summed up his findings by writing, "It is clear that Chasson got out of hand and that Officer Miller took the proper course of action."

Chasson's misguided quest to torment Officer Miller backfired. According to the decision rendered after the conference, "Chasson was found guilty of refusing to obey, profanity, disturbance and disrespect to an officer by the Disciplinary Board for the 7-29-1972 wake incident and given five days' isolation."

# SIX—HARD TIME

A model prisoner has been briefly defined as "someone who interacts well with other inmates." To take that a step further, this term also describes a convict who treats his caretakers—in this instance, the corrections officers—with the utmost respect.

Leroy Chasson, during assorted periods of confinement from 1968 to 1982, was the opposite of a model prisoner. His inmate record during that span is thick enough to fill a three-inch-thick loose-leaf binder to capacity. Chasson accrued eighteen disciplinary reports in one three-year span, taking place from 1972 to 1975, which were the early years of his seven-to-fifteen-year sentence for armed robbery. Many of the documented infractions involved threatening or disrespecting officers. Some included violent acts.

Massachusetts Corrections social worker J.A. Bedard drafted a number of classification reports, at one time comparing the temperamental inmate's personality traits to those of the infamous Dr. Jekyll and Mr. Hyde. In the classic novel of the same name, one man possessed two distinct personality traits, one good and the other evil. On the one hand, Leroy was thoughtful and helpful and "generally had an excellent work and attitude record." But as Mr. Hyde, the inmate "was prone to having a violent temper," according to Bedard. "When things aren't going his way, [the] subject's attitude toward other inmates and authority suffer."

One of those Mr. Hyde moments occurred on the morning of July 10, 1973. During breakfast on Block Two, Leroy Chasson suddenly became verbally hostile, yelling random threats at the corrections officers, or "screws" as they were insultingly known to the prisoners. "You fucking screws!" Chasson screamed. "I'm going to dig the motherfucking eyes out of the next screw that comes up here."

At 11:10 p.m. that same night, the belligerent inmate flagged Officer R. Furtado to approach his cell. Reaching through the bars, Chasson grabbed the man's arm and tossed a large amount of what appeared to be urine in his face. "Chasson called me to his cell, claiming he had some mail to be sent out," wrote Furtado after seeking medical treatment in the prison infirmary for "burning" eyes.

A week later, on a steamy, hot midsummer evening, Chasson teamed up with his Ten Block neighbor, Sam O'Brien. According to a report filed by Officer Charles Kenny, "O'Brien reached out through the bars of his cell, throwing papers into the corridor in front of his cell." Chasson then used a corn broom and swept the paper into a pile against the exterior wall. "At this time, I noticed a lit match being thrown from either room 42 or 43 (O'Brien's or Chasson's, respectively) into the pile of papers which ignited immediately."

Two months later, as breakfast arrived at Leroy's cell door, he grasped a full cup of milk from an officer and roared, "I don't want any!" Unprovoked, he threw the milk in the guard's face. It seems that this officer, Henry Gakowski, had earlier words with Chasson over the three-slice bread limit. "What the fuck am I?" Chasson shrieked. "I'm a man just as well as you! I'd like more than three pieces of bread! When I call you, you come to my fucking room with more bread!"

Several weeks later, on September 28, Chasson was attempting to gift a chocolate bar to an inmate friend who wasn't allowed to have candy because he was serving isolation punishment on Ten Block. According to Officer

Tenney's report, "Inmate Chasson refused to obey, and continued handing the candy over." Chasson was threatened with a ticket, which was similar to a demerit. He told the guard to "do what you have to do" and gave the isolated inmate a bag of cookies that were rapidly consumed.

The assaults on corrections personnel escalated in 1974. When Officer Henry Czaikowski delivered dinner on one January evening, Chasson threw an amount of an unknown substance at the well-meaning man. And in mid-March, Officer John Scarpaci confronted the inmate when he was discovered "wandering out of place." Chasson claimed he was heading back to Unit A1 to claim an item he had left behind during a scheduled meeting. Scarpaci promised a ticket for the violation.

"Fuck your ticket," said the short-tempered Chasson. "When you write your ticket, put *P.S.* on it for Piece of Shit because that's what you are." He then made matters worse for himself, jamming his fingertips into Scarpaci's chest.

Chasson was thought to be under the influence when he was charged with "creating a disturbance" in the visiting room on July 22, 1974. Officer James Wignall filed a disciplinary report stating that the inmate engaged in a swear-filled argument with a co-prisoner that soon turned physical. In this instance, a handful of inmates joined the fray and subdued Chasson until prison personnel took over.

One of the lesser documented charges was for "DESTROYING STATE PROPERTY" when Chasson, in a groundless fit of rage, smashed to pieces several plastic dinner trays in the mess hall. Along with a number of lost privileges, the loose cannon spent three days in isolation and was forced to pay restitution from his canteen fund in the amount of $3.75 for each shattered tray.

Chasson was also charged with attempting to bribe an officer in October 1974. In this instance, Corrections Officer Thomas Geiss filed a report with the MCI-Walpole Control

Supervisor regarding a brief conversation he had with the inmate.

"Hey, Officer?" Chasson called out through the bars of his cell as Geiss performed a head count.

"Yes?"

"If I ask you a question, would it be between just me and you?"

"It depends on the question," Officer Geiss replied. "Is it something illegal?"

"No."

"Okay, ask the question."

"Would you be interested in a C-Note to bring in contraband?" Chasson asked.

The prisoner subsequently lost privileges and was moved to isolation for the infraction.

In a twisted irony, Leroy Chasson somehow gained the support of a number of Walpole officers who drafted and signed a letter supporting the inmate in his endeavor to be transferred to MCI-Bridgewater. Despite the frequent ambushes on their brothers in blue, a dozen guards added their names to his request.

THE BELOW-NAMED OFFICERS ARE RECOMMENDING THAT INMATE LEROY CHASSON BE SENT TO A MINIMUM-SECURITY INSTITUTION. WE FEEL THAT INMATE CHASSON HAS MADE HIS SHARE OF MISTAKES IN THE PAST, BUT IT IS OUR CONSENSUS THAT HE HAS OVERCOME THESE PROBLEMS. THIS INMATE HAS ALWAYS APPEARED TO BE COURTEOUS, POLITE, AND CONSIDERATE OF OTHERS AROUND HIM, BOTH OFFICERS AND INMATES. WE'VE KNOWN THIS INMATE FOR APPROXIMATELY TWO YEARS AND THAT HIS MISTAKES WERE FROM THE CLOSED CONFINEMENT AND DEPRESSING SURROUNDINGS HERE AT WALPOLE. THEREFORE, WE CAN HONESTLY SAY THAT IF INMATE CHASSON WERE PLACED IN A MINIMUM-SECURITY INSTITUTION, HE CAN WORK HIS OWN WAY TO A PAROLE.

Oddly enough, the letter was made available without any redactions of the twelve officers' signatures but for the purpose of this narrative, their identities will not be revealed.

Leroy Chasson was transferred to MCI-Bridgewater to take part in a mandatory sixty-day drug rehabilitation program. While twenty-five-year-old Leroy was just three years into his seven-to-fifteen-year stretch for the armed robbery of Simpson's Drug Store, one of the corrections department social workers and institution's board members felt the young man could benefit from such measures.

"Mr. Chasson's extensive prior record caused close scrutiny of his current behavior and attitude," they wrote following a placement proceeding. "It appears that he is less volatile than in the past and that he has fewer periods of excessive drinking. These occasions usually result in criminal behavior, so alcohol control is a primary concern. His drinking brings on behavior that is irrational and sometimes out of character."

Leroy Chasson was transported from Walpole State Prison to MCI-Bridgewater and admitted on March 10, 1975. Built in 1855, Bridgewater was once home to Albert DeSalvo, the confessed infamous Boston Strangler.

Bridgewater was originally established as an almshouse, which was described as a temporary home for the local community's poor and infirm. As the decades passed, the isolated facility, which is located forty-five minutes south of Boston, expanded by adding a minimum-security prison, a state-run hospital for the criminally insane, an establishment to house sexually dangerous persons, and, Chasson's destination, a drug and alcohol treatment center.

His treatment plan continued well beyond the sixty-day requirement. The six-month effort on the part of the program clinicians was slow to yield discernible results. This was partly due to Chasson dragging his feet. Understandably, he preferred the relative comfort of the addiction center to the repulsive accommodations at Walpole. He slept in an actual bed and the meals were edible. He successfully manipulated the staff. He found the means to deliberately slow the process, gaining just enough ground to justify further treatment, but not enough to warrant return to maximum incarceration.

One of the most violent outbursts perpetrated by Leroy Chasson to date occurred shortly after a once-weekly family visit to MCI-Bridgewater.

On September 14, 1975, the irascible Chasson launched an unprovoked attack on his keepers, committing a violent assault and battery on a trio of officers who were simply carrying out their jobs. According to a detailed report submitted by one of his victims in the aftermath, Chasson refused to comply with the stern post-visit search protocol.

These stringent rules, which required a strip search and cavity check, were established to intercept contraband that visitors attempted to smuggle into the jail. Prohibited items, including drugs and paraphernalia, would often be conveyed during intimate contact, which was condoned. Many of the female visitors were exceptionally creative in finding the means to supply their husbands and boyfriends with narcotics.

It was just before eight o'clock in the evening when Chasson, having completed his visit with girlfriend Linell Travers and their son Derek, was ushered into the social services office to face what prison officials delicately termed a "skin search."

"All right, Chasson, you'll need to remove your clothing," Correctional Officer George Wentworth demanded, working the night shift with teammates Patrick McAuliffe and Robert Santos.

"I'm not taking my pants off and no motherfucker is going to make me!" the inmate snarled. A string of expletives followed.

Chasson's verbal blitz quickly turned physical. He launched himself at Wentworth, spewing, "You're a lousy cocksucker."

He then struck the guard in the mouth and, in rapid succession, connected three subsequent blows to the man's chest. Despite the painful barrage, Wentworth managed to grab one of Chasson's wildly flailing arms. Santos, who was in the office foyer, heard the commotion and rushed to the aid of his colleague. He was able to pin the inmate's free arm, which Chasson was swinging, trying to make contact. His upper body restrained by the two corrections officers, Chasson began using his feet as weapons, thrashing about and kicking at his captors as they struggled to move him to the corridor and the security of a spare cell. The inmate slumped heavily to the floor and kicked the office door shut.

The loud slam of the heavy door brought Officer McAuliffe into the fray. The three men raised Chasson to his feet and subdued him briefly. Far stronger than he appeared, Chasson broke free of their grasp and dove forward, slamming his head into the wire-reinforced glass panel at the top of the door. Santos pulled him back but not before Chasson smashed his forehead into the square window a second time, shattering the glass and drawing blood. The inmate would later need sutures for the injury rendered by the impact of flesh on steel wire.

Dazed and exhausted, Chasson paused his attack. A stream of blood trickled along the bridge of his nose, seeping from the ugly gash at his hairline. The prisoner looked at Wentworth and in a deep, unholy tone, hissed, "I'm going to kill you, motherfucker."

The corrections officer had been threatened before; it came with the territory. But the evil lurking behind the inmate's malicious gaze sent a chill up his spine. This man was beyond malevolent. As Wentworth adjusted his grip on the prisoner's upper arm, Chasson got in one final shot: a knee to the guard's groin. Wentworth was briefly incapacitated. The pain was excruciating, sending a shockwave through his body, triggering a bout of nausea. While Wentworth stooped at the waist, retching, Santos and McAuliffe redoubled their efforts to bring Chasson under control. They managed to wrestle the deranged man to the floor and temporarily stem the attack.

Joined by Senior Corrections Officer Alfred Goodman, the men dragged a kicking and screaming Chasson out of the confined space of the office and into the exterior corridor. The uproar had drawn a small group of roving residents, all who had taken part in the family visit day and were milling about, awaiting their turn for a strip search. They stood quietly, observing the confrontation. Those who knew him were not in the least surprised that it was tough guy Leroy Chasson clashing with the officers. Most gave him a wide berth.

Wentworth had recovered somewhat and rejoined his men. Surrounded now by four guards, the rampaging inmate broke free again. Before he could be taken down, the assailant struck resident John Harrison, a bystander, square in the face. He was also able to drop Goodwin with a solid punch to the head that sent the man sprawling to the concrete floor. Goodwin was later treated for a mild concussion by Dr. Kilinsky, the MCI-Bridgewater chief physician.

Forty-eight hours after the scuffle, Leroy Chasson was returned to MCI-Walpole for security purposes. The MCI-Bridgewater management claimed they lacked the means, or desire, to contain him in their minimum facility. Three of their men had suffered injuries in the brawl and officials insisted they weren't about to lose any more.

Once he was granted a hearing with the MCI-Walpole administration, Chasson explained that he was drugged without his knowledge. Under the influence, he had no control over his actions nor did he have any recall of the violent altercation. The Walpole prison officials tasked with deciding his fate, however, weren't buying the inmate's explanation. If he was, in fact, drugged by consuming "outside" food, why then did none of the women and children fall victim? They ate the same food. Five years were tacked on to Chasson's existing sentence for his aggressions.

In December 1975, Leroy met with social worker Leslie McKenna to further plead his case. He often found a sympathetic ear with the prison counselors and was hoping he could convince her to approve his return to Bridgewater, where he could resume his rehabilitation.

"The resident relates that he was visiting with his girlfriend and child and other inmates who were having a family day," McKenna wrote. "A visitor brought in food when he 'flipped out.' He attributes this incident to having been 'tabbed,' or having his food tampered with. He claims that he had a similar reaction when he used LSD in 1966. He further claims that he does not have memory of the incident. It is felt that he may have some enemies in the population at Walpole although he disclaims this."

Once again, Leroy Chasson was denied. He served his isolation time and soon returned to the routine of Walpole Prison. Save for a number of minor violations in 1976, which cost him exercise privileges and limited desirable work details, he was sedate. In January 1976, the inmate stumbled upon an interest in welding and enrolled in a program offered at Walpole's sister penitentiary, MCI-Norfolk, a minimum-security facility situated several miles to the north. Eventually, Chasson became a permanent resident of Norfolk, which opened in 1927.

Norfolk State Prison, located in a rural, woodsy town of twelve thousand, once housed renowned human rights activist Malcolm X, and in 2020, held more than twelve hundred inmates, including one hundred maximum-security inmates due to Walpole overflow. Some of these men, including longtime Mafia leaders, were housed in assorted step-down units on the thirty-five-acre property.

Adorning the walls of the unpretentious MCI-Norfolk lobby, where visitors would await FBI identity verification and prepare for entry processing, are the obligatory photos of past and present Massachusetts State governors, noteworthy prison leadership, and portraits of two corrections officers who were killed during an escape attempt on July 31, 1972.

Alfred J. Baranowski, sixty-four, and James R. Souza, twenty-nine, were gunned down by inmate Walter J. Elliott, whose wife, Katherine, had smuggled in a pair of guns during a visit. According to reports, Elliott, who was a Somerville man serving a life sentence for homicide, blasted his way through the prison. With his wife at his side, the convict first shot and killed Souza, a military veteran, and later, Baranowski, who managed the industrial shop. Elliott also fired at Corrections Officer David G. Mackey, thirty-eight, who was later treated at Massachusetts General Hospital for non-life-threatening neck wounds.

Trapped in a dormitory and facing a barrage of tear gas, Elliott attempted a murder-suicide, shooting his wife and then himself before a small army of corrections personnel could reach them. His wife survived.

With little fanfare, inmate #33706, Leroy Chasson, arrived at MCI-Norfolk on February 3, 1977. He had spent several months at MCI-Shirley, located in the hills of Central Massachusetts, as part of pre-release proceedings. He traveled through the system, from Walpole to Bridgewater, back to Walpole, then to Shirley, to Norfolk, and, eventually, to MCI-Concord, which was the final stop before early release.

The tolerance of the Massachusetts prison system and the Justice Department became evident following Chasson's escape with three other men from Shirley on October 27, 1976. He admitted to intoxication at the time of his flight to Somerville, where he hoped to visit with girlfriend Linell. A week later, he was picked up by the Somerville Police and returned to Shirley. Chasson faced minimal reprimand, which included three months at the Middlesex House of Correction (located in Billerica), and with only a minor delay, resumed pre-release steps. He continued his welding training, sought additional counseling for his substance abuse, and, possessing only a ninth-grade education, began studying to take the GED exam.

Despite his escape and serving only half of his term for armed robbery, Leroy Chasson was well on his way to parole.

"Since his incarceration here, he has displayed mature, responsible behavior," wrote counselor Mary Ellen Campbell in an early 1977 Concord classification update. "He strongly wishes to remain at MCI-Concord, and he is ready to prepare for the future. He has also stated that if he were allowed to stay, he would sign an agreement to willingly be sent to MCI-Norfolk if he did get in any trouble."

Campbell went on to document that Leroy Chasson "claims he has no problems dealing with alcohol and while he had a drug problem from 1964-66 and again from 1970-71, he feels that he will not become involved with drugs again."

In hindsight, Campbell's evaluation, and many others like it, missed the target in documenting this unpredictable inmate. Despite a criminal catalog that featured burglary, arson, gun charges, drug charges, assault and battery, and armed robbery, Chasson was soon to be awarded his freedom.

He was just a matter of months away from adding murder to his loathsome resume.

# SEVEN—PAGEANT FIELD

Quincy's Pageant Field was bustling with activity, typical for a late summer night. A dozen or more youths had gathered since dusk, as they often did, to drink a few beers and escape chronic boredom. Most were in their twenties and of legal drinking age and the police let them be. The school of thought was it was far better to allow them to loiter in the remote park rather than on the streets of downtown Quincy.

Several individuals were seated at picnic tables adjacent to the baseball diamond. Overhead, a canopy protected the seating area from inclement weather, but this night was warm and thick with humidity, normal for late August in the Coastal Massachusetts community, best known for shipbuilding and as the birthplace of a pair of early American presidents. John Adams was the second man to lead the country, following George Washington. Adams' son John Quincy was sixth, holding the office from 1825 to 1829. Former Massachusetts Governor John Hancock, a patriot of the American Revolution and the first Founding Father to sign the Declaration of Independence, also hailed from Quincy.

Pageant Field is shoehorned in the northeast corner of sprawling Merrymount Park. The Mount, as it is known to locals, is an eighty-acre community-run recreational space featuring playing fields, walking trails, an amphitheater, and a boathouse on the shores of Black's Creek. This narrow, dark water estuary carries the pungent scents from nearby Wollaston Beach and Quincy Bay. Boston Harbor and the deep waters of the Atlantic churn several miles further to the north.

During the summer, the park was often filled with Little League ball games. In the adjacent picnic pavilion, there were several permanent brick grills for public use and families would make a day of it, firing up a few hot dogs while the children played baseball.

Pageant Field was not really designed for nighttime activities, save for social gatherings like the one that was taking place this night, August 23, 1977. The park was poorly lit, to say the least. There were streetlamps arrayed in a distant parking lot, casting long, diffused shadows but offering little in the way of illumination for the ball field itself. Distant corners of the park, absent infrequent moonlight, were inky black.

Kevin Racette, standing beneath the backstop, was well into his second six-pack, perhaps third. He had lost track. When he was later questioned about his state of mind, Racette admitted to the authorities that he had been drinking steadily throughout the day, at least since the early afternoon. "Maybe I was drunk, intoxicated, whatever," was his reply when asked about his disposition.

"Hey, Toot, c'mon over here and sit with us," invited a female voice from the cluster of picnic benches. She was one of the few friends who used his longtime nickname. Racette glanced toward the source. While he couldn't see clearly in the darkness or through the artificial haze of alcohol, he recognized it was Laurie Schottmiller beckoning him to join them.

"Sure, in a minute," he replied as he kicked absently at home plate with a worn shoe. Racette raised his half-full can of beer and drained the remainder in a single slug. He then turned toward Schottmiller and the others, knowing that an ice-cold replacement would be waiting there to further quench his pursuit of total inebriation. Before taking a step forward, however, Racette paused as he caught sight of a familiar vehicle pulling into the distant parking lot. It was hard to mistake the bright-orange convertible, even in the low light. The car belonged to Bryan Fitzgerald, or at least it did until he transferred ownership days earlier to his girlfriend, Jeanne.

"Hey, Kevin..." urged Schottmiller, a slender, alluring twenty-two-year-old with wavy, waist-length brunette hair, known for her engaging smile and calm disposition.

"Yeah, yeah, just a second."

Racette didn't budge, however. His attention was elsewhere. He remained firmly anchored beneath the backstop, straining his eyes against the limited light cast by the one streetlamp in the vicinity. Fitzgerald emerged from the little orange sports car and, seconds later, a stranger climbed out from the passenger side and paused, scanning the layout. Across the distance, Racette couldn't distinguish who the figure was but assumed him to be "friendly." He was, after all, accompanied by one of their own in Bryan Fitzgerald.

Oddly enough, this wasn't their first visit to Pageant Field that night. They had arrived thirty minutes earlier, lingered for a few minutes, engaged in brief conversation, and then inexplicably departed. *Maybe they went to get some beer,* Racette thought. He discounted the odd behavior, but then noticed Fitzgerald and the unidentified man had returned and were now making their way toward the ball field.

In later interviews with the police, Fitzgerald explained that he and Chasson had arrived at Pageant Field earlier and spent a few minutes engaged in small talk with friends. Chasson, who seemed distracted, said he was hungry, so they returned to the car for a quick ride to the Southern Artery and Howdy! Beef n' Burger, a popular Quincy greasy spoon. Chasson showed little interest in food, however. "Let's go back," he said without further explanation.

Fitzgerald didn't say anything. He had only been with the guy for about an hour but it was long enough to understand that it wouldn't be wise to question him. It was obvious he had arranged for the ride from Chelsea to address unfinished business at the park. Without being asked, Chasson said, "I need to talk with this Racette character."

With that comment, alarms went off in Fitzgerald's head. But again, he refrained from asking. Instead, they took the short ride back to Pageant, parked the Fiat in the very same spot adjacent to the ball field, and began to walk toward the throng of people gathered in the picnic alcove. The night air had grown thicker with humidity, and the earlier cooling breeze had slackened.

As he emerged from the car, Fitzgerald immediately broke off and joined a group gathered near the fringes of the parking lot. Chasson, meanwhile, strode with purpose in the direction of Joe Marnell, who was sitting on the edge of one of the wooden tables, chatting with Schottmiller and several others. A small smoky fire had been built in one of the barbecue pits to ward off insects. As the man approached, conversation abruptly ceased.

Reaching the twenty-one-year-old Marnell, the stranger blurted, without introduction, "Hey, are you Kevin?"

Marnell, tall and lanky with dark, shoulder-length hair, wasn't known to take shit from anyone and he obviously didn't appreciate the man's lack of a proper greeting. He took a casual swig from his beer, set the can on the edge of the wooden table, and rose to his full height. Arms folded across his chest, the imposing Marnell answered in an equally hostile manner. "Who wants to know?"

The stranger hesitated, sizing up his potential foe, and said, "I just need to speak with him."

From a short distance away but within earshot, Racette observed with equal parts intrigue and trepidation. He sensed through the stupor of one too many beers that this guy might be a threat. It wasn't anything he could put his finger on—just a gut feeling. But as the outsider stepped away from an uncooperative Marnell and strode in his direction, Racette was able to get a better look at him. He was of medium height, six foot or so, with a thin, wiry build. At first glance, the stranger didn't seem to be much of a physical threat. Racette, who had done battle with far more formidable adversaries, relaxed, lowering his defenses. Sizing the guy up, he figured he could probably handle him in an altercation.

Before long, the man stepped in front of him, invading his personal space. Racette stepped back slightly, gaining separation and safety. The newcomer inched closer, once again narrowing the gap between them.

Smirking, the guy said, "Hey, Kevin." The greeting was later described as cheerful.

"Do I know you?"

"Yeah, you know me."

Racette took pause, growing alarmed. Despite the large quantity of beer he'd consumed through the day, he was sobering fast and gaining clarity. He could not recall where he had met this sinister character, but he did look vaguely familiar.

"I don't think so," Racette maintained, although still not yet certain where he knew him from.

"Yeah, you know me," the intruder repeated. He was insistent. "From jail… Concord."

"Concord?"

"Yeah, Concord," the man replied, his tone suddenly dark and impatient.

*Fuck,* Racette thought, coming to sudden, startling realization. *Now I know where I've seen him before. It's Leroy Chasson. We did time together at MCI-Concord. What the hell does he want from me?*

The drunken fog continued to lift. Racette's heart began to slam in his chest. He could feel the pulse in his neck. He tasted metal as raw adrenaline surged throughout his body and heightened his senses. His white cotton t-shirt soon became glued to his sweat-soaked skin and his breathing quickened.

He and Chasson and hundreds of others, he recalled, had served time in the early seventies at MCI-Concord for drug-related convictions as the cops clamped down on offenders. Some were locked up for simple possession while others served longer bids on distribution convictions. Racette was sentenced for multiple crimes, including larceny and dispensing controlled substances. He spent more than three years behind bars.

"Remember me now?" urged Chasson, as if he could read his thoughts. Racette shook his head, although he knew it wasn't convincing.

Would it be fight or flight? Racette resisted an urge to take a step back and wedge added space between them. He wouldn't be intimidated and wasn't about to yield to this guy. In the past, when faced with similar perils, he would always stand his ground. He'd been involved in his fair share of fistfights and prevailed in most of them. Physically, he was bigger and certainly stronger than the man who stood before him. There was nothing to fear.

On the other hand, he recalled that Chasson was a bad actor and prone to violent outbursts. While jails were a breeding ground for baseless rumors, Racette recalled hearing that this menace had killed another inmate, perhaps two, while incarcerated in the renowned MCI-Walpole Prison.

"What's on your mind?" Racette asked. He remained on full alert and proceeded with caution. This wasn't the time to let his guard down.

Chasson glanced over his shoulder, obviously to determine if the individuals seated at the picnic tables were listening to the conversation. He lowered his voice and uttered, "Look, I need a coupla bags."

"Sorry, can't help you," said Racette without pause, shaking his head.

"I was told you're the guy 'round here."

"You were told wrong," the former drug dealer insisted. "I'm not into that stuff anymore. You'll have to find someone else."

Racette was telling the truth. Upon release from prison the year before, he had enrolled in an outpatient drug rehab program. It was a condition of his parole but he was willing. He knew he needed help. And the program worked for him. Racette successfully kicked the drug habit. Certainly, he could drink most people under the table but heroin—both selling it and using it himself—was in his distant past.

"C'mon, man, it's just three friggin' bags," Chasson pleaded. The exasperation was evident in his voice. "You gotta help me."

In the foreground, Racette noticed Joe Marnell had taken a few steps in his direction, narrowing the gap. He had obviously sensed that the conversation between his friend Kevin and this uninvited stranger might escalate into something further, and he was preparing to intercede. Other friends began to gather as well, encircling the duo but keeping a safe distance.

Chasson put his arm around Racette's shoulder, as if they had been close friends for years, and began to guide him toward the backstop. It was an uncomfortable gesture and Racette recoiled. This guy was too close for comfort.

"Look, you gotta help me out," Chasson prodded as they walked together slowly. "You know how it is. I need a fix bad."

Racette shook his head. He was getting frustrated that his disagreeable companion, who removed his arm from his shoulder and stepped back, would not take "no" for an answer.

Without warning, Chasson took a swing at Racette, driving a rock-solid fist flush into his face. The assailant, as

Kevin learned, was much stronger than he looked. It was a stunning, unprovoked assault that flattened the unprepared recipient, knocking him heavily to the ground. He impacted with the hard-packed surface with a heavy thud. He groaned in pain. In later police interviews, Racette said, "I got cracked, you know; he punched me. He knocked my lights out."

Head spinning, a blurry-eyed Racette struggled to regain his feet. As he did, mass confusion erupted all around him. His friends, several of who had inched closer in anticipation of such an ambush, were now rapidly converging on the attacker and Racette. They were shouting unintelligible profanities. Several, including Albert Vasconcellos, Robert Hayward, and Paul Melody, were nearly upon the combatants. Meanwhile, Chasson hadn't budged after clocking Racette. Teeth bared like a vicious animal, he was crouched and ready to strike. His head whipped back-and-forth as he prepared to bring the attack to others.

Stunned, Racette glanced at Chasson and fearfully recognized the shiny blade of a knife in his assailant's hand. It glinted, reflecting off the muted light from a distant streetlamp. Seconds later, all hell broke loose at Pageant Field.

# EIGHT—STABBING VICTIM

Nathan "Buzzy" Shaw was first to reach the stabbing victim, who was bleeding profusely from what appeared to be a chest wound. Paul Melody's clothing was stained deep red and there was blood everywhere, including a rapidly expanding pool beneath the well-meaning casualty of a rescue attempt gone horribly wrong.

During a later statement, Shaw explained to Quincy Police Lieutenant Neil MacDonald that he was taking a leak in a nearby wooded area when he noticed what he described as a "little scuffle." The fight went down adjacent to the picnic tables. Specifically, it was taking place on a narrow strip of grass behind the chain-link backstop fencing. There was a small segment of concrete and the victim was sprawled out, bleeding excessively. His friend, Paul Melody, Shaw explained, seemed to be entangled in a violent altercation with an unknown assailant. "He was on the man's back, trying to take him down," was part of the description of the brief scrap between Melody and Racette's assailant.

Shaw rushed to his friend's aid just as the husky twenty-year-old dropped to his knees and fell backward near the edge of the backstop.

The attacker, meanwhile, was backing away. Damage done, he was withdrawing from the scene of his crime. Chasson turned away from the people who were gathering to render aid to his victim and strode toward the parking lot. He was seeking Bryan Fitzgerald and a ride out of Pageant Field. He did not discard the knife, gripping it in a threatening manner.

"Jesus Christ!" Vasconcellos shouted as he joined Shaw at Melody's side. "Fuck, there's blood everywhere!"

Vasconcellos scrutinized the victim, who was prone on his back and immobile. Vasco turned his palms upward and noticed to his horror that they were saturated red. He had been kneeling next to Melody, unaware that both of his hands were submerged in a deepening pool of his wounded friend's blood. It was difficult to determine in the darkness, but it appeared that Paul Melody had stopped breathing. His chest didn't seem to be moving. Vasconcellos by no means had any medical expertise, but he knew well enough that it was not likely that anyone, even someone as young and strong as Paul Melody, could survive very long after such substantial blood loss. Still, if there was a chance to save their friend's life, they had to move swiftly.

"We need to get him to a hospital!" he shouted. Shaw nodded in agreement.

At that moment, Vasconcellos recalled that Melody had driven a car to the park. Glancing over his shoulder, he spotted the vehicle in the distant lot, not far from where Fitzgerald's orange sports car was parked. Without further delay, he reached into Melody's pocket and found a set of bloodstained keys. Gripping the keys, he got to his feet and took off at a dead sprint.

In the meantime, Roger Gazzola joined Shaw at their friend's side. "Buzzy, anything I can do?" he offered, realizing they were wasted words as he sized up Melody.

"Vasco went to get Mel's car," Shaw informed.

"Guys, he stuck me too—"

The pair glanced toward the source of the comment and saw a man slowly emerging from the shadows. It was Bob "Hay" Hayward, who was from nearby Brockton, the sixth-largest city in Massachusetts, with just over a hundred thousand residents.

Hayward was a good-looking guy, of medium height and slightly heavyset. In better times, his friend Laurie Schottmiller, who was chatting with him just prior to the fracas, described him as "handsome and sweet as a teddy bear."

In obvious pain, Hayward shuffled closer to Shaw and Gazzola. As he drew near, they got a better look at him and were stunned at what they saw. Hayward was a ghastly sight, pale and ashen. He was hunched over, resembling a man far older than his twenty-seven years. He was guarding his flank and lower back.

"Jesus, Hay…" Gazzola uttered as he took stock of the new arrival. This was rapidly turning into a situation well beyond their capabilities. "What the f—"

He broke off when Hay grasped his blood-soaked shirt and slowly raised it, revealing a gaping wound on his lower back. It was several inches in length, deep, and still bleeding. Gazzola wasn't medically inclined, but he knew the kidneys occupied the lower back area. He wondered if Hayward had suffered damage to vital organs during the assault. A stream of fresh crimson blood trickled down the side of Hay's body as he twisted slightly, collecting at his waistline. Hayward lowered his shirt and applied steady pressure to the wound, using the material as a bandage of sorts.

Hay drew a strained breath with great difficulty and said in a near whisper, "Yeah, he stuck me too. I was helping Mel and he…" Hayward trailed off, unable to finish the comment. He was winded, as if he had just finished running a footrace.

He stood in silence, grasping his lower back and grimacing in pain. Blood oozed from between his fingers. In the low illumination at the edge of the field, his face began to turn a deeper shade of gray. It was obvious to his friends that Hayward had sustained a significant blood loss.

Gazzola, twenty-four, looked to Shaw as both men continued to kneel alongside the dying Paul Melody, who had celebrated his milestone twentieth birthday just three weeks earlier on August 3, 1977.

Words were not spoken but both were thinking the same thing: They came to Pageant Field that evening, a dozen or so long-time friends, to relax, drink a beer or three, and shoot the breeze. It was meant to be another in a series of mundane, forgettable summer nights in Quincy for this tight-knit group of twenty-somethings. But in a matter of minutes, all their lives had been irreversibly changed. Two of their friends had been stabbed in the chaos and while neither was confirmed dead, both could meet their end before daybreak.

Shaw rose to his feet and glanced toward the alcove and the tables. Something was happening. The savage attack by the unknown perpetrator, it seemed, was not over. "Rob Russell is in trouble," he announced. "He might need help."

Gazzola nodded but Shaw was already gone. While he understood the need to remain with Mel and Hay, Gazzola certainly wasn't comfortable being left alone with the two victims. There was little he could do to render aid; he felt helpless.

Hayward was still standing, in worsening pain. He remained silent. It was anybody's guess how serious his wounds were. From several feet away in the darkness, it did not seem that Hay's wounds were bad. There didn't seem to be as much blood, at least not as much as the volume draining from Melody's body. Gazzola thought he heard Mel gurgling, a sound you might expect from a drowning victim. It sent a chill up his spine. *This kid is far too young to die this way,* he thought. *Christ, Melody's dad is a Boston cop. How will he react when he receives word? He'll likely go berserk and hunt down his son's attacker like an animal.*

Gazzola looked desperately toward the distant parking lot. Across the thick, coastal air that wafted in from nearby ocean waters, he heard the muffled sound of a car roar to a start. Help for Paul Melody and Bob Hayward, thankfully, was minutes away.

# NINE—THE RETREAT

Near the edge of the baseball field, twenty-year-old Bobby Russell was rapidly making his way to join the others who were rendering aid to their friend Paul Melody when he unexpectedly crossed paths with a retreating Leroy Chasson. Russell stopped in his tracks. His breath caught in his throat and he broke out in a cold sweat. Backing up several paces, careful not to stumble, he glimpsed the blade. It was a sizable knife, as he later described to police officials. "It was big, like a hunting knife," he said during questioning.

"C'mon, punk!" Chasson urged, frenetically stabbing at the air between them with the blade. "You want some of this too?!"

Russell hadn't said or done anything to antagonize the aggressor. Like many of his friends under attack at Pageant Field, he began his night as an innocent bystander. He wanted no part of this madman, whose face was contorted in a threatening grimace.

"Take it easy, man—I got no beef with you," Russell said in a low, even tone, knowing his life could be at stake. In the distance, he could see others tending to a wounded man on the ground. This guy had already stabbed one person, perhaps more; he had nothing to lose in claiming another victim.

"You're nothin' but a bunch of fuckin' punks," Chasson hissed as he waved the knife side-to-side in a slashing motion. His brow was furrowed in rage and his eyes were squinted half-closed. His teeth were bared in a snarl like those of a cornered feral wildcat. "C'mon, I'll take you all on. I'll fuck up all of you! Gimme a reason!"

Not a moment too soon, Bryan Fitzgerald emerged from the shadows, distracting Chasson. There was an odd pause as the three parties weighed the evolving situation. Russell seized the opportunity and moved quickly to his right, maneuvering so that a picnic table was between himself and the slasher. Angered, Chasson lunged at his prey but the barrier proved effective, and Russell was able to shift from side to side, countering the assailant. If the situation had not been so dangerous, their moves could have been compared to a child's avoidance game, such as "Tag" or "Relievio." But Russell understood that this struggle was far from a game. If this psychopath managed to reach him, there could be more bloodshed.

Taking measures to diffuse the standoff, Fitzgerald put himself in harm's way. He positioned himself directly in the path of the raving lunatic, who continued to wield the deadly blade in a threatening manner. Bobby Russell thought it was a foolhardy decision to act as a human shield, but nonetheless, appreciated his friend risking his neck to protect him. If nothing else, he might have a chance to make a run for it while Rocky kept the attacker occupied.

When later questioned by the Quincy Police, Russell placed some of the blame on Fitzgerald for the hostilities. It was Bryan, after all, who drove this nutcase to the park. Therefore, some, if not all, of the culpability for the havoc should fall on his shoulders. If harm had come to Paul Melody and others, Fitzgerald should be held accountable. But the fault could be placed later. For now, it was all about survival and preventing further bloodshed.

"If you're going to cut anybody, you'd better cut me!" Fitzgerald shouted defiantly. As he spoke the words, it occurred to him that he hadn't put much thought into the irrational comment. To invite harm was suicidal, especially considering the assailant's obviously fragile state of mind. But both Fitzgerald and Russell, if not everyone taking part in the surreal scene at Pageant Field, were running on raw adrenaline. Nobody was thinking straight.

He considered charging at Chasson. At well over six feet tall, the physically powerful Fitzgerald would certainly hold the upper hand against Chasson, who was at least five or six inches shorter in stature.

"Most people loved him," later said Fitzgerald's sister Diane, who added that along with the nickname Rocky, he was also known to many as "Shane." "But at the same time, many others feared him because of his size."

Leroy Chasson slashed once more, this time at Fitzgerald, who recoiled. Russell couldn't be certain in the muted light, but it looked like the blade drew blood from his hand or fingers.

Brow furrowed in rage and snarling like a vicious junkyard dog, Chasson glared menacingly at Fitzgerald and shouted, "You're hanging around with a bunch of fuckin' punks!"

At that moment, Nathan Shaw, twenty-five, joined the fray, shouting, "Get away, you motherfucker, get away!" He had left Gazzola in charge of tending to Mel and Hay, figuring he could be of more use in the escalating confrontation near the picnic tables. Shaw stopped short of Chasson, however, when he spotted the knife.

Fitzgerald put aside thoughts of trying to overpower the attacker. Instead, he figured the best course of action would be to get the man out of the park.

"C'mon, Lee," Fitzgerald urged, glancing briefly at his sliced fingers. Small droplets of blood fell steadily to the crushed-stone surface beneath his feet. "We need to get the fuck out of here! Let's get to the car."

Chasson looked at Russell and then Shaw, contemplating his next step. He was outnumbered three-to-one, but he had the weapon. He glanced at Fitzgerald, scowled at his would-be adversaries, and began to withdraw. He briefly encountered Laurie Schottmiller, who was shielding herself from harm between a pair of parked cars. The attacker swore at her as he trotted alongside Fitzgerald toward the parking lot where the Fiat waited.

Reaching the car, Chasson grasped the passenger handle, pulled open the door, then paused. He glanced back at the scene unfolding in the space between the picnic structure and the baseball field. Just moments earlier, a group of friends was quietly enjoying the evening, chatting and drinking beer. And now, the typically pleasant park was strewn with mayhem and carnage.

Fitzgerald sensed that the man was reconsidering a continued assault but that just wasn't in the cards. Risking life and limb, he put his hands on Chasson's shoulders and forcefully guided him into the passenger seat. He braced, preparing for a knife penetrating his abdomen. Chasson was seated in the Fiat, and for a few treacherous seconds, Fitzgerald stood next to him, entirely exposed and vulnerable. He closed the door and drew a breath of relief.

Circling the little Fiat, Fitzgerald briefly considered making a run for it. A short distance to his left was a gravel roadway that he knew led to a small boathouse on the banks of Black's Creek. It was no more than a hundred yards from the parking lot. As children, he and his friends spent many warm summer days taking boating lessons, sailing along the winding creek. It was inky dark and he couldn't see the tree-lined road, but he knew it well. If he took off and Chasson pursued, Fitzgerald felt he could escape to safety even if it meant concealing himself in the thick strand of woods surrounding the park. He could remain there until help arrived. But to leave this madman behind—there would be nothing to prevent him from returning to the baseball field and inflicting additional trauma, nothing to prevent him from stabbing more innocent bystanders.

Fitzgerald opened the car door and slid into the driver's seat. Glimpsing at his gashed fingers, slightly dripping blood, he briefly considered pointing out the injury to the perpetrator but then thought better of it. He risked a quick glance at his maniacal passenger, wondering where he'd stashed the knife. He assumed Chasson still had it, concealed in some way, and there was nothing to stop him from using it again.

Firing the Fiat's throaty motor, he threw the shift and jabbed the accelerator. The powerful vehicle spewed dirt and stones as it gained traction. The dashboard clock glowed green in the middle of the gauge cluster. It was nearing eleven o'clock. Deep inside, Fitzgerald knew that by helping Chasson to escape the scene of the onslaught, the cops would probably charge him as an accessory. He'd likely land in jail. He felt certain he'd be linked to his passenger's crime in some manner. But he'd already made the commitment. There was no turning back now.

Perhaps the police would cut him some slack if he explained that throughout the night, he felt compelled to do as he was told. He wasn't a hostage but in hindsight, his life was certainly at stake. He hadn't known about the knife and he still didn't know the reasons behind Chasson's unprovoked attack on Racette that triggered the melee and the stabbings. But he had known that the man was dangerous by reputation alone. So, he did what he did—driving Chasson to and from Pageant Field—to save his own skin. He hoped the cops would take that into consideration.

Bryan Fitzgerald set aside the thought as he nosed the car onto the Southern Artery and Points North. He made a brief stop at his home and encountered his mother, but stayed only briefly. She was frightened at the sight of Chasson's bloodstained clothing. Soon, the pair was back on the road and crossing the Tobin Bridge. With the deranged Leroy Chasson at his side, Bryan Fitzgerald was heading back to Chelsea.

# TEN—HOSPITAL TRIP

Albert Vasconcellos wheeled Paul Melody's car toward the sweeping baseball field, coming to a hard stop adjacent to his friends, who were standing over Melody behind the backstop. The victim of the attack was prone and silent on the concrete slab. Viewed in the headlights of the vehicle, it seemed as if the hemorrhaging had slowed. But that wasn't an encouraging sign. It just meant his friend had bled out.

It wasn't lost on Vasconcellos that Mel lay dying merely a few feet from the popular field where, ten brief years earlier, they played baseball—batting, throwing, running, and sliding to their heart's content. Just a bunch of fun-loving kids in their grass-stained uniforms with their entire lives ahead of them.

The tires bit deeply into the dirt and soft gravel surface. Exhaust belched from the tailpipe, filling the warm, humid air with noxious fumes. He left the vehicle running, emerged, and quickly circled, opening all four doors as he passed to ready it for passengers.

His mind racing, Vasconcellos rushed to join Roger Gazzola at Melody's side and noticed the stabbing victim looked far worse than when he left to get the car only a minute or two before. Mel was pale and unmoving. Vasconcellos was afraid they were too late. The situation was grave.

Vasconcellos was acutely aware that an ambulance would have been a far more desirable method of transporting their friend to the hospital. But the available payphones were some distance away and there just wasn't time. They had no means to call for help. It would have been a perfect time for a Quincy Police squad car to make a pass. While the cops seldom bothered the kids hanging out in the park, they routinely included the Mount in their patrols. But there was no phone. There were no police. The car was the only method to get Melody the help he needed.

"C'mon," he urged. "We gotta get him in the car!"

In the background, in the picnic alcove, Vasco heard several strained voices. Across the span, he couldn't make out what was being said but it was obviously a tense exchange between his friends and the knife-wielding attacker. If this lunatic remained in the mix, none of them would be safe.

"What gives?" he asked Gazzola as he positioned himself at Melody's head and reached under his shoulders. His instinctively recoiled as his fingertips met the widening pool of blood that had accumulated beneath his friend. It was already starting to congeal. He shook off the aversion and gripped at the clothing.

"It's Robbie Russell and Fitzgerald," was his reply as he noticed the escalating standoff near the cluster of picnic tables. "I think they're arguing with the asshole who stuck Mel."

Vasconcellos visually inspected Hayward, who remained standing motionless, observing their effort.

"And Hay," added Gazzola as he shifted to Melody's feet and encircled his arms around both lower legs.

Lifting Paul was a task easier planned than done. He was a big, burly kid, easily topping two hundred pounds. They could certainly use more help. Vasconcellos glanced at Hayward, who was gingerly shuffling toward the waiting car; he certainly wasn't an option. The strain of lifting their strapping friend might worsen his knife wounds and trigger more bleeding. Thankfully, Racette and Marnell joined them, offering much-needed lifting help.

The youths half-lifted, half-dragged Paul Melody the short distance to the car and hoisted him into the back seat. A trail of blood followed. Gazzola then climbed in with his friend, positioned himself awkwardly in the cramped space, and pulled the rear door closed. Hayward, meanwhile, carefully climbed into the front passenger seat while Vasconcellos settled in behind the wheel and threw the shift lever into drive. He jabbed the gas pedal and the vehicle lurched forward.

The foursome sped to Quincy City Hospital, which was thankfully less than a couple of miles away. Vasconcellos skillfully maneuvered Melody's car along the winding Furnace Brook Parkway at a speed twice the posted limit. It was an undulating roadway linking the Quincy Shore area with Blue Hills and was known for numerous collisions at reduced speeds. But there was no other choice. Time, he knew, was rapidly slipping away for his friend—perhaps two of his buddies. He risked a look at Hayward, who was staring vacantly at the road ahead. His eyes were hollow. He was pale gray and grimaced each time they rounded a bend in the road or rumbled over a pothole.

"How're ya doing, Hay?" Vasconcellos asked.

"I just need a coupla stitches," Hayward replied, wincing in pain.

As he spoke, his words were garbled. He had not been drinking, at least not as much as some of the kids who were hanging out at Pageant Field. He was obviously delirious from the pain of the knife lacerations or blood loss or a combination of both. While his injuries did not seem as catastrophic as those sustained by Paul Melody, Vasconcellos gauged that his friend Hayward was in trouble. He took a deep breath and pressed harder on the accelerator pedal.

Reaching Adams Street, he guided Melody's vehicle into a sharp right turn and then a hard left onto Whitwell Street. Climbing the final hill, Quincy City Hospital was thankfully just ahead.

He angled the car through the entrance and turned toward the driveway adjacent to a brightly lit sign with red lettering that read "**Emergency**." He jolted the car to a hard stop at the apron adjacent to the sign. A wave of relief swept over him. There were people here who could provide the aid his friends so desperately needed.

"I'll be back with help," Vasconcellos announced to his companions as he burst from the car and dashed toward the emergency room entrance.

He was met by a uniformed security guard who gruffly shouted, "Hey, buddy, you can't park your car there!"

"I have two guys—they've been stabbed!" Vasco announced breathlessly.

Wordlessly, the guard turned and hurried toward the glass doors, which automatically parted as he neared. Vasconcellos followed him into the emergency department. A nurse and an orderly were passing the time chatting with a receptionist. It was a quiet night in the Quincy ER, or at least it had been a quiet night. Suddenly, bedlam enveloped the department as the Pageant Field wounded arrived. The staff turned to look as the security guard and a young man covered in blood rapidly approached them.

"Oh dear, where are you hurt?" the nurse asked, assuming it was Vasconcellos who needed help. He certainly looked the part. "There's blood everywh—"

"It's not me," Vasconcellos interrupted. "It's my friends. In the car. They've been stabbed!" He gestured toward the vehicle just outside the doors, still running.

Both the nurse and the orderly sprang into action, grabbing a gurney parked along the corridor wall. The receptionist, meanwhile, picked up the phone and made an announcement that reverberated from loudspeakers mounted in the ceilings throughout the hospital.

"Code Blue. Emergency room!" her voice clamored. "Code Blue!"

A Code Blue is typically reserved for patients in full cardiac arrest, serious trauma, and others requiring advanced resuscitation efforts. Within a matter of minutes, scores of medical personnel flooded the ER, streaming in through a number of entrances. All had immediately stopped what they were doing at the time and responded. Doctors, nurses, and support staff arrived and began to prepare the trauma room. When word reached the staff that there were two stabbing victims inbound, several rushed to ready a second chamber.

Vasconcellos, standing alongside the chest-high reception counter, watched helplessly as his friends were wheeled into the emergency room, one after another. He lowered his gaze and shook his head in anguish. The first stretcher to roll by held the limp body of Paul Melody. Beneath the fluorescent lighting, he looked even worse than he had in the dimness of the Pageant Field baseball complex. His skin was blue-gray and there were no signs of life. There was blood everywhere. Vasconcellos again shook his head in disbelief. Minutes earlier, this unassuming but friendly twenty-year-old was enjoying the company of a few friends and a beer or two. He was a good guy who worked hard and kept his nose clean. Paul had his whole life ahead of him, full of possibilities. But the decision to render aid to a friend in trouble likely cost him that life. As the medical staff pushed past with the next gurney, this one loaded with Hayward—who was thankfully still conscious—the ER receptionist spoke up.

"Excuse me, sir…"

"Vasconcellos," he answered without being asked. He turned to look in her direction and added, "Albert."

"Thank you, Mr. Vasconcellos," she said, smiling politely as she attached a document to a wooden clipboard and readied a pen. "Would you be able to provide me with some additional information about the vict— I mean, the two gentlemen? Your friends?"

He nodded and pivoted toward her as several grim-faced Quincy police officers entered and made their way toward the trauma rooms, their polished combat boots thumping loudly on the tiled floor. The receptionist's questions would prove to be of little difficulty for Vasconcellos compared with the police interviews that would soon follow.

# ELEVEN—POLICE RESPOND

Assigned to the standby detail at the Wollaston Center police callbox, Quincy Officers Thomas Frane and William Falco were gearing up for the end of their evening shift. It was nearing midnight. In another fifteen or so minutes, the duo would pull up stakes and make their way to headquarters on Sea Street to store their equipment and punch the clock. It had been a tedious Tuesday night, which was, thankfully, almost over.

Their light conversation was abruptly interrupted when a motorcyclist hastily pulled over to the curb, nearly losing control of his bike as he came to a stop. Frane noted the rider seemed to be in some form of distress. The youth aboard the bike killed the rumbling engine, violently deployed the kickstand, and stumbled slightly as he dismounted. Removing his helmet, he approached the two veteran cops, both now on full alert.

"My friends need help!" the motorcyclist pleaded. "Please hurry!"

"Take it easy, son," Frane calmly instructed. "What happened to your friends?"

"They've been stabbed!" shouted the animated young man, his face flushed bright red. "My two friends have been stabbed at the Mount!"

In his later report, Officer Frane wrote:

THE PARTY IDENTIFIED HIMSELF AS WILLIAM CORBIN, AGE 21, OF 201 BEACH STREET IN WOLLASTON. WE INSTRUCTED HIM TO WAIT AT WOLLASTON CENTER AND WE WOULD GO HELP AND THEN RETURN. WE NOTIFIED THE STATION OF THE REPORTED INCIDENT AND TO START AN AMBULANCE. UPON ARRIVAL AT THE FIELD, A GROUP OF YOUNGSTERS WAS STANDING AROUND AND THEY TOLD US THE VICTIMS WERE ALREADY TAKEN TO THE HOSPITAL.

Frane and Falco reached Pageant Field to find a full contingent of police already in place, seeking evidence and canvassing potential witnesses.

The two officers returned to their squad car and drove back to Wollaston Center. When they arrived, an anxious Corbin, who was a short young man possessing a head of closely cropped dark curly hair, was nervously pacing back-and-forth along the sidewalk in front of the callbox. Attached to the utility pole, the blue light indicating the callbox location cast an eerie glow on his troubled face. Despite his distraught state of mind, Corbin had complied with the orders from the police officers. He had resisted the urge to climb on his bike and rush back to Pageant Field.

"It was an orange sports car," Corbin blurted before being asked by the two officers. "My friends were drinking at the Field when two guys drove up in an orange sports car. They had the top down!"

"Slow down and tell me the whole story," Frane prompted, noting that Corbin was rambling. He was speaking quickly and was all over the place. "Did you know the guys in the orange car?"

Corbin drew a deep breath. His forehead was glistening with sweat. He wiped it away with the back of a sleeve. "Yes, I know the driver. Fitzgerald. I think the other guy was from Chelsea."

"Did you know him—this guy from Chelsea?"

"No, but it was so stupid! He just stabbed my two friends for nothing!"

"So, do you know this Fitzgerald, the driver of the orange car?"

"Yeah, and I can show you where he lives."

"All right then," said Frane. "Let's take a ride."

From the rear seat of the patrol car, Corbin directed the officers to 267 Wilson Avenue, which was just over a mile from Wollaston Center. When they pulled up to the residence, Corbin excitedly announced from the rear seat, "Stop, this is the house!"

They found the small but tidy Cape-style house to be well lit. The suspect sports car, however, was not parked in the driveway and didn't seem to be anywhere in the vicinity.

"Are you sure this is the house?" Falco asked their rider, wondering if they were wasting their time with this kid.

"Yeah," Corbin insisted, nodding frantically. "I've been here many times. This is where he lives."

"Stay in the car," Frane ordered as he and Falco climbed out and made their way toward the house. Darkness enveloped the neighborhood. A distant streetlight cast long shadows across vacant sidewalks and lawns. Both officers instinctively palmed the butts of their holstered service revolvers. While the orange car was not readily visible, it did not necessarily mean that Fitzgerald and the perpetrator had not stashed it out of sight and were inside the home, waiting in ambush.

The door opened as the officers approached. A yellowish interior glow spilled through the opening. Framed in the doorway was a middle-aged woman who reached to flip a nearby switch, bathing the yard with light from a porch fixture. She was wearing a nondescript robe that had seen better days. Her expression, the officers noted as their eyes adjusted, was one of deep concern. She looked tired and drawn. It was near midnight and a police visit could only spell trouble.

"Can I help you, gentlemen?" she asked politely, her voice trembling with the strain. Her arms were folded guardedly across her chest.

"Evening, ma'am," greeted Frane, removing his eight-point cap in respect. "Sorry to call at this late hour. We're looking for the Fitzgerald residence."

"I'm Theresa Fitzgerald," she acknowledged in a faint voice that was barely audible.

"I'm Officer Frane with the Quincy Police and this is my partner, Officer Falco." Falco nodded to the woman in greeting. "We're investigating a stabbing that took place at Pageant Field a short time ago." Mrs. Fitzgerald said nothing, remaining silent. When she failed to respond, Frane asked, "Do you know the whereabouts of your son, Bryan?"

"Haven't seen him since supper time," she replied nonchalantly. There was something in her tone that indicated she wasn't being truthful. There was also an air of defiance about her.

"Does Bryan drive an orange sports car?"

"He has an orange Fiat convertible," she confirmed flatly with little outward emotion. Most mothers would have been rattled by a late-night visit from the police and the prospect that her son might be implicated in a crime. But Mrs. Fitzgerald maintained a stiff, indifferent posture. Frane found it odd that she failed to ask about her son Bryan and what, if anything, he had to do with a stabbing. He sensed that she already knew and was being evasive.

"Would you know the registration number?" Frane asked.

"No," she replied, "but it has a new green license plate."

"All right, Mrs. Fitzgerald," said the officer. "Thank you for your assistance. We'll be in touch if we have any more questions."

As it turned out, the police did have further questions for Bryan's mother, who had been less than truthful about what she knew. In an obvious but ineffective attempt to protect her son, she had tried to be deceptive during the officers' visit and earlier questioning.

Frane and Falco later returned to persuade the woman to share what she knew. It didn't take long for her to relent, especially after the officers let her know one of the stabbing victims, Paul Melody, had succumbed to his wounds.

She revealed that her boy had, in fact, stopped by the house. "He was here," she said, lowering her gaze in shame for her earlier falsehood. "There was a guy with him. His shirt was covered in blood. Bryan had blood on him too—from a cut on his hand. I was hysterical."

"Did his companion have anything to say?" Falco asked.

"This guy was pretty upset when he saw me," she replied. "From what I understand, he thought Bryan lived here alone. I guess he just wanted to wash up."

"What did your son say?"

"He was trying to calm me down," Mrs. Fitzgerald recalled. "I kept asking him what the hell is going on, saying it repeatedly. My Bryan kept saying that he was in a fight and not to worry. He washed his hands in the kitchen sink. The guy with him just stood in the kitchen and didn't say a word. He wouldn't even look at me. They only stayed for a few minutes."

"Did they say where they were going?"

"No," she answered. "They got in the car and were gone."

\*\*\*

Quincy Police Sergeant James Buhl arrived at Pageant Field in Merrymount Park at 11:36 p.m. on August 23 to find scores of colleagues had reached the scene ahead of him. The parking lot, adjacent to the baseball field, was jammed with patrol cars, each with its rooftop beacons flashing intermittently. The lot and the surrounding fields, as well as the grim faces of the police officials and a number of curious onlookers, were bathed in the harsh blue light.

Buhl, a native of South Boston and a veteran of the US Air Force, had punched in for his graveyard shift thirty minutes earlier and made his way to a Texaco fueling station on the Southern Artery, a short distance from Quincy Police headquarters. He was topping off his assigned patrol car when the portable radio squawked, "Quincy Control to Sergeant Buhl." It was the familiar female voice of the midnight dispatcher.

Squeezing the last bit of gas to round off the amount at the pump, he returned the nozzle and reached for his two-way holstered on his gun belt. Triggering the microphone, he responded, "Buhl answering."

"Sergeant Buhl," began the dispatcher, her voice professional but pleasant, "would you respond to Pageant Field and assist with a report of a party stabbed near the baseball field?"

"Roger, on the way," the thirteen-year veteran of the force acknowledged.

He realized that instead of a quiet Tuesday night, he might be in for a long shift after all. *A stabbing call right off the bat*, he thought. His heart pounding from the rush of a true emergency, Buhl climbed into the cruiser, flipped the toggle for the blue lights, and pulled out of the filling station, heading north along the Southern Artery. It was a brief trip, less than a mile. Driving past the Mount Wollaston Cemetery, the entrance to the sprawling Merrymount Park complex soon appeared on his right. Buhl guided the patrol car into the familiar facility and followed the access road toward Pageant Field. He wedged his car between two others.

Emerging from the vehicle, Buhl noticed his associates had already established a perimeter with a bright yellow marking tape, which was wrapped around nearby trees in a large triangular pattern. One end of the tape—labeled

"POLICE LINE: DO NOT CROSS"—was tied off to the backstop and the other attached to a jutting tree branch. A pair of plainclothes Quincy detectives, along with scores of uniformed officers, had reached the expansive recreation complex moments before and immediately set to work protecting the grisly crime scene. It was essential that the site not be disturbed or contaminated.

Buhl was greeted by several officers as he circled the periphery. He began to make mental notes, which he would call upon later when he documented his observations in writing. In his report, Buhl wrote, "I observed a large pool of blood about twenty feet from the backstop of the ball field."

On the adjacent baseball field, a contingent of police officers was methodically marching across the dew-covered grass, shoulder to shoulder, in a grid pattern. Their flashlights were trained on the ground. The hunt for evidence was a painstaking task, particularly in the near-midnight darkness. Thankfully, the weather was cooperating with their search. It was mild with a light breeze wafting from the nearby Atlantic but there was no threat of rain to eradicate traces of wrongdoing. The collection of evidence, spearheaded by the Massachusetts State Police, could progress without the hindrance of inclement weather.

Standing just outside the yellow-taped boundary, watching the police activity, was an individual Buhl recognized as Kevin Racette. In recent years, the tall, strapping youth with a thick head of blond hair had been in trouble with the law—mostly drug charges—and was well-known to the Quincy Police.

As the sergeant approached, he noticed Racette's clothing was bloodstained in the flashing blue light.

"Kevin, I'm Sergeant Buhl."

Racette nodded wordlessly, realizing he did not need to identify himself; the officer obviously knew him.

"Where did all the blood come from?" Buhl asked, gently tapping the end of his flashlight on the front of the youth's shirt.

"Melody," Racette replied, his face dour. "After he was stabbed, they got hold of his keys and took him in his own car. To the Quincy City."

"Did you witness the attack?"

"Yeah," answered a sullen Racette. "A guy approached me and asked if I could get him three bags in a hurry. Meaning he was looking for three bags of heroin."

Buhl nodded. He had been on the streets long enough to grasp the lingo. He was no stranger to the drug problem in Quincy, much like other cities of comparable size and scope. And Racette, he understood, had been arrested a time or two and did a stretch for distribution, so this part of his story added up.

"And what did you say to him?" the sergeant asked, noticing that even in the low light, the swelling on Racette's face was obvious.

"The truth," Racette replied adamantly. "I told him I wasn't into that stuff anymore."

"Did you know who he was?"

Racette lied, stating, "He looked familiar, but I couldn't place him."

"Go on."

"He insisted I knew who he was."

"Where did he say you knew him from?"

"The joint."

"Concord?"

Racette nodded. "I asked if I knew him. He said, 'Yeah, I'm Lee from Concord.' I'd been drinking all day since the afternoon, just beer. But I was sober enough to know this guy was trouble. And suddenly, he sucker punched me. I went down hard. I don't recall but I think I hit my head pretty hard. I was seeing stars. And then I noticed a scuffle about fifteen feet away and saw Paul Melody fall to the ground."

As Racette was outlining what took place, a pair of young men emerged from the shadows of the park and joined them, identifying themselves as Joey Marnell and Bobby Russell. Both professed that they too had witnessed the attack on Racette and Melody. They added that another man—Robert Hayward—was stabbed during the brief melee.

"I think I know who the guy was," hesitantly offered Marnell, who explained that the perpetrator had approached him first, mistakenly believing he was Racette before moving on. "His name is Leroy."

Buhl realized that the field questioning of these youths was vital to the investigation and should be captured while events were still fresh in their minds. It was important that their comments were permanently recorded for a future trial. He knew detectives would need to collect this testimony on tape in formal interviews.

"All right, gentlemen," he said to the trio, "I'm going to give you a ride to police headquarters. The detectives will want to speak with each of you."

Buhl guided the youths to his patrol car and asked all three to slide into the rear seat. Nothing further was said during the brief drive to the Sea Street Police Station.

While Buhl was completing his report in a small office adjacent to the front lobby, the desk sergeant rounded the corner. It was after midnight. "Jim, got a phone call for you," he said.

"Sure, I'll take it in here." Buhl pressed the blinking extension, lifted the receiver, and said, "Sergeant Buhl, can I help you?"

"I think I can help you," stammered the excitable voice on the other end. "This is Jimmy Dobson."

Buhl knew Dobson. From neighboring Dorchester, he was the twenty-three-year-old doorman—sometimes bouncer—at the Beachcomber, a popular Quincy drinking and dancing nightspot located at 797 Quincy Shore Drive.

Established in 1959 by Jimmy McGettrick, the Beachcomber played host to up-and-coming music stars Johnny Matthis, Tony Bennett, Louis Armstrong, comedian Jay Leno, and countless others. According to *Patriot Ledger* reporter Joe DiFazio, who wrote a historical piece decades later, many of these marquee acts made a stop at the Quincy landmark after appearances in Boston. Scores of Quincy youths met their future wives and husbands during the club's heyday in the seventies and eighties. The Beachcomber later met with a wrecking ball in 2021.

"Sure, Jimmy, what do you have?"

"So, I saw Bryan Fitzgerald at the Beachcomber tonight at around ten o'clock," Dobson shared. "He was with a guy about six foot tall, one hundred and sixty-five pounds, blondish-brown hair, and wearing a shiny blue silk shirt. He had one of those handlebar mustaches."

The sergeant did not doubt the accuracy of Dobson's description. It was, after all, part of his job to recognize potential troublemakers and possess the ability to remember what club goers looked like. He had been instrumental during a number of past police investigations.

"Very helpful, Jimmy," said an appreciative Buhl, who was jotting notes that he would later add to his report. "Anything else?"

"Yeah, they took off in an orange Fiat Spider just a few minutes after they arrived," the door attendant recalled. "That's not a car I would forget."

"Thanks again, Jimmy."

"One last thing, Sergeant Buhl."

"Sure, go ahead."

"If you need it, I can identify the guy who was with Fitzgerald."

# TWELVE—CHELSEA REVISITED

The engine of the Fiat strained as it sped along Interstate 93, heading north. It had only taken several minutes to travel the distance from Quincy to Dorchester. Traffic was light on the three-lane highway, better known to locals as the Southeast Expressway. Those same folks would quickly point out that there was little "express" to this roadway, particularly during Boston's nightmarish rush hours. But the midweek morning commute was hours away and the roadway was clear.

Boston loomed ahead, and ten minutes further, after a pass through the Central Artery tunnel and over the monolithic Tobin Bridge, the limits of gritty Chelsea came into view near the terminating end of the mile-long span that carried vehicles over the Mystic River.

Fitzgerald, cognizant that he was speeding and risking a traffic stop, slightly eased off the pedal. Then again, he reconsidered—getting pulled over by the police would solve his dilemma. If ever he needed a cop, this was the moment. While the officer was checking for outstanding warrants, he envisioned covertly getting a message to him that the ruffian sitting in the passenger seat, calmly drawing on a cigarette, had just stabbed a number of people in Quincy. There had to be some form of broadcast sent out over the police radio by now. If that was the case, Fitzgerald might be off the hook. He imagined as the police handcuffed Leroy Chasson and carted him off to jail, he could point an accusatory finger and claim that the perpetrator had ordered him to drive to Quincy and then back to Chelsea under the threat of bodily harm.

He glanced at the reprehensible ride-along, who quietly observed the passing Dorchester scenery, made up mostly of row after row of triple-decker apartments. Fitzgerald noticed that Chasson's clothing was stained with blood. He had stabbed at least one person, perhaps more. His future was bleak. He was likely facing a trip back to prison. And yet, as Fitzgerald looked on, he noticed the man was grinning. Smiling, actually. It was a sickening sight and made his stomach churn. Chasson had a knack for bringing on bouts of nauseous anxiety.

Fitzgerald hazarded a comment, not sure of the ramifications. He envisioned what a knife to the abdomen would feel like, but pressed ahead, nonetheless. "Why the fuck did you do that?"

"Do what?"

"Stab those people? Why?"

Chasson's grin widened as he replied. "I *loved* it!" he declared, with emphasis on the word *loved*.

Fitzgerald did not clearly hear the comment amid the roar of the sports car's powerful engine. Or maybe he did hear what Chasson said and did not want to acknowledge it. This guy was clearly mentally unhinged. He had gone berserk at Pageant Field and hurt—perhaps killed—a number of people. The best place for him was behind bars or locked up in an asylum.

"I *loved* it," the offender repeated a little louder. With a venomous smirk and misguided pride, he added with a revolting nod of his head, "I got him good!"

At that moment, Fitzgerald wished he had the means to remove Chasson from the car, preferably as it sped along at sixty miles per hour. He wanted nothing more than to see this smirking lunatic in the rearview mirror, skinned alive on the unforgiving asphalt. Despite his rage, however, Fitzgerald contained himself. He had not seen Chasson dispose of the knife. It could still be concealed on his person. The man had nothing to lose by adding another victim, so Fitzgerald proceeded with caution.

"You loved it?"

"It's a debt I had to settle."

"What kind of debt?" Fitzgerald asked, wondering how an amount of money owed, no matter the circumstance, could drive someone to such an explosive attack. He couldn't wrap his head around it.

Raising his voice to be heard over the din inside the convertible, Chasson said, "Your guy, Racette, ripped off my friend."

"You stabbed people over a debt?"

"Yeah, fifty bucks."

"Fifty bucks, for Christ's sake!"

"It's a debt I had to settle, for Mark Bray. He's a friend from jail. I did it as a gift for him. He'll be happy to hear about it."

"If you wanted to take on Racette, you shoulda just took him somewhere and broke his jaw or something," said an exasperated Fitzgerald. "You didn't have to go around stabbing people."

The conversation paused for a moment before Chasson proudly declared, "I'm sure you've heard I was locked up." He treated his incarceration as if it were a badge of honor.

"Yeah, I heard." The more his passenger spoke, the more Fitzgerald understood this was one sick individual. He really didn't want to hear about the man's criminal exploits or his prison experiences. He understood that eventually, he would face questioning from the cops. The less he knew about this animal, the better off he would be under scrutiny.

"I killed a couple guys while I was in the joint," the remorseless slasher declared with a dispassionate shrug. "In Walpole."

Fitzgerald had no reason to doubt his passenger's claims. Chasson's tendency for violent outbursts had become obvious earlier when he indiscriminately spilled the blood of strangers. Human life, it seemed, was disposable in this guy's twisted mind.

The conversation ended as abruptly as it began. Under the circumstances, Fitzgerald thought it would be best to withhold further talk for the remainder of the trip back to Chelsea. He could only guess at Chasson's state of mind and what might trigger more hostilities.

Briefly taking his eyes off the roadway ahead, Fitzgerald examined his lacerated finger under the soft green glow of the Fiat's instrument panel. The bleeding had thankfully stopped but was replaced with a throbbing ache. He would likely need a few stitches. He wasn't about to complain, however, as a vision of his friend Paul Melody crept into his mind. The minor wound to his hand paled in comparison. He wondered if Mel had survived. He had hoped to reach the others rendering aid to their fallen friend and lend a hand, but he was compelled to intercept Chasson to do what he could to protect a defenseless Bob Russell.

As he navigated the Fiat along the Expressway, the familiar Boston skyline rose on the horizon ahead. Despite the late hour—nearing midnight—many of the lights in the office high-rises twinkled brightly against a dark backdrop. To his left, the Prudential Tower climbed fifty stories. Several blocks east in Copley Square, the Hancock Tower, New England's tallest, stood at sixty.

Bryan was so anxious to reach Chelsea and separate himself from Chasson that he hadn't given much thought to the people at the party. It was certainly risky bringing him back to the house on Warren Avenue. He was obviously capable of anything. He had already proven that on the baseball diamond in Quincy. What if he had a beef with someone at the party? He certainly had nothing to lose.

Fitzgerald assumed his girlfriend Jeanette Flanagan was still there and was probably worried sick. Or she was pissed off, wondering why her boyfriend had taken her car and more or less abandoned her. He had left the house party hours earlier to make what was supposed to be a quick beer run to Martignetti's package store. He vaguely recalled telling her he would be back in just a few minutes as he left with a virtual stranger. That was reason enough for her to worry. Fitzgerald was certain that by now, she had heard the party gossip.

A known criminal? An ex-con? A killer?

Fitzgerald wondered if word from Pageant Field had somehow reached the party. There were payphones within range of the sprawling facility but would anyone have thought to make the call? It was likely they were all heading for Quincy City Hospital with Paul and any others who were hurt during Chasson's rampage. It was also a certainty that the Quincy Police had been summoned and were canvassing the park and speaking with witnesses.

In that respect, Fitzgerald knew he would soon face intense police scrutiny. He'd been down that road before, under the hot lights of a police interrogation, although his troubles in the past were petty in comparison. Drug and alcohol charges. Fitzgerald had never played a role in a major crime.

Among other pointed questions, the Quincy Police would certainly want to know why he drove the attacker to safety. Why did he provide aid to the man who harmed his friends? It would be easy enough to explain the motives behind driving the ex-convict to Quincy. Fitzgerald felt threatened and feared for his well-being. But to drive this madman back to Chelsea after the knife attack could make him an accessory to the crime, at least in the eyes of the police.

Before long, the duo reached the home on Walnut Street where they'd begun their lethal journey hours earlier. As he climbed out of the Fiat, Fitzgerald paused briefly, allowing Chasson to scramble up the stairs ahead of him. He certainly did not want this man behind him, particularly if he still had the murder weapon.

Upon entering the house, Chasson stopped in the foyer and began to unbutton his blood-soaked shirt. Fitzgerald gave him a sideways glance and walked ahead. He noted the party was muted. There was no background music, and people were talking in strained voices as if they were attending a wake or a funeral. He could hear murmuring coming from the kitchen and made his way in that direction. It was obvious that word of the fight at Pageant Field had somehow reached the gathering.

Fitzgerald sought out his girlfriend. Finding Jeanne in the kitchen amongst a small group of mutual friends, he wrapped his powerful arms around her in an embrace. Out of the corner of his eye, he spotted Mark Bray standing alone in the shadows of the spacious kitchen. At six-foot-six, Fitzgerald towered over Chasson's sidekick, who stood barely five-nine. Bray, who was a Quincy native and familiar with Fitzgerald, cast a wary glance but quickly averted his eyes. The expression on his face was one of guilt, as if he were aware that the terrible events that had transpired earlier in Quincy were partly his fault. If he hadn't asked his lunatic friend to collect a debt—fifty bucks, no less—Paul Melody would not have sustained a stab wound.

Jeanne clutched Fitzgerald's arm. She wanted to talk, to ask questions, but he broke away and made his way to a phone mounted on the kitchen wall. With his girlfriend at his side, he dialed his mother's number. Obviously expecting his call, she answered on the first ring. The conversation was brief. He let her do the talking but assured her that he was fine and in a safe place, back in Chelsea with Jeanne. His mother explained that the Quincy Police had stopped by the house and were seeking him. She also confirmed his worst fears: the police were now investigating a murder; Paul Melody was dead.

Fitzgerald glared at Mark Bray. The look on his face said it all. It was obvious to Fitzgerald that Bray was aware that Melody had not survived the stabbing at Pageant Field. How he learned didn't matter. Chasson would soon find out as well.

"What is it?" Jeanne asked as he said his goodbyes to his mother and returned the phone to the cradle.

"He's dead," he answered, getting a little choked up.

"Who? What are you talking about?"

Just then, a shirtless Leroy Chasson rounded the corner and came into view. The room went entirely silent. He appeared to enjoy the command he held over the gathering. A sinister smirk appeared on his face. He seemed immensely proud that he could trigger such a reaction.

"Hey, Mark," Chasson said, gesturing with a tilt of his head for his twenty-one-year-old collaborator to join him. "C'mon, I need to soak my shirt."

Fitzgerald glanced at Chasson's shirt and, in the bright interior light, again noticed a patchwork of large blood stains on it. He had seen it while driving but now, beneath the kitchen lights, it was terribly obvious. The bare-chested Chasson had rolled the offending clothing into a ball, but he wasn't able to fully conceal the dried patches of blood from the spectators, who observed him guardedly.

Bryan Fitzgerald felt another wave of nausea take hold. *That's Paul Melody's blood*, he thought with revulsion. He fought off an urge to drive his fist into Leroy Chasson's remorseless face.

Following Chasson into the hallway, Bray lowered his gaze as he strode by observers in the kitchen. All eyes stared, silently shaming him. Nonetheless, he obeyed and dutifully followed. Both men made their way along the narrow hallway connecting the kitchen with the distant living room. There was a bathroom midway. Fitzgerald watched the two men, the killer and his accomplice, enter the room and close the door behind them.

"What happened to you?" Jeanne asked. He was thankful. Her question briefly relieved his tortured mind from the vision of Paul Melody lying prone on a cement slab.

Her expression was part-concern, part-anger for her boyfriend's unexplained absence. He had left for what was supposed to be a quick beer run but had been gone for hours. "I was worried sick. What happened at the park?"

"He stabbed a bunch of kids in Quincy," Fitzgerald blurted, pointing toward the closed bathroom door. Hearing the comment, a curious audience drew closer. They had heard the rumors and hearsay, but Fitzgerald was now sharing a chilling eyewitness account. "He killed Mel."

"Who? Who killed Paul Melody?" she asked, tears streaming down her cheeks. "Why?"

"The guy who just went in the bathroom with his buddy," he answered, nodding toward the now-closed bathroom door. Muffled voices could be heard, along with running water. Fitzgerald's stomach was twisted in knots. He thought he might vomit and swallowed hard to fight it off. He regretted the beers he had downed earlier in the evening before the fateful drive to Quincy. He again relived the vision of Melody, flat on his back, his life's blood pouring from his body. Only twenty years old and now dead.

"Bryan?" Jeanne urged.

He snapped out of his thoughts and continued. "Chasson is his name. Lee Chasson. Leroy, actually, but he gets pissed if you call him that."

One of the kids listening to the tale chimed in and uttered, "I've heard of that guy. He's bad news."

"His name is Leroy—Lee Chasson," Fitzgerald repeated, his expression as if he had tasted something sour. "He's in there washing the blood off his fucking shirt."

Jeanne's face was ashen. Her night, which was supposed to be a pleasant celebration among friends prior to her departure for school in Texas, had turned decidedly dark. Her boyfriend, from what she could gather, had driven a maniac to Quincy—in her car, no less—which led to a murder.

Fitzgerald again examined his lacerated fingers. The bleeding had long since stopped but the wound was obvious and deeper than he had first thought.

Jeanne followed his gaze. "Did he stab you?" she asked fearfully.

He shook his head and said, "Not really. Just a small cut while I was trying to break up the fight."

"Why did you bring him back to Chelsea?"

"I had no choice," he replied with a remorseful shake of his head. "He might have killed me if he thought I was going to leave him behind. Besides, it was up to me to get him out of there before he hurt anyone else. The only choice was to get him in the car and drive. What else could I do…" he trailed off as Chasson emerged from the bathroom with Mark Bray in tow.

Another man, Donald Bains, appeared and joined the duo. Chasson unfurled his shirt from the towel and slipped his arms through the sleeves, still dripping wet. He glared at Fitzgerald and seemed poised to make a comment. Instead, he just shook his head in disgust and strode for the front door. As Leroy Chasson stepped outside, Bray and Bains followed like a pair of obedient puppies.

# THIRTEEN—SOMERVILLE DETOUR

With his friends Mark Bray and Donald Bains trailing closely behind, Leroy Chasson hurried out of the Chelsea home where the send-off party for Bryan Fitzgerald and Jeannette Flanagan was rapidly winding down. After the partygoers learned of the stabbings in Quincy, there was little motivation to fraternize.

The three men made their way to a car that Bains had stolen earlier that evening in Quincy. He had helped himself to a 1969 Chevrolet Bel Air, which was good thinking on his part, according to what his accomplices said when they first saw it. They agreed it was not a car that would draw attention. Bains attached a set of stolen plates he'd also acquired earlier, hot-wired the Chevy, drove it to Chelsea, and parked it curbside on Warren Avenue. Not fully confident he could get it started again, Bains had left the motor running while he was in the house waiting for his two companions. Thankfully, the owner of the stolen vehicle had been kind enough to provide a full tank of gas.

The trio climbed in and with Bains at the wheel, began to make their way toward Somerville. With the earlier gossip reaching a fever pitch after word from Quincy made it to the party, it was likely someone would call the cops and tip them off to Chasson's whereabouts if they hadn't done so already.

As he drove along Warren Avenue, Bains flipped on the car radio, twisted the volume knob, and turned the dial in a hunt for a news channel. Chasson, sitting in the passenger seat beside him, lit a cigarette and took over the search so Bains could better focus on driving. The last thing they needed was to get into a collision. He paused on WBZ News, where he found a late-night talk show underway. Chasson stopped scrolling through the channels and remained tuned to the long-time Boston news network in case the broadcaster broke in with a bulletin.

"Where to? Your apartment?" asked Bains, who was described by many as a stocky man of medium height. At twenty, he had a ruddy complexion and a scarred nose, making him look twice his age.

"Yeah," Chasson answered as he intently listened for any news from Quincy. He turned the handle on the door panel, raising the window to minimize exterior noise. The dashboard array glowed a greenish hue and the clock at the center of the dial cluster now indicated that it was half-past midnight. "I just want to check in on Linell and my son before we leave town."

The roads were traffic-free and the trip over to Chasson's place at 87 Bartlett Street in Somerville was just a few short miles through neighboring Everett. Bains navigated the stolen Bel Air across the span over the Mystic River, through the Ten Hills neighborhood to Broadway, and took a quick left to Bartlett. Parking was scarce but he soon found a vacant spot. Once again, fearing he might not be able to restart the car in a time of need, Bains left it running. Thankfully, the vehicle ran quietly. An idling car would certainly raise the suspicions of nearby homeowners. Somerville natives were a cautious, wary lot. For many years, the hardened community was a stomping ground for organized crime.

In the fifties and sixties, the densely populated city of just four-square miles wedged between Cambridge and the historic Boston enclave of Charlestown was the home of notorious Irish Mob boss James "Buddy" McLean, who ruled the Winter Hill Gang. McLean led a faction during a protracted sixties gang war, which was apparently triggered by an angry suitor on Labor Day 1961. There are a wide variety of accounts as to what actually took place during a house party in Salisbury Beach, situated an hour north of Somerville. The most often-repeated version claimed that a Winter Hill man fondled the breast of a Charlestown hoodlum's girlfriend, who was not interested in the man's advances. A violent fistfight naturally followed the grievous act.

Over time, the altercation escalated into an all-out deadly feud between Winter Hill and the McLaughlin brothers out of Charlestown. When the lethal fighting finally ended six years later in 1967, more than sixty lives had been claimed, including both crime bosses. Charlestown's Bernie McLaughlin met his end on October 31, 1961, gunned down by Buddy McLean in front of the Morning Glory Café. According to police accounts, one hundred people witnessed the shooting, but none, understandably, came forward. Exactly four years later, also on Halloween night, McLean was assassinated near his Somerville home, shot multiple times by Charlestown hired killer Stevie Hughes.

Following McLean's death, Howie Winter assumed control of the Winter Hill Gang and the Somerville rackets thrived. Winter, whose name was coincidentally the same as the gang he commanded, was a close associate of McLean and had earlier been released following ten years in federal prison for horse race fixing. In later years, he faced yet another decade in prison on a trumped-up drug charge. The FBI approached him with a deal, seeking to add Winter to their band of informants in exchange for a reduced sentence. Specifically, they were hoping he would agree to provide "dirt" on Whitey Bulger, the infamous mobster who claimed the Somerville rackets in Winter's absence. To his credit, Howie Winter served his time, refusing to rat out his colleagues to the FBI—he even spared the reprehensible Bulger an indictment and likely prison time. The FBI got nothing from him. In organized crime circles, the honorable Winter was known as a tight-lipped man of unmatched integrity.

Uncommon in the often-cutthroat world of organized crime, Howie Winter died of natural causes on November 12, 2020, at the ripe old age of ninety-one.

In an odd twist to the Irish Gang War story, the man whose girlfriend suffered the groping misdeed that incited years of death and bloodshed was Alex Rocco, who successfully transitioned from the role of real-life hoodlum to portraying one as Las Vegas gangster Moe Green in the award-winning 1972 organized crime film, *The Godfather*. For viewers who did not like the Green character, he took a bullet in the eye, rubbed out on orders from Godfather Michael Corleone. But Rocco, formerly known as Alexander Petricone, was active in film until his actual death in 2015 of natural causes.

***

Chasson carefully examined both the rear and side-view mirrors to make certain that they were not being tailed by the cops. There was no sign. Either the police had not been notified by any of the kids at the house party or the authorities had yet to learn that their prey had made a pit stop in Chelsea. Very few people knew he lived in Somerville so perhaps they had not yet made the connection. His apartment would certainly be of interest but to that juncture, the police seemed slow to react.

The rental apartment was a third-floor walk-up in a three-family home, which was tightly sandwiched between similar structures on a cramped street in the Winter Hill neighborhood. With a glance at the windows above, he noted the lights were on, but his girlfriend, Linell Travers, twenty-four, often left a lamp lit for his benefit and his frequent late comings and goings. Too many times, he had stumbled noisily into the apartment and woken their three-year-old son, Derek.

The three men exited the car and gently clicked the doors closed, careful not to make any unnecessary noise. Even the slightest sound echoed in the quiet of the deep night. The trio entered the small foyer of the triple-decker and climbed the narrow staircase. Bains, who walked with a noticeable limp, trailed slightly behind. Months earlier, he had lost control of his motorcycle, sustaining a fractured lower left leg. The injury earned him a cast, which he tolerated for most of the summer. But he soon tired of the prohibitive anchor and cut away the plaster himself, paying little heed to the fact that his leg might not be fully healed.

Chasson keyed the lock and entered the apartment. He was not surprised to find his girlfriend and his son both fast asleep, huddled together in the master bedroom. He leaned in to give each a kiss on the forehead and then stealthily made his way to the bureau he shared with Linell. Quietly opening the bottom drawer so he did not disturb the sleeping pair, Chasson pushed aside some of his clothing to reveal a pair of handguns, including his favorite, a .38-caliber Colt revolver he had concealed days earlier. He checked both pistols to make certain they were fully loaded before stuffing the weapons in the waistband at the small of his back.

Before closing the drawer, he grabbed a fresh shirt and quickly changed. He made sure to keep the bloodstained original, which was still slightly damp from the earlier attempt at cleaning in the bathroom at the Chelsea party. Despite his effort to rinse away the offending blood, there were still traces. He made sure to keep the shirt; with the cops undoubtedly closing in on his Somerville apartment, he was not about to leave evidence behind. He would have to find a place to dispose of it where it would not be found. Maybe he would have the means to burn it.

With a parting glance toward his slumbering loved ones, he returned to the living room to rejoin Bray, Bains, and a new arrival, Patricia Landon, who had been sharing the apartment with Leroy and Linell. She glanced warily at her roommate as he entered the living room. Most of the time, they were civil but, on this night, she felt he looked uneasy.

"Hey, Patricia," he said in a low tone. His greeting was half-hearted. He had not noticed her when he first arrived. He assumed she had been out of sight in the kitchen when they entered the apartment.

"Hi, Lee. How's it going?" said the petite twenty-year-old strawberry-blonde, forcing a weak smile. The hot-tempered Chasson made her anxious.

She recalled a time in the not-too-distant past when she had overdosed in this same apartment on his watch. "He was really pissed off," she recalled years later. "They thought they were going to have to call an ambulance for me and the cops would show up. With all the drugs in the apartment, that would have been a problem. Instead, Lee gave me a cold shower, a mug of coffee, and slapped my face a few times. Another time, he jabbed his fingers hard into my stomach, but I don't remember what I did to deserve that."

It was obvious to Leroy Chasson that Patricia had no knowledge of the events that took place hours before in Quincy or that he was a highly sought-after fugitive. Had she been aware, her reception might have been even more subdued.

"Going well," he lied as he signaled to his companions that it was time to get moving. They had remained in the apartment far too long. The law would soon be at the door and he did not want to risk a gun fight with a bunch of trigger-happy cops and put his girlfriend and son in harm's way.

Donald Bains gestured to Chasson that he wanted to speak in private. The two men moved to the kitchen while Bray remained in the living room with Patricia, who knew him from their years at Quincy High School. They dated briefly but a meaningful relationship never materialized.

She divulged that, weeks earlier, after his escape from the Concord Reformatory, Mark Bray had reached out to her. She explained that, starved for companionship, he was seeking to hook up with her. "'Sure,' I said, agreeing to meet him at a restaurant on Cambridge Street in Boston, opposite the Massachusetts General Hospital. I guess that explains where I was in my life at that point. Great! Running off to meet an escaped convict."

According to Patricia, the only thing she had in common with Mark Bray was drug use. Along with most of their friends, they were frequently seeking the next high. As she chatted with her childhood friend in the living room, Bains was in the kitchen with Chasson.

"Look, Lee, I'd rather not go any further," his friend implored. "You know I don't really want to go into hiding. I'll just stay here and face the music when the cops show up."

"Donnie, you know they're gonna work you over," Chasson warned, placing a concerned hand on his friend's shoulder.

Bains nodded in agreement. His friend was dead on—once the police learned that he had driven Chasson from Chelsea to Somerville in a stolen car, essentially aiding and abetting a wanted fugitive, all bets would be off. He was now an accomplice to murder. But he insisted he would say nothing to the police. That was part of the code. His silence was assured. In fact, he might be able to feed the police a line or two of bullshit to impede their hunt for his friends. He agreed with Chasson that he would undoubtedly receive a beating and get locked up for a stretch. But he had done short time before. He had been at the receiving end of police brutality in the past, as a youth. Whatever the cops dished out, he could handle it.

# FOURTEEN—SOMERVILLE SIEGE

Just before three o'clock in the morning, a heavily armed detachment of police arrived at the Somerville apartment Leroy Chasson shared with his girlfriend Linell Travers, their son Derek, and Patricia Landon. Bartlett Street was awash with the flashing blue lights of a half-dozen patrol cars. Despite the late hour, several curious homeowners stepped out to their porches and sidewalks, some in their robes, to observe as the uniformed storm troopers gathered in front of No. 87 and readied their weapons.

The police armada entered the cramped foyer single file and climbed rapidly, scrambling up the narrow staircase to the third floor. Their heavy combat boots, pounding on two flights of wooden stairs, woke the tenants in the apartments on the first and second floors. As the occupants stepped out to determine the source of the ruckus, cops gruffly ordered them back inside. Doors slammed, one after another, as the fearful tenants complied.

When the insistent knock came at the door to Chasson's apartment—actually, it was better described as a hammering fist—Bains calmly tamped out his cigarette in an ashtray, rose from the sofa, and shuffled across the living room to answer, bracing for the inevitable.

Linell had long since awoken and was perched on the edge of a kitchen chair opposite Patricia. Both had steaming mugs of coffee in front of them. Three-year-old

Derek remained sound asleep in the bedroom, although not for much longer as the unsettling rapping at the door grew louder and more insistent. Linell made her way to the bedroom to retrieve the boy. The little toddler would certainly be frightened by the chaos that would soon erupt in the apartment.

Minutes after his companions had departed for points unknown, Donald Bains shared with the two young women what he knew about the Pageant Field brawl. His knowledge was limited, however, to the nominal discussion between Chasson and Bray during the brief ride from Chelsea to Somerville. Linell lowered her gaze and gently shook her head when she learned that her boyfriend of several years had stabbed a young man to death. Her friend Patricia, a native of Quincy, was a former classmate of Paul Melody's.

"The kid who got killed, I graduated from Quincy High School with him," she remarked while recounting the tragic murder of Paul Melody decades later. "My brother was at the park but had gone home before the fight. Paul Melody had driven him home earlier that night."

Patricia joined Linell as Bains unlatched the door. He was barely able to step back as a pair of Massachusetts State Troopers violently forced the door open, bursting through the narrow opening. They were shouting for everyone to put their hands up. The first two men through were armed with what Patricia described as "long-ass rifles." They pointed the barrels menacingly at the apartment's four terrified occupants. A steady column of men, some uniformed and others in plainclothes, filed into the room like scores of angry wasps pouring from a damaged hive.

"Where's Chasson?" barked one of the troopers, who respectfully lowered his shotgun when he caught sight of the little toddler trembling in his mother's arms. "Is he here?"

A scowling Donald Bains, defiant to the last, said nothing.

The lead officer, a brawny man with a square jaw and trademark high-and-tight haircut, set his teeth and slowly repeated the question, pausing between each word for added effect. "Where. Is. He?"

Linell answered meekly, "He's not here."

One of the lawmen, obviously a detective, dispatched men to give the apartment a once-over. From the racket they were making in the bedrooms, the invaders paid little mind to preserving Linell's belongings. When the rooms were found clear, police conducted separate interrogation sessions. What followed was grueling questioning that went on until daybreak. The police scrutiny was primarily directed at Donald Bains, once it was learned he had been at the house party in Chelsea. But Patricia, who was one of nine children, also garnered added interest when the detectives found out she was from Quincy and knew the victim.

"You knew him, you were there," insinuated one of the Somerville cops. She admitted to the gruff detective that she knew Paul Melody from school but had not seen him since graduation—three years earlier in 1974. Nor had she visited Quincy in some time.

"I think I did have mixed feelings on the whole thing," Patricia shared, years later. "I could not give the police any answers because I didn't know anything at the time. I could tell them that Leroy was not known to the Quincy crowd. It was the first and only time any of them even heard his name.

"The cops were disgraceful—just plain nasty—in their treatment of me," she recalled. They put that guy Donald in one room, Linell in another, and me in a third. I don't remember for certain but there may have been drugs stashed somewhere. But the cops were mostly interested in a cache of guns they believed were kept in the apartment. I guess that's why Lee came back to the house. To get his guns."

The light of dawn arrived as the police packed up and left the apartment, departing with an ominous promise for the exhausted trio that more questioning would follow as the search for Chasson and Bray progressed. Oddly enough, Donald Bains was not arrested, partly because he had no outstanding arrest warrants. In addition, police failed to determine that he was behind the stolen getaway car, then in the possession of the fleeing fugitives. Had that information been available to the cops, he would likely be occupying a six-by-nine in a dreary Somerville jail—or worse, put under lock and key in a far-flung state police precinct.

But again, it was a bitter pill he could swallow if it meant his longtime friends would have more time to make a run for it.

\*\*\*

Chasson, now behind the wheel of the stolen sedan, drove slowly and with caution, following the rules of the road. He didn't have a license but if the cops pulled him over, the lack of credentials would be the least of his problems. He skirted the high-speed lane and observed the posted limit, never exceeding fifty-five miles per hour as he progressed along Interstate 93 southbound.

Before long, the outlaws rounded the sharp off-ramp to Route 95 in Canton, known affectionately by locals as Dead Man's Curve because of the number of crashes and overturned trucks that occurred over the years. The duo then settled in for the twenty-minute trip to the Rhode Island border.

Chasson was aware that the Massachusetts State Troopers could be concealed anywhere along this stretch of roadway, parked in a rest stop, or camouflaged behind outgrowth on the median strip, ready to pounce on an unsuspecting speeding motorist. It was nearing the end of the month, after all, and citation quotas had to be met. It was also after two o'clock in the morning, which made the possibility of police meddling more feasible. As the popular saying goes, "Nothing good ever happens after midnight." The police, particularly those on the graveyard shift, would undoubtedly agree.

But the brief twenty-mile jaunt along I-95 was without interruption or incident. Soon, a large roadside sign appeared at the edge of the roadway announcing, "WELCOME TO RHODE ISLAND, THE OCEAN STATE." Minutes later, the two men reached the Pawtucket city limits and Chasson urged the car to the first available off-ramp. Bray, who had been dozing, woke as they rounded the turn to join US Route 1 South, which was also known as Broadway.

"Let's get a room," Chasson suggested as they made their way south. The road was the main artery through Pawtucket and crammed with strip malls and box stores, although nothing was open at the late hour. "I'm fuckin' beat."

Bray nodded in agreement. He could certainly use a little shuteye. Since his escape, he had been crashing at friends' homes on assorted couches. Earlier in the week, on Sunday, August 20, he had moved into more comfortable digs, renting a room at the Milner Hotel in Boston. His room was still available on this night, paid for in advance, and he debated urging Lee to head there. But when they left Somerville, his friend began driving south without indicating where they were going or what he had in mind. Days earlier, Bray recalled mentioning the Milner room but in the excitement of their hurried escape from Somerville, it must have slipped from his comrade's mind. He decided to remain quiet about the Boston hotel for the time being.

The pair soon pulled into a seedy, no-name motel on the outskirts of Providence. In the near distance, the high-rises of the city rose into a murky gloom, indicative of approaching rain. The air in Pawtucket was mild but damp with humidity.

The neon sign suspended from a rusting stanchion at the motel entrance declared "Vacancy" in loud blue lettering. Chasson guided the Bel Air into a spot at the distant edge of the parking lot, out of view of many of the side-by-side guest room doors and windows.

"I'm going to shut it off," he said to his companion as he reached under the steering column and manipulated the ignition wiring. There was no other choice. It had been running nonstop since Bains had stolen it hours earlier. Leaving it running all night while they slept would certainly draw unwanted attention. As he pulled the twisted wires apart, the engine went silent.

A concerned Mark Bray asked, "Will you be able to get it started again?"

Chasson surveyed the lot, spotted several idle cars, and said with a grin, "If not, we'll just help ourselves to another."

While his accomplice considered their transportation needs, Leroy made his way to the motel office. A small bell positioned above the door jingled as he entered, alerting the clerk. A scrawny kid, barely past his teens, was working the front desk. He looked up from the pages of a tattered comic book and muttered, "Help you?"

"Can we get a room?"

"Just one?" asked the motel clerk as he gazed out at the parking lot. He craned his neck and took stock of the man leaning against a Chevrolet. "You don't want a room for each of you?"

Business had obviously been slow at the little rundown motel and the kid was trying to boost revenue, either for the owner or himself by pocketing the difference.

"No, just one," snapped his impatient customer in response.

"Twenty-nine," the clerk said.

"Here's thirty," said Chasson as he slapped a crumpled wad of cash on the counter. "Keep the change."

Without a word, the clerk slid the guest registration book across the smooth counter surface and added a pen. He then retrieved a room key from a cabinet mounted on the wall. Chasson, meanwhile, scrawled the name "Walter Travers" in the book. *Travers* was his girlfriend Linell's last name and *Walter* was her dad. It was the first name that came to mind. He grunted a "thank you" to the kid as he collected the key and made his way toward the room.

Before the men turned in for the night, they briefly discussed their next destination. Bray thought getting back on I-95 and continuing south to Florida would be the most prudent. "I have friends in the Miami area," he explained. "They'll give us a place to stay and some cash."

"I think we should head for Canada," Chasson said.

"Canada?" Bray asked, disbelieving.

He did not say it aloud but felt it was an unwise decision. Florida, he felt, was a far better choice while they were on the lam. There would be added isolation from the Massachusetts-based authorities seeking them, as well as ample resources from his Florida contacts for as long as the duo remained in exile. And with winter on the near horizon, he thought selfishly, it was a far warmer choice. Besides, if they were Canada-bound, why then did Lee drive south on I-95 to Rhode Island? They were heading in the wrong direction. He chose not to mention it.

"Yeah," Chasson said. "Canada is closer to home and help from friends if we need it. Maybe Montreal. But first, we need to make a stop in Boston."

"Boston?" Once again, Bray thought about his room at the Milner. If they had driven there, they would already be in the city. But again, it wasn't worth bringing up. He knew it was fruitless to protest.

"Yeah—I'll explain after we get some sleep."

"Sure, I guess," Bray agreed reluctantly.

"C'mon," Chasson said, dangling the key and gesturing toward their room. "Let's get some sleep. We need to get an early start."

# FIFTEEN—POLICE INTERVIEW

The narrow metal chair was far too small for Bryan "Rocky" Fitzgerald's considerable frame. He twisted slightly, to his left, then right in an attempt to find a more comfortable position but to no avail. He resigned himself to the discomfort and tried to block it from his mind. Perhaps it was intentional on the part of the police. Just another method to disarm their subject during questioning, Bryan surmised. Warm, airless interview room, garish overhead lights, nothing to eat or drink, and... and an awful steel chair. Hopefully, whatever the cops had in mind for him wouldn't take long and he would soon be on his way.

Fitzgerald glanced at the adhesive bandage he had placed to cover the small laceration he sustained on his fingers when Leroy Chasson was wildly swinging the blade during the melee. He glanced up to see five police officers observing him—or were they glaring at him? They were looking at his hand. The stare felt accusatory, as if he had something to do with the stabbings. Perhaps they were on to something. He had, after all, driven the perpetrator to Pageant Field—twice.

Fitzgerald slid the offending hand beneath his thigh, out of view. Why were they looking at him like that? He hadn't killed anyone. If he was guilty of anything, it was being misguided enough to drive that madman to Quincy. It made him sick to think about it, but he and Chasson had split a hamburger at Howdy's minutes before...before the deranged killer indiscriminately carved up Melody and Hayward. Fitzgerald's heart began to race and beads of sweat broke out on his broad forehead. *Man*, he thought, *these lights are hot*. Of course, that was just in his tortured imagination. Fluorescent lights gave off less heat than standard incandescent bulbs.

It was after two o'clock in the morning, according to the clock mounted on the wall. It would be daybreak in a matter of hours. He and Jeanne were supposed to be leaving for Texas, where she was slated to begin classes at Sam Houston College in early September. Now she would be making the trip alone. It was doubtful the police would allow him to leave the Quincy area during an ongoing murder inquiry.

The car was also a problem, it seemed. The couple had originally planned to drive to Houston first thing in the morning. Earlier, Fitzgerald had been informed by the police that the Fiat would be impounded as evidence. Learning that, he reached out to Jeanne and suggested she book a flight to Houston—and purchase only one ticket. He was not sure what his immediate future held but he was almost certain it wasn't Texas.

The police read Fitzgerald his rights and then the lead investigator, Lieutenant Neil MacDonald, began the interview in earnest. *Interview, or was it an interrogation?* thought Fitzgerald, who was suddenly regretting his decision to report to the Sea Street police headquarters voluntarily. If these men were going to treat him like a common criminal, he should act like one and not cooperate. Then again, it was his mother who urged him to talk with the police. The cops visited his home soon after the murder, seeking him for questioning. They also spoke with his mother on two occasions, and he later found that she had assured officers that he would turn himself in. She was certain her loyal son Bryan was not about to go against her wishes.

MacDonald, tall and thin with a thick shock of graying hair, friendly eyes, and a warm smile, was joined by several Quincy PD colleagues and Massachusetts State Trooper Robert Masuret. The lieutenant cleared his throat, rechecked the spinning tape recorder positioned in the middle of the table, and began the questioning.

"Bryan, your mother said you drove the suspect back to Chelsea. Did you drive him back to Chelsea?"

"No, I dropped him off at the train station," Fitzgerald lied without hesitation. He swallowed hard, realizing too late that he should have been honest with these guys from the outset. It was a mistake on his part, but he wasn't certain at that point how to untangle himself from the lie. He tried to avoid eye contact with the probing lieutenant but was rapidly losing the battle. He submitted to a stare down; yet another police tactic to rattle witnesses.

"Why didn't you drive him back to Chelsea with you?" his interviewer asked. "Why didn't you take him back to the party?"

"I didn't want to have no part of him."

"Did he ask you to take him to the train station?"

"Yeah," answered Fitzgerald, his gaze downward toward the tiled floor below, trying to avert the cop's unblinking stare. "He said I got to get him out of there."

"And he got on the train, all covered with blood? Really?"

"Yeah, that's right," Fitzgerald insisted, realizing by the looks on their faces that the cops weren't buying it.

Lieutenant MacDonald paused for effect and scribbled a few notes on a lined yellow legal pad. He looked up from his writing and, for a tense moment, Bryan Fitzgerald felt the man's eyeballs boring a hole in him. It was the lieutenant's way of letting his subject know that he could read between the lines and see through the lies. Fitzgerald sensed it. Sooner or later, he was going to have to come clean and tell the cops that he did, in fact, drive Chasson back to Chelsea and not the train station as he continued to profess. The longer he carried on with the lie, he realized, the more difficult it would be to undo the damage rendered. He had nothing to gain and everything to lose with the compounding mistruths. Before Fitzgerald could confess, however, MacDonald abruptly switched his line of questioning.

"Bryan, did you see the knife?"

"Yeah, I seen it in his hand," he answered truthfully. There was no reason to do otherwise in this instance.

"What hand was he holding it in?" the seasoned cop asked.

"I have no idea," Fitzgerald replied, shaking his head. "It all happened so fast. I was just trying to calm him down."

"You got in between when he was going after Rusty and—"

Fitzgerald interrupted and said, "Right and that's when he cut me." He slid his bandaged hand from concealment and held it upright to illustrate his comment.

"And?" said Lieutenant MacDonald, pressing for more details.

"And he took a slice out of me—I should need a stitch or two, but I have this Band-Aid on it. And then I was freaking out when I seen this one kid keel over."

"What kid was that?"

"I don't know," Fitzgerald answered, shrugging his broad shoulders. "I think it was Melody. He just slumped and then went right on his back. That was all that I seen."

"Who else was in the ruckus besides Melody?"

"Somebody started a fight and they were all beating on him?"

"Who?"

"Chasson," Fitzgerald replied. "I went over there and there was a big kid named Hay—I don't even know his real name."

"Hayward?" MacDonald offered.

"Yeah, Hayward. I went over and pulled him off the pile. He was a big kid and there was blood all over the place."

"Hayward is a big kid," said the lieutenant.

"I'm a big kid too," said Fitzgerald, pointing out the obvious.

MacDonald nodded in agreement.

"Lee started running around the parking lot screaming and yelling and shit. And I could see the knife in his hand. The light wasn't very good but I could see it flashing."

Lieutenant MacDonald, who was days shy of his forty-fourth birthday, shuffled his notes and glanced at his colleagues, who were jotting on their legal pads. There was murmuring between two of the other investigators in the small room, which Fitzgerald noted was not much larger than a typical jail cell. He hoped he would not see the inside of an actual lockup before the night was out. In the not-too-distant past, he had spent time behind bars on drug charges. He wasn't proud of it and had since cleaned up his act. He might be drug free but there were other reasons to get pinched by the cops. Lying during an interview, for instance.

"Bryan, so far you've been terrific," said MacDonald, who was a nineteen-year member of the Quincy Police Department and a decorated Korean War veteran. "Now tell us what he did with the knife."

"I think he has it in his pocket."

"Did he stash it in your car?"

"No," said Fitzgerald, knowing it was just a guess on his part. He really didn't know the whereabouts of the knife but he certainly did not want the cops ripping apart Jeannie's car looking for it, especially when she still planned to set out for Texas in the morning.

As if the man could read his mind, Lieutenant MacDonald asked, "Where is the car now?"

"With Jeannie. We left Chelsea and came back to Quincy right away. She dropped me off here. She's at home and knows nothing about any of this."

"Bryan, I'm sorry but we may have to take the car for a while."

"I heard," he responded glumly. "One of the other officers mentioned impounding it as evidence."

In a further effort to deter the police from searching Jeanne's Fiat and disrupting her life, he went on to explain that there was little space in the tiny car to hide something, even something as compact as a knife. The vehicle wasn't equipped with a center console or a glove box. The two bucket seats, Fitzgerald explained, were attached to the floorboards. There wasn't any space beneath. There was an obscure area behind the seats, but a knife placed there would have been immediately obvious. Fitzgerald also surmised that Chasson could not have thrown it out of the car as the two men drove back through Quincy. While the convertible top was down during the trip to Martignetti's and later, the brief visits to Bobby Dodd's and the Beachcomber on Quincy Shore Drive, Fitzgerald had restored the vinyl covering and rolled up the windows prior to returning to Pageant Field the second time.

"Maybe he tossed it at the Mount—I never seen him throw it anywhere," he suggested.

MacDonald nodded and scribbled more notes. Fitzgerald wondered what he could be writing, if anything. It was all part of a carefully crafted interrogation methodology. Never allow the candidate to relax. Constantly raise the level of anxiety or paranoia. Put him or her on the defensive and wait for a mental lapse or an omission. Warm room, uncomfortable chair, making fake notations. Wait for the mistruths.

There was another pause in the questioning but Fitzgerald knew the interrogation was far from over. It was nearing three o'clock and he had been up since early the previous morning, twenty hours nonstop. He was hoping MacDonald and his sidekicks would signal for a break or at least offer him something to drink. There had to be a vending machine somewhere in this cavernous police headquarters, which had opened for business in 1925. The interview room was growing warmer, if that were at all possible. *Were the cops, in their buttoned-up collared shirts and neckties, as restless as he was? Didn't these guys ever need to take a piss?*

"Did he go into your mother's house?" the lieutenant asked.

This question came as a surprise. It was obvious the cops had talked to his mom and already knew that he did, in fact, pay a visit to his home with Leroy Chasson in tow. In hindsight, he knew that was a mistake. He wished he hadn't involved his mother. But Fitzgerald wanted to wash up and his house was just a brief drive from the scene of the crime.

"Yeah, and she totally freaked out," he recalled. "Chasson wasn't happy either. He thought it was my house, not my parents'. He didn't expect to see my mother when we got there."

"Your mother seen him?"

"Yeah, she was totally hysterical," Fitzgerald stated, raising his voice slightly as he described his mother's emotions. "She saw all the blood on him and me. She kept yelling, 'What the hell is going on? What the hell is going on?' over and over."

"He didn't ask for a change of shirt or wash up?"

"No, he was too out of control and just wanted to get out of there," he replied. "I just told my mother I got in a fight, and we left. She was pretty worked up."

"Where did you get a new shirt?"

"Chelsea, when I got back to the party. The kid who lives there found one that fit me."

"Where's the other shirt?"

"I don't know," said Fitzgerald. "I tossed it in some bushes. In Chelsea."

"Did Lee ever go back to the party? Do you know?"

Fitzgerald lied again, understanding that he was digging a deeper hole. "No," he answered, lowering his gaze.

He sensed Lieutenant MacDonald knew he was being dishonest. There were at least a half-dozen people who were aware that he drove Chasson from Quincy back to Chelsea, including his mother and his girlfriend. He would never ask either of them to cover for him. But regardless, when the detectives eventually got around to questioning partygoers, Fitzgerald would be in serious trouble. He wasn't on parole or anything like that, but he did have a criminal history. How much more time would he get for lying to the police? Worse still, would he be charged for driving Leroy Chasson away from the scene of a murder? Aiding a killer? *What the hell had he done?*

"What did you tell them?" MacDonald prodded.

"Tell who?" he asked, losing his train of thought as he contemplated his fate.

"The people at the party?"

"I said I was with a nut and he started a big fracas and stabbed a few people. I could see one person he stabbed because my headlights were on Melody as I was leaving. I could see he was cut right here," he recalled, pointing.

"You're indicating his left side," the lieutenant said for the benefit of the tape recorder.

"Yeah," Fitzgerald continued. "He was on his back and I could see the cut. On his shirt, I could see blood. But Lee said he stabbed a few people."

"He did? Did he, uh, did he know he stabbed Melody or…"

"He thought he stabbed Racette," Fitzgerald said, correcting the lieutenant. Considering the series of questions that he had answered during the two hours he had spent in that sweatbox without so much as a simple glass of water, he was beginning to grow impatient with Lieutenant MacDonald and the four silent idiots surrounding the table. He was buckling.

MacDonald continued with a round of questions seeking more details about the stabbings but while Bryan Fitzgerald was a firsthand witness to the events that took place at Pageant Field, he was not involved in the actual melee that resulted in Paul Melody's death. According to his statement, when the fight began, he was a short distance away, speaking with Nathan Shaw. As a witness, Fitzgerald seemed to have reached an impasse. There were others sitting in the station foyer, under the watch of the desk sergeant, who would be able to provide more damning statements about the actions of Leroy Chasson. Kevin Racette, for instance, would certainly be able to furnish details of the brawl.

Turning to his colleagues, MacDonald asked if they had any additional questions for Mr. Fitzgerald. Each of the four officers indicated they had nothing further. The lead investigative detective then sternly said, "Bryan, I think you've been pretty truthful with us except for one point about the knife. I don't think—"

"The knife?"

"And driving to the train station," MacDonald persisted. It was obvious he knew that Fitzgerald had lied about dropping off a blood-covered Chasson at the train station. "You're sure you didn't take him back to Chelsea? Now is the time to tell us, you know. Let's tell the truth."

"Okay, all right. The knife."

"Where is it?" the lieutenant asked, sensing a breakthrough.

"I have no idea." Fitzgerald sighed, shrugging in frustration. "It's probably in his pocket, like I said before."

"You're sure it's in his pocket?"

"It's in his pocket," the witness insisted. The pressure of the questioning was building, like a leaking gasket about to blow.

"How do you know it's in his pocket?"

"Because I didn't see him throw it out of the car, like I said."

"Okay, and driving him to the train station," repeated Lieutenant MacDonald. "Are you sure you didn't drive him back to Chelsea? Now is the time to tell us."

Fitzgerald straightened up in the uncomfortable chair, drew a deep breath, and said, "I've been honest all the way. Look, I lied once. I didn't take him to the train station. I drove him back to Chelsea. Okay?" While he was embarrassed to admit to his falsehoods, it was a relief to finally get it off his chest. He braced for the reaction of the police but surprisingly, it was subdued. That led him to believe they knew all along that he was lying and they were just waiting for him to come clean.

"You did?" said Lieutenant MacDonald, feigning surprise. He knew the witness would eventually cave.

"Yeah, but he didn't stay long," Fitzgerald said, hoping they could quickly move to another line of questioning. "Lee left the house with two other guys. One of them was his prison buddy, Mark Bray. I don't know the third guy. They left in a stolen car."

"They had a stolen car?"

"Yeah, I heard they stole a car in Quincy and then attached stolen plates."

"What model was the car?"

"I have no idea."

MacDonald paused, glanced at his notes, and then asked several pointed questions regarding the party, such as the presence of drugs. Shaking his head, Fitzgerald explained that there was a basement apartment where the event was held. The homeowner, Mr. Joil Heichman, was there the whole time and frequently came up to check in on the kids. Beer drinking was allowed but there were no drugs on the premises. Had there been any such activity, the homeowner would have promptly brought an end to the event.

"Was there any conversation you recall about Racette owing Mark Bray six hundred dollars?"

"Six hundred bucks?" Fitzgerald replied, shaking his head. "No, no, it was only fifty."

"Where did you hear that?"

"In the car, on the way to the train sta—" Fitzgerald began and then abruptly stopped, realizing as he spoke that the cat was out of the bag on his lie about dropping the murderer at a train station. "I mean, on the way back to Chelsea. Chasson said it was fifty bucks."

While the amount of the debt owed to Mark Bray varied from one witness to another, the majority agreed that it was only fifty dollars. Not that it mattered. In MacDonald's opinion, a young life was lost over an unpaid debt. Fifty, six hundred—in hindsight, what difference did it make?

"So, this Bray character asked Chasson to seek out Racette to collect fifty bucks owed to him, and as a result, Paul Melody is dead," stated MacDonald, condensing the entire interview into a single concise comment. Fitzgerald shrugged, acknowledging his agreement with his interviewer's summary.

The lieutenant gently shook his head. He had investigated a number of murders during his time with the Quincy Police force, all a waste of human life, but none as senseless as that of Paul Melody. He felt pity for the Melody family, particularly the young man's dad, who was a brother in blue who had recently retired from the Boston Police Department.

"Bryan, have you spoken with Mark Bray since the night of the incident?"

"Yeah, he called me."

"What did he have to say?"

"He asked me to get word out to the kids who damaged the shrubs on his mother's property," Fitzgerald recalled. Bryan understood that some of the kids from town were harassing Bray's mother in order to indirectly punish her son. "He said if they bothered her again, he was coming to Quincy with a gun and shoot the place up."

"Anything else?"

"Yeah, just that they were leaving the state immediately and he would call me in a month."

MacDonald decided to wrap it up so he and his colleagues could catch up on desperately needed sleep. The probe was just getting underway and a short break would keep them sharp. Bryan Fitzgerald could be brought in for follow-up questioning if necessary, and there was also the possibility that he would be charged with aiding a known criminal and lying to the police. As it turned out, there were no charges against the youth. The police were lenient.

"Bryan, would you mind removing that bandage?" MacDonald asked, pointing to the tightly wrapped lacerated fingers. "We want to see the extent of the cut and take a photo."

"Do you have another one, in case it starts bleeding again?"

One of MacDonald's colleagues climbed from his chair and left the room to seek out a first-aid kit. Fitzgerald, meanwhile, began to carefully peel away the bandage, which had grown soiled and needed a change anyway. It didn't bleed. In fact, the wound had signs of early healing.

"Hmm, not as bad as I thought," said Fitzgerald. "It was bleeding all over me when he slashed me."

"All right, this is the cut you sustained when you put your hand up when Lee was swinging?"

"Swinging in midair."

"With the missing knife?"

Fitzgerald could read between the lines. The detective was insinuating that he was not telling the truth about the location of the murder weapon. He had lied once, about driving Chasson to the train station. But he was truthful about the knife. He really didn't know the whereabouts of the offending blade.

"Yeah, with the missing knife," Fitzgerald answered slightly sarcastically.

MacDonald glared at him but shook it off. He picked up a Polaroid camera, walked over to the witness, who held out his hand. A brilliant flash lit the room and with a familiar mechanical whine, the device ejected the photo, which would later be introduced into evidence.

Returning to his chair, Lieutenant MacDonald sat heavily, fatigue clutching at him. He had worked through the day on another case and now he was into what would prove to be an all-nighter. A dozen or more interviews were scheduled. He hoped he and his colleagues would have a chance to grab a little shuteye, even for an hour or two. Clasping his hands on the table, he turned to his colleagues.

"Okay, any more questions, Bill?" he said to Detective William Curran.

"No."

"Well, this concludes the interview—"

"I'm not under arrest or anything, am I?" Fitzgerald interrupted.

"No, you're not."

*\*\*\**

In early September 1995, Bryan "Rocky" Fitzgerald tragically took his own life at the age of forty-two. Twenty years earlier, his father, John, had become ill and passed away. Bryan, the eldest child, stepped into the role. But according to his sister Diane, the pressures of a difficult childhood took their toll. "Bryan became our parent even before my father passed," she said. Diane said that Bryan was "distraught" following the murder of Paul Melody. "I never saw my brother as upset as he was the next day," she said. "He felt guilty that he couldn't stop it—it all happened so fast."

# SIXTEEN — BOSTON DETOUR

A steady drizzle met fugitive Leroy Chasson as he stepped outside his Pawtucket motel room to grab a quick smoke and clear his head. The sky overhead was steel gray. Before closing the door, he glanced inside at his sleeping companion, who was tightly wrapped in blankets against the chill of the air conditioning wall unit.

The television, volume muted, flickered with a morning news show. There were no other furnishings to speak of save for a rickety nightstand wedged between matching twin beds against the back wall. It was covered with empties and an overflowing ashtray. The room stank of stale beer and nicotine. As Chasson recalled, the room was foul smelling before he and Mark Bray added cigarettes of their own. Certainly not the most comfortable of lodging but both men had done jail time over the years, sleeping on rancid, inch-thick mattresses. In comparison, this fleabag motel room, with its dime-store paintings hanging from stained walls, was a five-star accommodation.

Despite a decent night's rest, Chasson was still dog-tired. He lowered his weary frame into a metal chair sheltered beneath an awning. The chair creaked under his weight, disturbing the quiet of the surrounding parking lot. He lit a cigarette and drew deeply, dispersing the smoke in lazy blue circles toward the covering above his head.

In the still of the early morning, he could detect the telltale gurgling of a stream he stumbled upon the night before. The bubbling brook emerged from a culvert beneath the parking lot and wended toward the rear of the motel. Before turning in, he retrieved his bloodstained shirt from the car and made his way toward the water. His head was on a swivel, making certain he wasn't being watched. Reaching a slick, grassy embankment, he scooped up a softball-sized stone, tied the shirt in a knot around it, and tossed it in the water. As expected, the evidence sank from view. He had briefly considered burning the clothing but set aside the thought, realizing an open flame would draw unwanted attention.

It was just after seven o'clock on a gloomy Wednesday morning. August 24, 1977. Eight hours earlier, Chasson had plunged a knife into the chest of twenty-year-old Paul Melody, a perfect stranger, and ended his life. He had slashed another man but Mark Bray, who supplied the news he learned in Chelsea, had not heard anything about the second victim's condition.

It felt like days had passed since he and Bryan Fitzgerald sped out of the Pageant Field lot in the little orange sports car, leaving carnage and death in their wake.

Fifteen minutes passed before Bray emerged from the motel room. With a quick greeting nod, he made his way to the stolen Chevrolet to fetch a fresh pack of cigarettes. Chasson observed as his friend climbed into the burly sedan. Upon his return, Bray slid into an adjacent chair and fired up a smoke.

"Morning," he muttered, wiping the sleep from his eyes.

"Morning, friend," Leroy said as he stomped out his half-smoked cigarette on the narrow concrete patio. "Sleep well?"

"Uh huh," Bray said unconvincingly.

"Ready to go?"

"Guess so." Truth be told, in that moment, Bray might have preferred returning to stress-free incarceration. Three squares and a room, even one enclosed by iron bars, were preferable to running from the cops. He didn't have faith that he and Leroy could evade the authorities for very long.

"Look, we got to make a stop when we get to Boston," Chasson declared. "I might need a favor from you."

Bray was confused. "Boston?" *Why did we drive to Rhode Island? None of it made sense.* He thought this might be a suitable time to change his friend's mind about heading north to Canada. Just get in the stolen car, get back on Interstate 95, and continue south to the Sunshine State. If they took turns driving, they could be there in twenty hours, ditch the car and find a beach.

Leroy soon cleared the air about needing help with some tasks in Boston. "I thought a night or two here, away from the search, would give me time to gather my thoughts," he explained.

"Okay."

"I made a call last night while you were sleeping," Chasson imparted, pointing to an isolated phone booth near the edge of the motel parking lot.

"Yeah?"

"So, now we have to go back to Boston to pick up a package, before heading to Canada."

"Package?"

"I'll explain later," Chasson said, resuming the mystery.

Bray simply nodded. While he was curious to learn what type of *package* so interested his companion, he hoped that retrieving it did not involve prolonged exposure in cop-filled Boston. It was certainly unwise. Granted, Bray had been a guest at Boston's Milner Hotel for a week. He had checked into the out-of-the-way hotel after spending several nights with friends. But he seldom left the confines of his tiny room. If he did venture out into the city, it was only for brief trips to pick up a meal or provisions. But now, the same cops who were seeking him for his escape from jail were now on his trail for his role in the Quincy killing.

Florida or Canada, it didn't really matter, the more he considered the options. They just had to get out of the area.

Without further delay, Bray stood and made his way toward the waiting Bel Air. Chasson followed, after a quick visit to the motel office to return the room key. The teenager from the night before was still there but said nothing as he claimed the key.

The men resumed their original positions in the car—Chasson behind the wheel and Bray riding in the passenger seat. Chasson reached beneath the steering column, located the ignition wiring, and rubbed the two exposed ends together. The friction created a spark and the engine roared to life. Before long, they were retracing the previous night's drive, heading north and crossing state lines into neighboring Massachusetts.

Less than thirty minutes later, they transitioned onto the Southeast Expressway, passing through Quincy. As the duo drove past the Furnace Brook Parkway off-ramp, Chasson realized they were only a few short miles from the scene of the melee.

As the wipers rhythmically swept the light rain from the broad windshield, he imagined that Pageant Field was still bustling with police activity. Yellow caution tape certainly encircled the crime—his crime. Glancing out the window at the distant Quincy homes and businesses, he withheld comment from his passenger. There was nothing to say. Mark Bray was not with him when he cold-cocked Kevin Racette, igniting mayhem.

Chasson absently shrugged. Bray glanced at him but said nothing. There was no turning back or undoing the deeds of the previous night. Paul Melody was dead by his hands and he was on the run. He lit another cigarette, leaned back in the seat, and blew smoke that buffeted off the windshield and wafted through the car's interior.

Reaching the city limits of Boston, Chasson took the Morrissey Boulevard exit in Dorchester and soon, wheeled the trusty Chevrolet into the Howard Johnson's parking lot. He expressed the need to rustle up some grub. His own stomach rumbling, Bray agreed. Neither man had eaten much of anything since the day before.

"I'll meet you inside," Chasson announced as he made his way toward a row of neatly lined-up newspaper boxes in front of the popular roadside restaurant with its distinct orange-tiled roof. HoJo's was known everywhere for its multiple flavors of ice cream and deep-fried clams.

In the eighties, the landmark eatery also became known as the "office" of notorious South Boston Mob boss Whitey Bulger, who often conducted business meetings with associates and made calls from the bank of payphones. The FBI recorded footage of Bulger's scandalous activities at the restaurant.

"Grab me a coffee, will ya?" Chasson added as Bray pulled open the glass door and entered the establishment.

Sliding a quarter into the slot of the green-colored *Boston Globe* dispensary, Leroy ignored the block-lettered sticker that read "ONE COPY PLEASE" and pulled out several. Tucking the papers under his arm, he entered the HoJo's and rejoined his friend, who was seated in a booth some distance from the row of windows facing the front parking lot. *Good idea*, he thought. *If any cops walked into the restaurant, we might have time to slip out the back undetected.*

As he slid across the vinyl seat, Chasson handed a copy of the *Globe* to Mark and then spread his across the table. Sipping from the coffee mug waiting for him, he began to scan the front page. Before long, his face began to burn crimson with anger. Irate at what he saw, or rather what he didn't see, Chasson growled, "Not a fucking thing! Where's the story?"

Bray began rifling through his copy of the *Globe*, page after page. "Here it is!" he finally exclaimed, catching the attention of patrons seated nearby. Lowering his voice, he jabbed a finger at a page add-several deep in the morning edition. "It's on page four, in the Mass News Brief section."

"Page four?" Chasson snarled. "That's the best they could do?"

"It's early, Lee. I'm sure they don't have much to work with."

While he certainly did not agree with him, Bray understood the reasons behind his friend's outburst; Lee was all about the notoriety, as sick as that point of view was under the circumstances. His ego was obviously bruised by the lack of coverage of his wrongdoings. Bray wouldn't risk saying it aloud but he felt the less attention paid to the unsavory events of the previous night, the better off they were. What if the story had been splashed on the front page and the police had decided to add a photograph of Chasson? There were certainly mugshots available to the authorities and the newspapers would publish his likeness if asked. That would have put a huge target on their backs anywhere they went. The added publicity would have made it near impossible to move about freely. While Chasson felt he deserved a front-page story, Bray thought it was best they remained out of the spotlight, at least until they were able to get out of the Boston area.

Bray glanced at the headline again, which read "QUINCY POLICE SEEK MAN IN FATAL STABBING." The third paragraph of the brief article hit close to home: "A young man in a group at the park apparently owed Chassons money," the reporter wrote. "He said a fight broke out when Chassons allegedly swung a knife at the young man."

Reading that, Mark Bray felt a slight twinge of guilt. It was at his urging, after all, that Leroy Chasson made the trip to Quincy to retrieve money owed. Bray could have gone himself but felt it was too much of a risk at the time. As a Quincy native, he was well-known to most of the kids who were on hand at the Mount. He was on the run from the authorities after his foolhardy escape weeks earlier. There would be too many questions from friends about his jail status and "early" release. Chasson, meanwhile, was legally a free man, paroled a month earlier in July. He could move about at will.

Bray also didn't dare point out to his annoyed friend that the *Globe* reporter had misspelled his name as "Chassons." It was obvious he hadn't noticed when he read the article. That might send him over the edge.

Pushing the paper aside in disgust, Chasson reached for a breakfast menu. He was famished.

"Take your order, gentlemen?" asked a plump, middle-aged waitress who pulled a pencil from her hair bun and prepared to write. Each man ordered in turn and she soon sauntered off to the kitchen. She returned in less than ten minutes with two heaping plates of steaming breakfast food.

"So, this package I'm picking up?" Bray began as he sliced a breakfast sausage with a butter knife.

"My girlfriend," Chasson blurted without changing his expression.

"Your *what*?" Bray asked incredulously. He stared at his friend in disbelief, at a loss for words.

Chasson shook his head, smirking. He scooped up a forkful of scrambled eggs, delaying his response deliberately, for effect. It was one of his quirks that often irritated Mark. For Leroy Chasson, it was all about the drama, even when it came to something mundane like sharing information. After a pause, he said, "I need you to meet up with my girlfriend Kathleen and bring her to me."

"Kathleen? Do I know her?"

"You haven't met her," said Chasson. "I'm not sure if I've ever mentioned her to you. She wrote letters and visited me while I was in the can."

"Where?"

"Walpole," he answered, gnawing on an overcooked sausage link.

Bray shook his head. Knowing Chasson as well as he did, he refrained from asking about the *other* girlfriend—Linell. The mother of his child.

"You'll like her," Chasson said as he shoveled more food in his mouth and washed it down with a slug of coffee. "Sweet girl."

Mark Bray paid the check. The pair left the HoJo's, which in four short years would be the site of a vicious killing of an innocent woman who was just trying to make a little extra money to put food on the table. Kathleen Downey, a Worcester schoolteacher, was working as a part-time desk clerk at the Howard Johnson's Motor Lodge connected to the restaurant. On Easter Sunday 1981, Downey was gunned down during an armed robbery that yielded $385 to her ruthless killer.

Angel Toro, a known criminal and drug dealer, was convicted of the slaying and spent twenty-three years in prison. New evidence surfaced in 2004, however, of a report from May 1, 1981, pointing to a different perpetrator who was subsequently killed during the commission of a nearby drug store robbery. Found to have been the recipient of an unfair trial, Toro was later exonerated of the Downey killing but continued to serve a long sentence for an unrelated Florida murder.

Chasson and Bray walked briskly across the expansive lot, reaching an obscure parking spot that was not in view of the roadway. Chasson climbed into the driver's seat and once again worked his magic with the ignition wiring. Soon they were back on the expressway, heading deeper into the city. The weather brightened as they drove the short distance from Dorchester to downtown Boston.

He urged the burly vehicle around the Kneeland Street off-ramp and then drove slowly through the densely populated enclave of Chinatown, with its scores of restaurants, groceries, and assorted businesses, most featuring a Southeast Asian flavor.

Reaching the intersection at Washington Street, they rolled to a stop at a red light. Both men instinctively turned their heads to the right, glancing up the heavily traveled thoroughfare and the spectacle known to locals as the Combat Zone. Even during broad daylight, garish flashing neon signs dominated the landscape of Boston's notorious red-light district.

In the sixties, as part of the Government Center redevelopment project, Boston's West End was razed. Thousands of indignant residents and their businesses were forcefully relocated and scores of buildings and homes were demolished. Scollay Square was also displaced. Boston's political leaders understood the need for such debauchery and nightlife, particularly because of the numerous sailors and soldiers on leave out of the nearby Charlestown Navy Yard. The Combat Zone—with its peep shows, X-rated movie theaters, pornographic bookstores, strip joints, and nude dancing venues—grew out of this demand. A tempered attitude from law enforcement, a result of obvious payoffs from the Mob-controlled businesses, led to a rise in prostitution and organized crime. The "live and let live" attitude, however, soon led to murder.

The Combat Zone gradually met its end after the 1976 stabbing death of Harvard University football player Andrew Puopolo on the grimy streets. Along with negative publicity, the pressure from neighbors, and a sea change in the attitudes of Boston's leadership, the police were ordered to begin cleaning up the district. Rising property values also contributed to the Zone's demise as the city soon found more lucrative commercial uses for the valuable urban land.

The traffic signal glowed green and Leroy Chasson moved forward with the traffic flow toward Stuart Street. Before long, the two men reached the intersection at Tremont Street and pulled over to the curb.

"We'll get out here," Chasson announced as he disengaged the ignition wires. The car fell silent as he reached for the door handle and emerged. Ever wary that the cops might have learned he possessed the stolen Chevrolet, Chasson gave the interior a quick once-over to ensure nothing incriminating had been left behind. He would have preferred ditching the car in a less visible location; torching it would have been the best bet. But setting the car ablaze in this prominent location would draw far too much attention. Abandoning the car was the best option—it might buy precious time.

"I have a room a short walk from here," Bray informed his companion. "I've been staying there."

"Not yet. C'mon," said Chasson, gesturing toward a throng of tourists gawking at the array of theatre district marquees advertising off-Broadway shows. "Let's get off this street. Too many friggin' eyeballs 'round here."

The two men made their way north without pause, quickly covering the two city blocks to the southeast entrance of Boston Common, where Tremont met Boylston Street. Soon, the outlaws entered the sprawling fifty-acre park, ever watchful for roving cops and Boston Police patrol cars.

In comparison to bustling Tremont Street, few people were taking advantage of the peaceful city center preserve, which at more than three hundred years in age, was the oldest such green space in the U.S. Bostonians often imparted stories of how, in the sixteenth century, when the Common was first established as a public park, families would use the land to graze their cows. Centuries later, it was a law that remained on the books. Along with peaceful uses, Boston Common also held a grim history, namely in the form of public executions.

One of the most macabre episodes in the narrative can be traced back to 1676, when angry Bostonians executed fifty Native Americans for their roles in King Philip's War, which was an armed hostility fought between the Southern New England colonists and the indigenous inhabitants.

Many of the accused were shot while others were put to death by hanging from a prominent tree known as the Great Elm. Also left suspended by her neck from the infamous tree for alleged crimes was Ann Goody Glover, who met her demise for performing witchcraft and conversing with the Devil. Pirate Rachel Wall, who joined her husband George in a crime wave at sea, was found guilty of highway robbery. She maintained her innocence as officials snugly fit her with a noose. On October 8, 1789, thousands of spectators stood beneath the elm to watch the accused pirate sway from a sturdy branch.

For centuries, concealed beneath the lush green lawns of Boston Common was an unmarked graveyard discovered during excavation for subway construction in 1895. The graveyard contained more than a thousand bodies. These disturbed souls were believed to be American soldiers and British Redcoats who perished in battle or died from illness. The remains were moved to the Central Burying Grounds, adjacent to the existing subway. Ghost chasers and melodramatic Boston tour guides insist two women, dressed in Victorian-era clothing, had been seen parading about the Common. Over the years, a number of trolley passengers maintained they caught a glimpse of a musket-wielding Redcoat standing on the tracks.

Leroy Chasson and Mark Bray walked past the markers designating the graveyard without a second glance. Their pace quickened as they spotted a Boston beat cop meandering toward them from the west. Thankfully, he was walking slowly, biding his time, and the fugitives had a chance to divert to an alternate pathway and avoid detection. They soon emerged from the Common, exiting through a wrought iron gateway to Beacon Street.

Chasson climbed the staircase fronting the entrance of the Park Street Church and said to his friend, "This is a good spot."

Bray nodded and joined him on the wide granite stairs at the church entrance. Passersby gave them little notice. After receiving brief instructions, Bray climbed to his feet and gave his comrade a half-hearted salute as he departed to retrieve the "package." Chasson, meanwhile, moved to the shadows of the church exterior and lit a cigarette. It had yet to reach ten o'clock in the morning, but it had already been a long, exhaustive day.

It was much longer, however, for the Melody family who, ten miles to the south, were busy making arrangements to bury their beloved son, Paul.

*** 

To a person, Paul Melody's friends had nothing but good to say about the quiet, unassuming youth, who was born in Boston and raised in Quincy by his parents, Mary (Canavan) and Thomas. He had four brothers.

Paul had worked as an apprentice electrician for Comer Electric out of Quincy. According to his friends, he was dedicated and plugged away to advance his career.

"Mel worked his forty hours a week and never bothered a soul," said Joe Marnell, a friend and witness to the Pageant Field slaughter.

Paul Melody was buried in Braintree's sprawling Blue Hills Cemetery on August 27, 1977.

# SEVENTEEN—INTERVIEWS RESUME

The Quincy Police headquarters was bustling with activity on the morning of Wednesday, August 24, 1977. Mild, blustery ocean breezes buffeted in from the summer-warmed waters of the nearby Atlantic Ocean. Forecasters pledged an ideal day ahead for a pleasant stroll on scenic Wollaston Beach, either along the paved boardwalk and seawall or the hard-packed gray sand at the edge of the gently encroaching surf. There were few summertime activities more enjoyable than picking up fried food from the Clam Box on Quincy Shore Drive and dining on the wall overlooking the beach, the Boston skyscrapers serving as a distant backdrop.

Less than a mile to the southeast at Pageant Field, wide ribbons of bright yellow tape stretched between the baseball backstop and adjacent trees. The caution tape, in a telling triangular pattern, fluttered against the gentle winds that steadily cascaded across the thick green turf. The tape read, "POLICE LINE: DO NOT CROSS," indicating to curious passersby that something had recently occurred at the site— something heinous, perhaps.

In the nearby Sea Street police headquarters parking lot, reporters were jockeying for position. All the available spaces were occupied by vehicles marked with one television logo or another. Technicians raised the transmission booms atop their trucks, preparing to send live feeds back to their respective networks, while correspondents rehearsed their delivery. Channels 4, 5, and 7, the three major Boston-based television news agencies, had all sent reporters, and each impatiently waited for police officials to furnish a statement. It was explained to them that witness interviews were underway and there were few details to share at the time.

Inside the station, the lobby was standing room only, filled wall to wall with newspaper reporters and other journalists. Other than a generic briefing, however, the Quincy Police remained tight-lipped. All they would say when asked was that a thorough investigation was ongoing and a press conference would be forthcoming.

Meanwhile, witnesses to the events of the previous night were ushered through an alternate entrance, avoiding the media gauntlet. A steady parade of Quincy youths, each with a story to tell, showed up as the day wore on. Some reached the station by their own means while others were dropped off by family or friends. Each had previously received instructions to arrive at a designated entrance at the rear of the building. They were temporarily sequestered in the patrolmen's lunchroom, isolated from the clutches of probing reporters.

Second to pay a visit to the interview room was Nathan Shaw, who took the seat previously occupied by Bryan Fitzgerald. Like Fitzgerald before him, Shaw was escorted to the cramped, stifling room sparsely furnished with several chairs spaced around a square steel table. Shaw pulled his chair slightly forward, closer to the table, and brushed a shock of unruly hair off his forehead. According to a recently submitted handwritten police report, Shaw nearly became the third stabbing victim as he rushed to the aid of his injured friends. In fact, he was still wearing his bloodstained clothing.

Shaw was welcomed by Lieutenant MacDonald, who, in preparation for the interview, shuffled through the papers stacked in front of him. The pile of documents had grown considerably since he first began the interview process hours before, and there were still a number of witnesses waiting to be heard. In addition, several Quincy officers who had responded to the crime scene had filed their individual reports, adding to the available evidentiary material. He soon located the memo he was seeking, which listed key demographics for the young man sitting before him.

"Good morning, Mr. Shaw," he began, speed reading through the information detailed on the document.

"Good morning," Shaw replied, stifling a yawn.

"I understand one of my colleagues read you your Miranda Rights when you first arrived?" verified MacDonald, gesturing toward the three police officials seated around the table. Shaw scanned their faces and nodded a greeting. Each man—Detective Lieutenant Joe MacDonald (no relation) from the Massachusetts State Police, along with Quincy Police Representatives Angus McEachern and Detective Captain Frederick Tighe—acknowledged the witness in kind.

"Yeah, I'm all set," said Shaw, futilely seeking a position of comfort in the chair, wondering how anyone as big as Rocky Fitzgerald could have sat for any duration. He hoped the interview would be over quickly.

"All right, Mr. Shaw," Lieutenant MacDonald began. "Could we have your date of birth and address?"

"August 21, 1952," Shaw answered. "45 Lund Street, North Quincy."

"Hmm, recent birthday, I see. Your twenty-fifth."

"Uh huh," Shaw confirmed with disinterest.

"Okay, we'll get right to it," said the lieutenant as he withdrew a mugshot of Leroy Chasson from a manila folder and slid it across the table. "Did you see this man stab Paul Melody?"

"No, I didn't. Mel was already stabbed when I got up to him."

"Okay, when you got up to him, what did you do? You said this man confronted you because you tried to help Melody?"

"Yes, well, Mel was blood from head to toe and I could see his eyes were all… you could see he was gonna die," Shaw stated as he described the macabre scene. "He was that bad. So that's why I rushed toward the cars because I wanted to, uh, you know, get a car to give him a ride."

"Go on."

"This guy here," the witness indicated, tapping his index finger on the photo of Chasson, "was coming the other way between the cars. He told me to back off and I did. I didn't want anything to do with him."

"And Robert Hayward; did you see him get stabbed?"

"No," Shaw answered, shaking his head. "When we were trying to put Mel in the car, we asked Hayward for help. Mel was a big kid, but Hay is big too. Hay just said, 'I'm stuck too. I'm stuck too.' Everybody had blood on them. It was hard to tell who got stabbed and who didn't."

"When was it that he pointed the knife at you?" asked Lieutenant MacDonald. "Did he take a slice at you with the knife?"

"No, he just kind of put it in front of him," recalled Shaw as he demonstrated how Chasson was holding the knife at waist level. He also went on to briefly describe the weapon, claiming the blade was at least five or six inches in length, maybe more.

"What were his exact words to you?" Lieutenant MacDonald asked.

Shaw sat upright in the stiff chair, stretched his back, took a deep breath, and said, "He was yelling, 'Get away, motherfucker! Get away, motherfucker!' He must have said it five times."

"And you backed off?"

"Yeah. I mean, he had that look of fire in his eyes," Shaw explained. "I mean, Christ, you know, after somebody stabs somebody, they're gonna look a little crazy, you know?"

"This all started with Kevin Racette, am I right?"

"Yeah, over fifty bucks."

"Who told you that?"

"Kevin did."

"Did you question Kevin about why your friend Mel got stuck?" the lieutenant quizzed.

"Uh huh," replied Shaw. "It was over money owed, I guess."

"Fifty bucks?"

Shaw slightly lowered his tone and glanced at the floor as he answered the lieutenant's question in the affirmative. The painful realization came to him that his friend Paul Melody was dead, murdered over an insignificant amount of money. The thought turned his stomach.

"Was it involving drugs?"

Shaw shrugged his broad shoulders and remarked, "Kevin didn't actually say that—I just assumed it was."

Lieutenant MacDonald nodded and leaned back, testing the limits of his chair. He laced his hands behind his head and, for a moment, stared at the garish fluorescent lights suspended above. The windowless interrogation room had grown considerably warmer. The air conditioning was not keeping up with the climbing exterior humidity seeping into the building. MacDonald loosened his tie and took a deep breath as he collected his thoughts.

Based on the evidence gathered to this stage of the probe, there seemed to be little doubt it was a drug deal gone bad that led to the death of Paul Melody, as well as the near-fatal attack on one of the young man's would-be rescuers, Robert Hayward.

In his twenty years of service to the Quincy Police Department, Lieutenant MacDonald could trace many of the crimes he'd dealt with back to drugs, violent or otherwise. The murder at Pageant Field was no exception.

Quincy, like similar cities across the country, was awash in drugs and drug-related crimes during the sixties and well into the seventies. The worldwide War on Drugs, led by the United States Federal government, officially began six years earlier in 1971. During a press conference, President Richard M. Nixon borrowed a familiar slogan once coined by FBI Director J. Edgar Hoover. While Hoover used the term to describe ruthless bank robbers of the Depression era, Nixon described the runaway proliferation of drugs and drug abuse as the country's "public enemy number one." At the time, it was believed that ten percent of American troops fighting in Vietnam were battling another enemy: heroin addiction. They sought the means to diminish the near-constant fear of death—or worse, capture. And it wasn't much better on the streets of cities across the nation. In 1973, the Drug Enforcement Agency was created to combat the scourge, but despite stringent new laws for offenders, as well as sweeping changes to the treatment of addicts, the DEA proved ineffective.

After just a pair of interviews, Lieutenant MacDonald understood that a former heroin dealer by the name of Kevin Racette, who was known to Quincy Police, owed a party named Mark Bray a small sum of money (fifty dollars) and Bray had asked Leroy Chasson to run an errand—to collect the debt. The pair had been incarcerated at MCI-Concord and struck up a typical prison friendship, often based on bartering and trading tasks both inside and outside the walls. Chasson was out on parole, released after serving time for armed robbery, while Bray had recently escaped from a work assignment at the Fernald State School for the developmentally disabled in Waltham. He was on the run and therefore, it was far too risky for him to surface. It made more sense for Chasson, a free man, to oblige his friend and settle the score.

Racette, Lieutenant MacDonald gathered, was not fully cooperative when Chasson approached him at Pageant Field, which triggered a confrontation that grew into an all-out brawl and two stabbings, one deadly. MacDonald anticipated that his upcoming discussion with Racette, if effective, would unveil constructive information. Meanwhile, based on the statement from Bryan Fitzpatrick earlier, Chasson, Bray, and a third party left the Chelsea house party in a stolen vehicle. Their whereabouts were unknown, but the lieutenant had a suspicion the murder suspects were still in the general area.

There was a knock on the door of the interview room and a uniformed officer poked his head in. "Excuse me, detectives, but there's a Kevin Racette who has been waiting to see you."

"Thanks, we're wrapping up here," Lieutenant MacDonald said. He straightened out his stack of paperwork and returned the Chasson notes to the folder. Glancing at his colleagues, he asked if they had any further questions for Nathan Shaw. All three men shook their heads.

"All right, Nathan," he said. "We appreciate your time and honesty. You've been very helpful."

"Anytime," Shaw replied, visibly relieved that his grilling was over. He rose from his chair and proceeded toward the door. As Shaw exited, he spotted Kevin Racette standing in the narrow corridor, leaning against a wall. His expression was gloomy. As Shaw passed him, he muttered, "Best of luck in there, Kevin."

Racette nodded and slowly made his way into the interview room.

# EIGHTEEN—PLAIN SIGHT

In a brazen move, Leroy Chasson lingered in the Boston area after taking the life of an innocent young Quincy man and severely wounding another. Instead of quickly gaining a safe distance from the all-hands police dragnet that sought him, the wanted desperado and his escapee cohort Mark Bray remained within arms' reach of the local authorities and the FBI agents who scoured the Greater Boston region and beyond.

A printed photograph of the two fugitives could be found tucked in the tunic pocket of every officer walking the beat, while each patrol car had Chasson's likeness affixed to the dashboard. At regular intervals, Teletype updates were distributed and received by police agencies, both large and small, across the Commonwealth. The Quincy Police represented the administrative lead in the search for the outlaw, but Boston also assumed a significant role. Chasson had, after all, killed the son of one of their own highly respected Boston Police officers. It certainly was not spoken aloud, but when the wrongdoer was eventually apprehended, the arresting officers would likely dole out a serious beating when Chasson resisted arrest—whether he resisted or not.

And yet, despite the obvious risk, the two men roamed the streets of Boston, defiantly taunting the police, daring capture.

Mark Bray had set off thirty minutes earlier to meet Kathleen MacDonald. This woman, Chasson explained to his friend, was the "package" he had earlier alluded to.

It was Wednesday, August 24, and nearing midday as Bostonians enjoyed a comfortably mild seventy-five degrees. Pleasant breezes infused with the scents of salt and brine wafted in from the nearby Boston Harbor, where a year earlier, dozens of tall ships had gathered to commemorate the nation's bicentennial. The weather conditions were uncommon for Boston during what were commonly described as the "dog days of summer." Baking temperatures and the typically oppressive August humidity often made outdoor activities unbearable. A thin gray blanket of clouds prevailed but thankfully, there seemed to be no threat of rain. They could always head for Bray's room at the Milner but immediate shelter from rain would have been a problem for the two fugitives. Soon to be three when Kathleen joined them.

Examining the near-empty pack of cigarettes stuffed in his shirt pocket, Leroy Chasson realized it might be a suitable time to buy more. He wasn't certain how long it would take Bray to deliver Kathleen but figured he had at least an hour to kill.

Stepping off the wide granite steps of the Park Street Church, he made his way toward a small Tremont Street grocery mart he had noticed earlier. Ever vigilant for Boston cops walking the beat, he weaved through the lunch hour foot traffic. Scores of workers hurried past on the wide sidewalk, heading for a quick meal, meeting, or appointments unknown. Teeming commuters poured from the egress of the hectic Park Street MBTA station like an army of swarming ants. As the intersecting point of the often-chaotic Green and Red subway lines, it was one of the busier depots in the city.

Lowering his head and wishing he had a baseball cap or some other form of concealment, Chasson began to second-guess his choice of this location as a rendezvous point. Then again, most of the people scurrying about could not be bothered with their surroundings. Nobody gave the wanted killer even a cursory glance. And besides, media coverage of the events in Quincy had, to that point in time, been limited. His likeness was not yet known to the public. He recalled griping to Bray about the lack of news attention during breakfast at the HoJo's earlier that morning. As twisted as the thought might be, Chasson felt his actions at Pageant Field warranted a front-page news story. But now, as he watched workers racing back-and-forth with daily newspapers tucked under their arms, he understood a photo splashed on the front page for all to see would have made it far riskier to move about in public. He realized an obscure column on page four of the *Boston Globe* morning edition was actually a blessing in disguise.

Chasson bought a couple packs of smokes, grabbed a candy bar to gnaw on, and, as an afterthought, added a can of soda. Despite a filling breakfast only hours earlier, he felt the pangs of hunger returning. He made a detour to the newspaper rack and scanned the assorted front pages. An updated edition of the *Boston Globe* was still hours away and the *Boston Herald American* showcased an article about popular rock n' roll superstar Elvis Presley, whose death a week earlier at age forty-two had stunned the nation. None of the papers, thankfully, had yet reported the Quincy murder in depth.

He paid the clerk and exited the cramped market. Minutes later, the wanted man was comfortably perched on a wrought-iron bench opposite the ornate Park Street Church just inside the Beacon Street side of the Boston Common. His new vantage point was advantageous. Not only would he be able to see the return of Bray, but he could keep a watchful eye for approaching police. He had a decent view of Tremont Street in both directions.

Chasson cracked the soda and gulped half the can. He balanced the container on the bench and lit a smoke. Across the street, a pair of tourists snapped photos of the large glass-paned double doors of the Park Street Church, which was known for its nineteenth-century role in human rights and antislavery movements. To the rear of the historic brick place of worship was the Granary Burying Ground, which held the graves of Samuel Adams, Paul Revere, and Crispus Attucks, the first American colonist killed at the start of the Revolutionary War. Mary Goose, known to most as Mother Goose, was also interred in the Granary. The Freedom Trail, which traverses two and a half miles from Boston Common to Charlestown, features seventeen historic locations, including both the Park Street Church and the Granary Burying Ground.

Gazing to his left, toward the west and the Back Bay of Boston, Chasson admired a pair of Boston's tallest skyscrapers, the Prudential and Hancock Towers.

The Hancock Tower Observatory, which treated visitors to a white-knuckled, high-speed elevator ride followed by commanding views of Boston and scenic points as far north as the White Mountains of New Hampshire, was once a threat to pedestrians and passing motorists. Soon after the building opened for business in 1976, scores of the five-hundred-pound azure glass reflective windowpanes were found to become dislodged by high winds and tumble up to eight hundred feet to the streets below. Until repairs were completed, police were forced to close nearby streets, including St. James Avenue and Clarendon Streets, when the prevailing wind speed exceeded forty-five miles per hour.

Each of the two buildings stood sentry over the historic three-hundred-and fifty-year-old coastal city, which a year earlier, had been the centerpiece of the nation's 1976 bicentennial celebration. Chasson might have enjoyed the events, including the fireworks and the historic Tall Ships' visit to Boston Harbor, which drew millions of tourists. But to his chagrin, during the momentous celebration, the repeat offender was once again behind bars on what he felt were trumped-up drug charges.

Leroy Chasson trained a watchful eye on the steps of the Park Street Church and before long, spotted his friend Mark Bray standing beside the woman Chasson had first met two years earlier while he was incarcerated at MCI-Walpole. He grinned as he rose from the bench, exited the Common, and made his way across the street to greet her.

"Kathleen, I'm so happy to see you," Lee uttered as he drew her firmly into his arms.

She warmly returned the embrace and replied, "I've missed you too."

Chasson looked to Bray, who was nervously surveying the landscape and the throngs of passing pedestrians, many emerging from the nearby Park Street subway station. Bray was not about to express his concern aloud or point out to his often-hotheaded friend that there were far safer, less conspicuous places to meet up with this woman if that was, in fact, necessary. In his opinion, there was absolutely no need for Chasson to reunite with his girlfriend amid their flight from justice. They were fleeing to Canada, another potential disaster in the making, and getting out of the area should have been their priority. But if Leroy Chasson was adamant about meeting with her and doing so in the risky Boston location, he should have at least considered an arrangement after dark.

The mounting apprehension must have shown on Bray's face.

"You okay?" Chasson asked.

"There must be a million cops around here," his co-conspirator said, gesturing toward the Massachusetts State House a city block away at the top of Beacon Street, its prominent gold leaf dome visible throughout the city. Eight years earlier, in 1969, the dome had been regilded with actual gold at a cost of thirty-six thousand taxpayer dollars.

It stood to reason that Governor Michael Dukakis and politicians of all shapes and sizes, some unpopular, would require a considerable law enforcement detachment to protect them. A handful of the Massachusetts State Police detailed to guard the State House and its occupants were attired in plainclothes and not readily detectable, which compounded Bray's unease.

Chasson nodded in agreement and said, "Look, Mark, go grab a bite to eat and we'll catch up with you at the Milner later, okay?"

"Yeah."

"Five, six o'clock?"

"Yeah, yeah—sure," Bray agreed. "I have a room waiting."

"Need some cash?" Chasson asked, pulling a few loose bills from his pocket and offering them.

"No, I'm good," Bray replied. Lee had obviously forgotten that Bray's mother had, days earlier, sent him an envelope stuffed with cash for expenses.

"Thanks again for bringing my girl here; I really appreciate it. I'll properly introduce the two of you later at the hotel."

"Sure, not a problem." With a quick wave in parting, Bray strode toward Tremont Street, turned left, and soon blended into the dense crowd of midweek workers.

Chasson turned to his companion, gently grasped her by the arm, and ushered her toward a nearby entrance to Boston Common. "C'mon, let's walk."

"Sure," said Kathleen with a strained smile.

The couple started out briskly and then slowed their pace. Despite the perfect weather, there were few people enjoying the expansive park. There was certainly no need to hurry. They strolled wordlessly along the wide concrete walkways that crisscrossed the park. Chasson broke the silence. "I'll be leaving soon," he disclosed.

"Leaving? Where are you going?"

"Heading north," Leroy imparted. "To Canada, I'm thinking."

The couple reached the western limits of the Common, crossed over traffic-free Charles Street with other pedestrians, and entered the Boston Public Garden, home of the world-famous century-old Swan Boats. There were a handful of tourists snapping photographs of family members posing in front of the flower beds growing in abundance. Chasson guided Kathleen to a secluded bench. He lit a smoke and offered one to her. She shook her head.

"So, Canada?" she asked with a quizzical look on her face.

"Yeah," he answered, pausing to take a long draw on his cigarette. "But I have to make a stop in Maine."

"Maine?"

Chasson paused again, deciding whether to share the reason for his Down-East detour with Kathleen. But he trusted her and knew that she wouldn't fold under the pressure of police scrutiny or interrogation. Besides, he needed her help, specifically with renting a car. He certainly didn't have the credentials. Nor did Bray.

"A little town called Fryeburg," he shared.

"Why Fryeburg?" she persisted.

"There's an antique store," Chasson answered. "It's in the middle of nowhere. They have antique clocks, I'm told. Expensive clocks." Kathleen MacDonald nodded, letting her boyfriend know that she understood. "We need the money," he added without being asked.

"Lee, I'm going with you."

He began to speak, likely to talk her out of it, although that's not what he really wanted. She put her fingers to his lips, silencing him. Chasson grinned and shrugged his shoulders in resignation. Among other attributes, Kathleen MacDonald was a stubborn woman. She wouldn't take *no* for an answer.

"C'mon," he said, rising from the bench and grasping her hand. "Let's find a bite to eat."

Near the southwest corner of the park, they stumbled on a street vendor selling hot dogs. Grabbing a couple of dogs and sodas, the couple returned to their original park bench in the flower-filled botanical gardens and wiled away the afternoon watching tourists riding the nostalgic Swan Boats on the lagoon.

At dusk, they left the Boston Public Garden. In no hurry, they meandered along the wide sidewalks toward Boylston Street. An early autumn breeze ruffled the leaves overhead, leaves that would soon turn brilliant reds, yellows, and oranges to mark the New England seasonal change to autumn.

The carefree pair, their arms locked in an awkward embrace as they strolled, made their way to Charles Street. They walked past the historic landmark birthplace of noted nineteenth-century writer Edgar Allan Poe without a second look and soon reached their destination. Passing beneath the wide red awning with simple block lettering depicting the hotel's name, Chasson moved ahead of his companion, grasped the ornate handle, and pulled open the heavy door. Kathleen strode past him, tipping her head in thanks, and entered the lobby.

"Welcome to the Milner, Mr. and Mrs. Travers," said the pretty desk clerk as she fetched the room key from a cabinet mounted on the wall. "I see you'll be guests of Mr. Roach in his room."

Leroy found it humorous that Mark Bray had used the phony name "Roach" but his own choice of Mr. and Mrs. Travers, the parents of his *other* girlfriend, was no less amusing.

"Thank you," said Chasson as he clutched the key and guided his girlfriend to the elevator.

# NINETEEN — MILNER HOTEL

After leaving Leroy and Kathleen at Boston Common, Mark Bray made his way along Tremont and then to Cambridge Street. He was still digesting the breakfast he'd wolfed down at the Howard Johnson's hours earlier, so instead of eating again, he stopped at a convenient mart adjacent to the Massachusetts General Hospital to check the newspapers. Little had changed in the late editions.

Circling back to the Common, Bray made his way toward Charles Street and turned south, headed for the Milner.

A week prior to helping Leroy Chasson reunite with his previously undisclosed girlfriend, Mark Bray found lodging at the historic Milner Hotel. Compared to some of the other establishments in the area, he sensed the Milner was the best hideaway following his escape. It was a low-key place, tucked away on the northern fringe of Chinatown. Guests and employees kept to themselves. In addition, Bray had an ace in the hole. He knew the front desk clerk, Karen McLaughlin. Several years earlier, before he was sent away to the Concord Reformatory, the pair had attended classes together at North Quincy High School. He felt their connection would fuel her loyalty, and her silence, if the police should happen to pay a visit to the hotel in their canvas of the city.

"Welcome to the Milner Hotel," McLaughlin greeted when Bray first checked in to the establishment on Sunday, August 20. He approached the small desk in the tiny lobby, which had little space to spare and few furnishings to speak of. Mark returned the attractive young woman's smile. "Checking in?" she asked, spinning the registration book in his direction.

Nodding, he picked up the pen and without putting a great deal of thought into it, scribbled an alias, James Roach.

"Welcome, um, Mr. Roach," she said with a girlish giggle as she glanced at his falsified signature. "It has been a long time."

"Three years," Bray agreed, counting backward in his head to their high school days.

They traded pleasantries, but he soon broke off the conversation. Paranoia, a frequent visitor since his escape, crept back into his mind. He anxiously scanned his surroundings. As he turned to scrutinize the tiny lobby, Bray half expected to see the police standing behind him, dangling handcuffs. To his relief, there were no cops, nor were there any other patrons. He assumed business would pick up later in the evening, as theatre guests arrived for a night's stay following a show and dinner.

With another warm smile, McLaughlin slid a room key across the waist-high polished wooden desktop. "Well, Mr. Roach, I certainly do hope you enjoy your stay with us."

Nestled in the heart of Boston's vibrant Theatre District at 78 Charles Street, the two-star hotel was aptly described as a "quaint brownstone" by a Boston-based travel periodical. Walking distance to the five-hundred-seat Charles Playhouse, which was established twenty years earlier in 1957, the Milner was an imposing century-old five-story brick structure known as one of the most enduring small hotels in the city.

The Milner later became known for its dark history. In 2001, terrorist Abdulaziz Al-Omari was reported to have spent his final night in the hotel on September 10 before joining al-Qaida hijack ringleader Mohammed Atta in launching deadly suicide attacks on New York City, Washington, DC, and Pennsylvania from Boston's Logan Airport. Prior to their stay at the Milner, the terrorists also checked in to the Days Hotel in Brighton and the Charles Hotel in Harvard Square.

Decades earlier, the Milner Hotel housed scores of reporters from around the world who descended on Boston to cover the trial and subsequent executions of Nicola Sacco and Bartolomeo Vanzetti. The pair was put to death on August 23, 1927, in the Charlestown Prison for a murder committed during a botched armed robbery of a gas station in 1920 in the Massachusetts South Shore community of Braintree, which neighbors Quincy.

Two days prior to their executions, twenty thousand flocked to Boston Common, marking one of dozens of worldwide protests of the questionable verdict. Overseas, the outcry turned violent, and lives were lost in riots with the police. According to accounts, the Italian immigrants were led to the Charlestown electric chair, which had claimed sixty-five lives between 1901 and 1947, following a sham trial and politically tainted convictions. Sacco and Vanzetti were admitted anarchists. Bias and prejudice played a significant role in their deaths, according to legal historians.

In an unrelated but certainly ironic twist, the executions of the two wrongly accused Italian men took place exactly fifty years to the day prior to the murder of Paul Melody at Pageant Field.

Mark Bray settled into an inexpensive but comfortable room on an upper floor. There was an elevator but he chose the stairs. Furniture in his room was sparse. A bed, a well-worn chair, and a chest of drawers with a television resting on its top filled the small space. It was cramped, but compared to his six-by-nine cell in the Concord Reformatory, this lodging was comfortable.

He gazed out the window and noticed the wrought-iron fire escape attached to the side of the building like patterned lattice. In later years, it was pointed out by a hotel employee that the escape framework was accessible from all rooms for obvious reasons but also allowed a Peeping Tom, if so inclined, to peer through the single window of each dwelling. The staff suggested that each guest pull their curtains before retiring for the evening. For Mark Bray, however, the escapeway provided just that—a means to vacate in a hurry if he sensed the cops were on the way to his room.

Weeks before, Bray had indirectly escaped from Concord. He took flight from a work detail at the Fernald School in suburban Waltham, a bustling community situated eleven miles northwest of Boston. Through good behavior, Bray had earned the privilege of working a day shift as an attendant at the Fernald. It was a dreadful sanatorium established in the late nineteenth century to house the mentally ill, thinly disguised as a school but most of the *students* had been forcibly ripped from their families and admitted to the Fernald School based on tainted IQ tests.

Prominent author Michael D'Antonio wrote a detailed account about the Fernald School and its reluctant occupants. In *The State Boys Rebellion*, D'Antonio described in depth the eugenics debate, which resulted in the confinement of many children who were thought unfit to be part of society. Those earning an IQ score between 30 and 50 were rated as "imbeciles" and were often treated like common criminals and placed under lock and key. In custody, some of the children were abused and beaten. In today's testing, a score below 70 is considered impaired but obviously does not trigger mandatory institutionalization like it did a half century ago. An average IQ result today is between 85 and 115.

In the 1920s, misguided scientists believed that by permanently filtering out the "feeble-minded" individuals from society in general, eventually, the gene pool could be improved across humanity. Nazi Germany leaders adopted eugenic concepts in their efforts to eradicate certain peoples and develop a "superior race."

As bad as conditions were at the Fernald, Bray would have accepted any task just to detach himself from the dreary confinement of Concord. In hindsight, he understood he would have been far better off completing his sentence. He was serving time for armed robbery and assorted drug charges, but at the time of his escape, he was within sight of a parole and a chance to reclaim a normal life. A few more months, even a year, at the Concord Reformatory would have been a cinch compared to what lay in store for him if authorities managed to successfully hunt him down. As a result of his rash decision to bolt from the work detail at the Fernald, he faced an all-but-certain return to captivity and the likelihood of a far harsher existence for years. Few escapees were ever returned to their original placement. Typically, the Massachusetts Department of Correction transferred these individuals to more secure facilities—jails with higher walls, thicker steel doors, and, most fearsome of all, a population rife with violent hardcore criminals. The worst of the worst in Massachusetts Correction was, in this instance, the dreaded Walpole State Prison.

Mark Bray spent several restful days and nights at the Milner Hotel. He dined on assorted takeout meals from restaurants within walking distance. Fearing the police, he seldom ate at the diners themselves and instead ferried the food back to his room. When he risked travel, he did so after dark. He skimmed the local papers, watched a little television, and read a tattered paperback he found abandoned in the hotel lobby.

On a pair of occasions after his flight from the Fernald, he met up with his former Concord cellmate, Leroy Chasson. On one early August night, while drinking at an out-of-the-way watering hole in the depths of the Combat

Zone, the discussion turned to Quincy and a man named Kevin Racette.

"What about him?" Chasson had asked.

"He owes me money," Bray answered. "He had some stuff smuggled into the joint for me but he hustled me on the amount. Bastard owes me fifty bucks."

"Want me to get it from him?"

"Yeah, if you don't mind," Bray agreed, nodding vigorously. "I can't go to Quincy. Too many people would recognize me."

Chasson raised his beer for a slug and nodded that he would accept the errand, setting the wheels in motion for a night of chaos in Quincy.

"Consider it done," he said with a grin.

# TWENTY—RACETTE'S TURN

While the earlier interviews were certainly productive, it was the statement from Kevin Racette that most captivated Lieutenant Neil MacDonald and his associates. From the information gleaned from their earlier discussion with Bryan Fitzgerald, police officials had learned that Racette was at the center of Leroy Chasson's assault at Pageant Field. Racette, according to Fitzgerald and other witnesses, was at Ground Zero. He was the unwilling trigger point. After a brief conversation with the perpetrator, Racette was knocked senseless in an unprovoked ambush, which ignited a chain of events that led to the homicide of Paul Melody and the near-fatal stabbing of Robert Hayward. Hayward, the lieutenant learned, was recovering from his stab wounds and faced surgery at Quincy City Hospital. Obviously, Hayward's statement would be gathered when he was coherent enough to answer questions.

"Kevin, would you give us your name and spell your last, please?" In a practiced action, Lieutenant MacDonald positioned the cassette tape recorder to ensure it would pick up his guest's comments.

"Kevin Racette," the respondent grunted in a low, barely audible voice. He slumped forward in his chair and seemed visibly annoyed. He was apparently less than interested in speaking with the police, even though he had nothing to hide. "R-A-C-E-T-T-E."

Lieutenant MacDonald eyed the all-important recorder, which had been in near-constant use since the investigation began. The cassette tape was new and the batteries had recently been changed, but in this instance, he was not certain if the witness was speaking loudly enough for the built-in microphone to pick up his comments. Inhaling deeply, the usually patient lawman instructed his witness to move closer to the device, speak louder, and repeat his answer. Racette reluctantly sat upright in the rigid chair and complied.

Several of the officers who had aided MacDonald in the earlier interviews had left the station, driving to their nearby homes to grab a catnap. Only State Police Detective Bob Mazaray remained. As was the standard in homicide cases, the Massachusetts State Police Lab was lending a hand with crime scene preservation. Mazaray was primarily tasked with the collection of physical evidence and other related aspects of the rapidly developing case. But while his capable crew was laboring at Pageant Field, he felt he could contribute in other ways, such as analyzing witnesses. Like MacDonald, he knew Racette was far too important an interview to miss while napping in a bunk room.

"All right, Kevin, that's better," MacDonald said. "What's your date of birth?"

"January 11, 1952. I'm twenty-five."

MacDonald nodded, jotted a note on his yellow pad, and said, "I'm told you've been read your Miranda Rights—do you understand those rights?"

"Am I under arrest?"

"No."

"Okay then, I understand my rights," agreed Racette who, in recent years, had occasion to hear those same rights during arrests for drug use and distribution charges. As a long-time junkie and dealer, he was well-versed in that respect.

"Kevin, I assume you know the reason for this interview?"

"Yeah," he said, nodding.

"Would you relate to us what you know about the incident when you got there?"

To that point, the recalcitrant witness hadn't spoken more than a dozen words. He was evasive and slipped back into a slouch in the steel chair, arms folded defiantly across his chest, offering little. It was a bit of a surprise to both MacDonald and Mazaray when suddenly their obstinate subject suddenly veered off on a verbal tangent, speaking nonstop for a moment or two. The questioning of Racette, it seemed, might not be as trying as the two investigators first thought.

"I was there most of the night," Racette began. "From about nine o'clock to whatever time it was when it happened. And, uh, I had been drinking. I had been drinking most of the day. I was drinking that afternoon. I was drinking that night. Maybe I was drunk, intoxicated. Whatever. And, um, from what I remember, somebody said, 'Kevin, come here.' And this guy took me off to the side and everything. And I looked at him and I says, 'Do I know you?' And he goes, 'Yeah, you know me from Concord.' And as I'm looking in his face, I got cracked; you know, he punched me. And uh, I went down and then I heard, like, what I could see, I saw stars and mass confusion going on. I do remember seeing this kid, Paul, my friend, Paul Melody. He kinda sticks out, he's two hundred pounds, blond hair, you know? And, uh, I'm seeing him kind of hanging over this guy. The next thing, I'm trying to get up and I walked over and there was all kinds of yelling. Everyone was in a panic and we saw Paul there on the ground. Everybody thought he was knocked out or something."

"Describe what happened next."

"It was mass confusion," Racette repeated. "Like I said before, Paul Melody was standing over this guy. Everything happened so fast and everyone was in a panic. I heard a car door slam and then a car sped out of the lot. There was a big pool of blood under Mel."

Racette paused, shook his head in disbelief, and took a swig from a soda can that had been placed on the table. He rubbed his sleepy, bloodshot eyes and continued. "So we grabbed the keys out of his pocket and one of my friends went to get his car. Paul was lifted into the back seat and a couple of my friends piled in. Hayward, the other kid who was stabbed, went with them. We were still trying to get our thoughts together about what had just happened when the police came up in the ambulance."

MacDonald understood that the ambulance arrived just minutes after the boys had left the park, heading for Quincy City Hospital in Melody's car.

"We told the cops what happened," Racette added. "They were looking at me kind of funny because I was covered in blood. I told them I had helped lift Mel into the car and his blood got on my clothes."

The lieutenant asked the witness if he saw a weapon of any sort; his response was that he saw something *shiny* but wasn't certain it was a knife. MacDonald then asked Racette if he knew Bryan Fitzgerald. "Yes, but I didn't see him arrive at the park."

MacDonald moved on to a new line of questioning, targeted toward his assumption that Racette knew more about his attacker than he was disclosing.

"You were in Concord?" MacDonald said, which was more statement than question. He already knew the details of Racette's Concord Reformatory incarceration thanks to the condensed version of his rap sheet, which was fanned out on the table in front of him. But the investigator wanted to hear it directly from the target of the accused killer, hoping to draw out details of past prison strife between the men or something that might have fueled the attack. MacDonald still could not grasp that a young man lost his life over fifty dollars.

"Yeah, I was in for a long time."

"How long?"

"Forty months. I was released July last year. I've been out for thirteen months. I finished rehab on March 8, about six months ago. I've stayed clean."

MacDonald nodded, disappointed that an evasive Racette failed to elaborate on his association with Leroy Chasson. The cop figured that if the witness spoke more about his time spent behind bars at MCI-Concord, it might jar loose more information about the perpetrator. "Do you remember this guy, Leroy?"

"The name? Um, no."

"Did you recognize his face?"

"Uh, maybe—can't be sure," Racette replied hesitantly, swallowing hard. "But in jail, you see a lot of different faces."

"I mean, from when you saw him last night?"

After a long pause, Racette finally answered, "Um, no, I didn't recognize him. I don't know him." He absently rubbed at the red welt on his right cheekbone, the visible remnant of his attacker's fist. The swelling had worsened and a dark black bruise was forming beneath his eye. It was painful to the touch but he was thankful the guy hadn't hit him in the mouth and knocked out a few teeth.

MacDonald glared at the witness. His patience was wearing thin and he did not believe Racette was telling the truth. He was certain that Racette knew Leroy Chasson, but for reasons unknown, was unwilling to admit it. Racette placed his hands flat on the table surface and stared at them, avoiding the accusatory stare. MacDonald decided not to dwell on the subject of Racette's relationship with the killer. He was certain that the young man before him would change his tune under pressure, like Bryan Fitzgerald had when he lied about driving the perpetrator to a Quincy train station.

MacDonald decided it was time to tighten the screws. "Okay, Kevin, you do realize that Paul Melody is dead by a homicide. We're talking about a murder."

"Yeah," Racette acknowledged after a pause, squirming in the uncomfortable steel chair. The interrogation room, poorly ventilated, had grown stifling. He wasn't claustrophobic but at that moment, he felt like he was shoehorned in a crowded elevator. He glanced at the door of the interview room, the only exit, and wondered if it was locked. If he bolted, could he get past a gauntlet of police officers scattered throughout the building? Not likely.

"Kevin, you've been in a number of jams in the past, am I right?" asked the lieutenant.

"Yeah," Racette admitted, understanding this probing cop was already fully aware of his criminal history. He realized the papers spread out on the table were part of his criminal jacket.

"And now we're talking about a homicide," MacDonald repeated, a decided edge in his voice.

"I know," Kevin concurred, now on full alert amid the sudden insinuation that he was partly responsible for Paul Melody's murder.

"We want the truth from you. All right? It's time to get down to brass tacks. Let's not kid around with each other. We've talked to a lot of people here tonight. We've got a good idea why he was out there. Chasson comes out here for a particular reason and you were a big part of that reason. Now, let's have the truth."

"I'm trying as best I can—" began Racette, his face turning a shade of crimson. There was a note of arrogance in his tone, carefully measured.

The cops, to that point, had treated him with fairness and respect. They had been patient with him. But that could change at any moment. He certainly did not want to invite their wrath. He had been on the receiving end of that treatment in the past, as a youth when he refused to divulge the names of his drug dealers—that would have been a death sentence once word leaked that he had ratted out the dealers.

"Go on, Kevin," Lieutenant MacDonald urged.

"I can only speculate," the witness proceeded. "But there's a good chance a story spread from jail, and when this guy Chasson got out, he was asked to do it."

"So, you're saying someone sent him out here after you?"

Nodding, Racette replied, "I've been thinking about it since I left the Mount. I'm a lot more sober now and thinking straight."

"Any idea who sent him?"

"No."

"Does the name Mark Bray ring a bell with you?"

Hearing MacDonald mention the familiar name, Racette sat bolt upright in his chair, at full attention. Suddenly, he realized who was behind the violent attack. And obviously, the police were also aware. It all made sense to him now.

"Yeah, I know Mark Bray. I owe him money."

Racette claimed it was the same paltry amount the investigators had heard about throughout the night from Bryan Fitzgerald and other witnesses who had knowledge of the debt. Fifty dollars. The witness nodded in agreement when asked if he was certain that was the reason behind Leroy Chasson's visit to Pageant Field. Racette went further, explaining that he was supposed to deliver, through a courier, one hundred dollars' worth of heroin to Bray at MCI-Concord but only had fifty available at the time. He had earlier been paid the C-note and promised to return with the other half of the stuff but failed to do so. As time passed, Bray obviously grew enraged over the shortfall. He sent messages, ignored it seemed, that he wanted the money or the drugs. When neither arrived, he arranged for Chasson, newly released from jail, to deliver the message to Racette in person. Bray, a native of Quincy and widely known in the city, could not do it himself. And besides, his friend Leroy had a knack. He could be *very* convincing.

MacDonald nodded in agreement at the scenario Racette laid out for him but continued his line of questioning, seeking confirmation.

"Do you think Bray might have mentioned to Leroy that you ripped him off and he took it upon himself to go after you?"

"Ripped off?"

"Well, you ripped him off of fifty bucks, didn't you?"

"Oh, you mean go out and get revenge, right?" Racette agreed, ignoring the insult. "I guess he could have. It's a good possibility."

"Did you know that Mark Bray is an escapee now?"

"No, I didn't."

"You didn't know that?"

Racette hesitated, realizing that it made more sense to be truthful with the cops, at least with certain aspects of the story.

"Yeah, actually, I knew he was out," he said, changing his response.

MacDonald was annoyed with the inconsistent answer and made his displeasure known. "You better get your values straight here," he said, raising his voice. "We're not concerned with his escape or your drug activity. We're investigating a murder. Possibly two. Now this guy, Leroy, he came out here expressly for you."

"That's what I figured."

"Well, he was apparently convinced that it was you that he stabbed," MacDonald imparted. "He was very happy about it."

"Oh yeah?"

"Yeah. That was his intention in coming out here."

"But he punched me," Racette said, emphasizing his narration with a jab of his fist. "If he wanted to stab me, why didn't he just stab me?"

"Can't say I know," the lieutenant admitted. "So, the amount? Fifty? Are you telling me that Bray would put a contract out for you for fifty dollars?"

"I don't believe it either. We were pretty good friends in jail. But Mark is very vindictive."

"Yeah, I guess so," the lieutenant agreed. "Somebody is dead as a result of Mark being vindictive. They came after you and got somebody else."

"I've been thinking about this whole thing, saying to myself, 'That fuckin' punk, all this over fifty bucks,'" said Kevin, growing animated. "Fifty lousy fuckin' bucks."

MacDonald determined that neither of his colleagues had any further questions. He dismissed the witness. Racette rose from his chair and made his way to the door and suddenly paused. After a moment, he returned and sat again. MacDonald watched and waited.

After deep contemplation, Racette said, "I need to come clean about something."

"Go ahead," the lieutenant prompted.

"I lied earlier," admitted the witness. "This is the first time in my life I've ever sat down in a police station and said shit like this. You know, rat people out."

"Well, Kevin, you've got to admit, this is the first time in your life that your friends—"

Racette interrupted the man, finishing the comment. "Yeah, I know, got croaked like that."

"So, we were talking about Mark Bray, the guy who lives here in Quincy?"

"Yeah."

"How do you know he's the one who sent Chasson out here?"

"Well, because Chasson was out—paroled from Concord—and Bray had escaped," he explained. "A couple weeks ago, they were seen together in a bar. It was one of those situations where, you know, they were talking and—"

"And Bray told this guy Chasson he was bullshit at you over fifty bucks?" MacDonald said, filling in the details of the alleged transaction. "You're sticking with that amount—fifty?"

"Yeah."

Racette recapped his testimony, claiming that ten months earlier, in October 1976, he was filling an order for Mark Bray who, at the time, was still behind bars at MCI-Concord. Bray was seeking one hundred dollars' worth of heroin. Racette sent a partial order of the drugs with their mutual friend, Bobby Russell, along with a message that supply was short and the remaining half would be delivered in a matter of days.

At the time, Racette fully intended to follow through, either with the additional heroin or a refund. He failed to send either, triggering a deadly chain of events.

"So, Leroy Chasson," MacDonald began. "Earlier, you told us you didn't know him."

"I lied," Racette sharply admitted, lowering his eyes in shame. "I knew him in jail."

"Thank you for your honesty," the lieutenant said as his colleagues nodded approvingly.

"Uh huh," Racette muttered, unable to shield his embarrassment.

"Do you know if he ever stabbed anyone before?"

"He might have, in the can," the witness replied with a shrug. "He wasn't afraid of anyone. He could handle himself. The guy has balls, that's for sure."

"How long have you known him, would you say?"

"Two years. I met him while doing time in Concord."

"And then you saw him last night?"

"Right."

"And what did he have to say when he come up to you?" MacDonald asked.

"He wanted me to go to a party over in Chelsea, with him and another guy," Racette replied, sharing a fact that was being heard by the police for the first time. "I thought nothing of it but as it turned out, it would have been a death trap."

"Is that what you think?"

"Yeah, I would have been found in Chelsea, either mutilated or dead."

"So, you could say that your friend Paul Melody really bailed you out by jumping in to help you," stated MacDonald as he prepared to wrap up the interview—a second time—with his subject.

"Yeah, Mel saved my life."

"Well, it definitely cost him his," the lieutenant said morosely.

# TWENTY-ONE—MORE INTERVIEWS

Quincy Police Lieutenant Neil MacDonald sipped a lukewarm coffee as he awaited the arrival of his next interview subject, Albertine Vasconcellos. On hand to lend their expertise were two highly experienced colleagues, Quincy Detective Paul Smith and Lieutenant Joe MacDonald (no relation), who was representing the Massachusetts State Police. The hope was that Vasconcellos and several others slated to pay a visit to Quincy Police headquarters would mark the conclusion of the interview phase of the ongoing inquiry.

Guided by a uniformed officer, Vasconcellos entered the room and claimed the vacant chair at the far end of the table, which was littered with empty cups and soda cans. The tape recorder, which had been used nonstop for hours, stood at the ready in the center of the table. Lieutenant MacDonald had made certain that a set of fresh batteries and a new cassette tape were installed in the trusty device. Each discussion was subsequently transcribed by the Quincy Police clerical staff.

"Welcome, Mr. Vasconcellos," the lieutenant greeted as he sized up the witness. According to the documents spread across the table, their current guest was a twenty-three-year-old Quincy native, residing at 157 Newbury Street. MacDonald understood, based on earlier interviews with the youth's friends, this individual had commandeered Paul

Melody's car and driven the two stabbing victims to Quincy City Hospital.

"It's very late," he said. "So, we'll try to make this as brief as possible."

Vasconcellos nodded as he shifted in the chair, seeking a comfortable position. Like those who had visited the interview room before him, the effort was in vain.

"Okay, getting back to earlier this evening, which would be August 23, 1977, were you at Pageant Field in Quincy?"

"Yes, sir, I was."

"And could you tell me who you were with?"

"I was with a number of people."

Vasconcellos failed to elaborate. It was not a good start to the interview. MacDonald leaned back in his chair, folded his hands behind his head, and glared menacingly at the young man who, for reasons unknown, had chosen to test him. The lieutenant drew a deep breath and audibly exhaled for all to hear. It was obvious that his patience for the witness' antics was wearing thin. He had been quizzing these kids for hours and cooperation had been hit or miss; far more *miss* than he anticipated. Bryan Fitzgerald and Kevin Racette, both key witnesses, told falsehoods during questioning. Eventually, each man was persuaded to come clean. And now, Vasconcellos was being obstinate, answering a simple question with an empty reply.

The mounting frustration evident in his tone, Lieutenant MacDonald insisted, "Just give me some of the names, please."

"Paul Melody and Hay," Vasconcellos blurted.

"Who is Hay?"

"Hayward. I believe his first name is Robert. I think he's from Brockton. The rest of the people, um, I really don't want to mention any more names."

MacDonald slapped the surface of the table with the flat of his hand. The sound reverberated off the walls of the compact, windowless interview room. He startled his associates, who would admit they could not recall a time when they had seen the longtime Quincy law enforcement officer lose his self-restraint. His calm demeanor was usually a constant. These insubordinate kids were clearly getting under his skin.

"Well, Mr. Vasconcellos, let me mention a name for you," he snarled. "You were with Kevin Racette."

"Yes," was the tentative reply, a slight tremble now evident in the subject's voice.

"Approximately what time did you arrive at Pageant Field?"

"Um, I'd say early. Eight o'clock. I was there by myself at first, but others began to show up thirty minutes later. Maybe quarter to nine."

"Okay, and can you tell me what you were doing up there this evening?"

"We were just, you know, talking and having a few beers," replied Vasconcellos, who was more cooperative following the lieutenant's theatrics. "That's about the extent of it."

MacDonald was content that he had regained control. He shifted to the heart of the matter, asking Vasconcellos questions related to his role following the stabbings. "Something occurred up there, is that correct?"

"Yes, it did," the youth answered ruefully.

"Can you tell me what you saw and what you heard?"

Vasconcellos launched into his depiction of the events, stating he had not seen the actual assault but was deeply entangled in the immediate aftermath. He was approached by Hayward, who said he had been stabbed and needed stitches. The witness noted that he would need far more than that—a substantial blood stain had formed on the man's lower back in the kidney area. The witness went on to say that as he stood over Paul Melody, the young victim wasn't talking or moving at all. Vasconcellos told investigators that he took Mclody's keys from the pocket of his trousers, retrieved his car—which was parked directly adjacent to the picnic pavilion—and backed in next to the prone stabbing casualty, who remained motionless.

"I can't remember who helped us get him in the car," Vasconcellos said, "but they threw him in the back seat. Robert Hay and Gizza got in the car, and we took off for the hospital."

"Gizza?"

"Gazzola—Roger Gazzola. We were the only ones in the car. Me, Gazzola, and the two guys who were stabbed—Hayward and Mel. When we got to the hospital, the emergency people took over. That's the extent of my involvement."

"What did you do after you got to Quincy Hospital?"

"I gave the receptionist any little information I knew about Paul Melody," Vasconcellos answered, shaking his head. "After that, I just went outside and walked around. Thirty minutes later, someone found me to say Melody was gone."

***

Michael Cleary, based in Hawaii and on thirty-day leave from the US Army, was not present at Pageant Field when the murder took place but did spend considerable time at the house party in Chelsea. He had a great deal of information on Mark Bray, which he willingly shared when he was summoned to police headquarters.

"Mark called me nine or ten days ago and asked me to pick up an envelope from his mother," Cleary recalled. "It had money in it. He told me to meet him with it near Government Center. I took the train into Boston and met him on Charles Street at Harvard Gardens."

On his notepad, MacDonald wrote "HARVARD GARDENS," which is one of the older restaurants in Boston, first established in Beacon Hill in 1930. Notably, Harvard Gardens was one of the first bars to earn a license when Prohibition was repealed in 1933 and liquor once again began to flow in the United States.

"What did his mother have to say to you?"

"She said he was in trouble," answered Cleary, referring to Bray's escape from jail. "She said he had access to money from an inheritance."

"Did she give you two thousand dollars?"

"She gave me an envelope," Cleary replied. "I knew there was money in it but didn't know how much." He went on to explain that Bray chose not to visit Quincy to retrieve the cash himself because he wanted to avoid the possibility that someone might see him, drop a dime to the police, and share his whereabouts. While Bray had a lot of friends in Quincy, he also had a number of enemies.

Several days after their meeting in Boston, Bray called Cleary and asked if he would be interested in joining him on a job in Maine stealing antique clocks.

"Mark has asked me to do other jobs with him," he admitted without elaborating on the details. "I never did any of them. I was working and had my own money and didn't have a need to rip things off or beat people."

When asked if he knew Leroy Chasson, Cleary shook his head but then told the cops that he had seen the murder suspect once he and Bryan Fitzgerald returned to the Chelsea house party. "There were a lot of dirty looks between them but nothing verbal," recalled Cleary. "The Chasson guy ordered some kid to get him a towel. He used it to wrap his shirt after he came out of the bathroom."

Joseph Marnell, twenty-one, of 479 Sea Street, was a reluctant eyewitness. In a classic chess match between cop and former criminal, Lieutenant MacDonald questioned Marnell but reached a stalemate. The youth feared his Quincy friends would label him a rat if he said too much to the cops. Recently released from MCI-Concord, where he served a sentence for drug charges, he felt that his statement might in some way trigger his return to prison, where rats were often dealt with severely.

"I'd like to tell you everything you want to know as long as nobody can find out," said Marnell, who was one of the first to encounter Leroy Chasson as the predator approached Kevin Racette. "Can this be used in court?"

MacDonald nodded and said, "Eventually, this will reach the district attorney. It's not some picayune case. We're talking about a murder."

"I had better wait then," Marnell countered. "I'll get a public defender."

"Joe, you can exercise that option if you want," the lieutenant said. "And again, it is recorded. For the sake of the recorder, you refuse to answer any more questions?"

"Yup."

***

Early on the morning of August 24, 1977, Quincy Police Sergeant Kenneth Borst and Detective Sergeant Guido "Budsy" Pettinelli were dispatched to Quincy City Hospital to interview Robert Hayward, twenty-seven, who was recovering from surgery.

According to Dr. Anthony Dragone, Hayward was admitted to QCH with two stab wounds to his lower flank. The first was described as a "three-inch jagged wound," while the second was a "two-inch smooth cut." Hayward was placed on the danger list, although his condition was not considered life-threatening.

Hayward, understandably drowsy from anesthesia and frequent doses of post-operative pain medication, was coherent enough to answer questions. His story, according to a report filed by Sergeant Pettinelli, was closely aligned with several of the other witness accounts.

Standing bedside, the sergeant said, "Mr. Hayward, we'll keep this brief so you can get some rest."

"I'm all right."

"Okay, what do you recall about the incident at Pageant Field last night?"

"I saw this guy Chasson arrive and start a discussion with Kevin Racette," Hayward began. He paused to draw a breath, grimacing in obvious pain. "Chasson punched Racette, and Paul Melody went over to the aid of Racette. I saw Chasson take a swipe at Melody and noticed that Melody was knocked to the ground from the blow."

"Did you see a knife?"

Hayward shook his head and winced as the sutures in his lower back dug into the surgical incision.

"What happened next?" Pettinelli asked.

"I ran to Melody—I thought he was just punched and went to the ground," Hayward recalled. "Chasson came at me and I threw a punch but missed. He then took a swing at me with his right hand, and I felt a sharp, stabbing pain in my lower back."

Sergeant Borst took notes of the interview as his partner continued with the questioning. It was obvious to both men that Hayward was running out of steam.

"Where did Chasson go after he stabbed you?"

"He was chasing some of my other friends near the picnic tables."

"What did you do at this time?" Pettinelli asked.

"I went to Al Vasconcellos and told him I got stabbed."

As the investigators wrapped up the brief discussion, Hayward explained that he and Vasconcellos dug the car keys out of Melody's pocket and readied his car.

"Melody was just lying there," he said. "He couldn't move and he wasn't talking. Nobody was doing anything so we did what we could to help him."

***

In the depths of Quincy City Hospital, Massachusetts State Pathologist George Katsis was joined in the morgue by Medical Examiner William Ridder and a pair of state troopers, George McDonough and Arthur Bourque, to witness the autopsy of Paul Melody. Little surprise to those in attendance, Katsis determined the cause of death to be a stab wound to the left chest of a depth of five or six inches. The duration of the autopsy, in Quincy Police Department Case #77-112-0904-0211, was thirty-seven minutes.

Officially, Paul Melody was pronounced dead at 11:30 p.m. on Tuesday, August 23, 1977. According to the medical examiner, the young homicide victim suffered fatal stab wounds to the left side of his chest, as well as traumatic penetration to the left ventricle of the heart.

# TWENTY-TWO —
# SCHOTTMILLER VISIT

On Thursday morning, August 25, 1977, Lieutenant MacDonald summoned Laurie Schottmiller to the stuffy, airless interview room. She made the trek to Quincy Police headquarters on her bicycle and had done the same to reach Pageant Field two nights prior. The bike was her primary means of transportation. MacDonald had already held a toned-down conversation with her on the night of the fight.

At the time, a patrolman had placed her bike in his trunk and given her a ride to the station. MacDonald, understanding the uphill climb before him with the number of witnesses to interview, had released Schottmiller to go home, get some sleep, and return on Thursday. Before she left, however, he did ask several questions, limiting the scope to ensure he captured her responses on tape. MacDonald asked Schottmiller if she got a good look at the suspect. At the time, she nodded in the affirmative.

Settling into his chair two mornings later, the lieutenant organized his growing stack of documents and scribbled a few questions on a notepad. Schottmiller soon arrived, guided by a uniformed officer who offered her a coffee or a can of soda. She was an attractive young woman, just shy of twenty-two, and it was not surprising to MacDonald and his colleagues that the officer extended a special welcome to her. Laurie politely declined the refreshments with a knowing grin.

"Good morning, Miss Schottmiller," MacDonald began, greeting his fifth witness with a welcoming smile. She was the first, and only, woman to witness the events at Pageant Field. His notes read that Laurie's twin sister had been with her earlier in the evening, but she was irrelevant because she had left for home long before the perpetrator arrived at the park. "Just for the tape recording, may I confirm your last name is, in fact, Schottmiller?"

"Right," she confirmed, spelling it out. "S-C-H-O-T-T-M-I-L-L-E-R."

"And your address?"

"109 Waterston Street, Quincy."

"And your date of birth?"

"September 12, 1956."

"Okay, Laurie, you've had some time to reflect on what happened up at Pageant Field the other night," the lieutenant said. "Could you tell me what took place, step by step?"

"Um, Bryan Fitzgerald pulled up in his orange MG with another kid that I didn't know, and Bryan got out to talk for a while," she recalled. MacDonald chose not to correct her with the make of the car. He was aware that the English-made MG was similar to a Fiat. She had the color right. "There were maybe ten or twelve people up there. I saw this stranger talking with Joe Marnell and others, but he didn't talk with me. I thought Bryan was leaving for good because he was going to Texas in the morning and seemed to be saying goodbye to people. The guy left with Bryan after a few minutes but then they came back."

"What did they do when they returned?"

"This guy took Kevin Racette over near the parking lot and was talking with him."

MacDonald asked if she heard what was being said between the two men, but she claimed she was standing adjacent to the tables and wasn't close enough to hear the conversation.

"A fight started," Schottmiller continued. "It was just a scuffle between the stranger and Kevin. And then Paul Melody ran over right away, and then others ran over. I heard a bottle break."

"What else did you see?"

"He had a knife—the kid was trying to cut people," she narrated with added emotion.

"Could you see who he was trying to stab?"

"He was trying to stab anyone who was there, anyone who went near him. Everyone was backing away. I thought I saw him slash at Vasco."

"Vasconcellos?"

"Yeah."

The lieutenant asked Schottmiller to demonstrate the stabbing motion. She stood from her chair and with an imaginary blade in her hand, drove it forward, piercing a feigned victim, then withdrew. She then began swinging it back-and-forth in a savage ripping motion.

"Was he holding the knife in his right hand?"

"Yes, I believe it was in his right hand," she acknowledged.

"And can you describe the knife?" MacDonald asked.

Schottmiller paused for a moment, conjuring up what she saw, and visualizing the weapon wielded by Leroy Chasson. The stabbings had occurred only days before, but she wanted to get it right for the police.

"I just saw the blade," she replied. "It was about five inches long and very shiny, even in the dim light."

"Did you see Paul Melody get stabbed?"

"No."

"Did you see Robert Hayward get stabbed?"

"No," she repeated, shaking her head. "Hayward came over and thought he was stabbed with a broken bottle. He was bleeding badly. And Paul was on the ground."

Schottmiller went on to explain what her friends did for Melody in an effort to save his life. She described to investigators how they retrieved his car and loaded him for the trip to the hospital. She mentioned the foursome—Robert "Rusty" Russell, Al Vasconcellos, Kevin Racette, and Joe Marnell—as the men moved Melody from the ground to the back seat. All of them were covered in the boys' blood, both their hands and their clothing. She could not imagine how someone could survive after all that blood loss; it didn't seem possible. She heard more than one person say Melody might die as the car, driven by Vasconcellos, sped out of the Pageant Field lot.

"Were you friends with Paul?" MacDonald asked.

"Yeah," she replied, "for a couple of years."

MacDonald nodded and said, "So, Paul didn't start any trouble, he just ran over when—"

"I was just talking with him," Laurie interrupted, "when he heard a fight. He just ran right over to help. I think he had a beer in his hand."

"A beer?" asked MacDonald. "Was it a bottle or a can?"

"I don't know... we were mostly drinking from cans."

"Okay, Laurie, do you recognize this man?" MacDonald slid a mugshot of Leroy Chasson across the table surface. "I believe earlier when we spoke, you said you could identify him."

"No, I didn't say that," Schottmiller denied adamantly. It was a complete reversal from what she had said to the lieutenant when they crossed paths in the corridor.

"You didn't say that?"

"I didn't say I could recognize him. I'm not sure I could."

"You said there was a streetlight up there," MacDonald reminded his witness, rifling through notes. There was an edge in his tone. Schottmiller had to perceive his increasing frustration with her.

"Yes, and I did see him when he came after us near the picnic tables," she elaborated. "But I was looking mostly at the knife."

The lieutenant began to pressure Schottmiller. Based on what she said earlier, she agreed that she could identify Chasson. MacDonald hoped she would be able to pick the suspect out of a lineup if it came to that. It was understood that Bryan Fitzgerald had spent a great deal of time in the Fiat with Chasson, driving to and from Quincy. And Fitzgerald had seen the knife in the perpetrator's hand. In fact, he sustained a minor laceration when Chasson slashed him madly with it.

But the lieutenant knew from countless hours spent in courtrooms that a single witness was never enough, especially a tainted witness such as Fitzgerald. He needed someone to corroborate the eyewitness testimony of others. Another person, particularly the likes of Schottmiller, with a near-flawless reputation, would need to identify Chasson and say she had seen him brandish the deadly knife. Her testimony would augment the case against the alleged murderer.

"When he approached the picnic area, didn't you get a good look at him?"

Repeating the question had the desired effect. "I never really stared at him or got his looks straight in my head, but I did see him."

"Go on," MacDonald urged. "What did he look like?"

Laurie nodded, paused briefly, and said, "He had short-type wavy hair, light-colored but not blond," she said. "He was about four inches taller than me—I'm five-foot-six—and he was skinny and he had light-colored eyes. He didn't have a mustache; maybe it was a goatee, I don't remember clearly."

"He might have had a goatee?" a displeased MacDonald asked. "That's completely different from what others have said. Apparently, you didn't get a good look at him. How long did you actually look at his face?"

"Not long. Less than a minute."

"Do you recall his clothing? What he was wearing?"

"Yeah," she said. "He had on a navy blue short-sleeved shirt with white stripes and a white rectangular square pattern."

"Pants?"

"Dungarees."

"Well, that seems consistent with what others have said," MacDonald said.

The lieutenant asked Schottmiller a series of questions to determine the assailant's state of mind. He asked if Chasson seemed drunk or high on drugs. Schottmiller shook her head, stating that he wasn't stumbling or slurring his words in any way; he seemed fully coherent. When asked if she was seeing anyone, she said she was dating Roger Cappola, who had been at the park with her earlier in the evening. She told MacDonald that she was getting ready to leave when the fight started. She also mentioned that, at first, the stranger and Kevin Racette were congenial.

"They were congenial?" he repeated.

"Yeah, like they knew each other," Laurie replied. "But then the guy went mad. He was slashing at everyone and screaming that he was going to kill everyone who was up there."

"Okay, Laurie, we want to thank you for your time," MacDonald said, reminding her to reach out if anything else came to mind.

"Yeah, definitely."

# TWENTY-THREE—LEAVING BOSTON

On the morning of Monday, August 29, after several days and nights sharing a single room at the Milner Hotel, the intrepid trio—Leroy Chasson, Mark Bray, and Kathleen MacDonald—were prepared to leave their Boston refuge.

While the three of them had been shoehorned in a room designed for one, Kathleen and Lee spent much of their time traipsing around the city, dangerously carefree. They weren't as cautious as their roommate had been about showing their faces during daylight hours. The pair frequently roamed Boston Common, visited a number of Combat Zone establishments, and dined at Bob Lee's Islander, a landmark Chinatown restaurant that opened in 1951. All were a brief walk from their hotel.

While their stay was uneventful, there was one event worthy of mention. On the first morning, Saturday, Chasson rose early. He had a quick errand to run. He rousted Mark from his slumber. Kathleen stirred in her sleep but did not wake. He let her sleep; it was better she remained behind.

"C'mon, Mark," he whispered.

"Where to?" asked his half-asleep friend as he pulled on his clothing.

"I'll explain on the way."

Their destination was Boston Common, a city block away. They walked briskly, reaching a cluster of park benches in the southwest corner in a matter of minutes. No sooner had Mark Bray asked Chasson why they had come to the park when Linell Travers and Patricia Landon strolled through a nearby gateway.

"Good morning," Chasson said, greeting his *other* girlfriend with a light embrace.

Fearful that she and Patricia had been followed by the police, Linell anxiously surveyed their surroundings. There were a few pedestrians making their way along Boylston Street, but none paid any attention to the foursome gathered just inside the gates of the Common.

"Good morning," she replied, her smile strained.

"Derek?"

"With my parents."

"Good to see you," Leroy said. "Hi, Patricia."

"Hello," she replied but said nothing further.

"Will you be okay?" Linell asked.

"We're good," he said, unsure what else to say. He wanted to apologize for the police raid on their Somerville apartment a week earlier but couldn't find the words. "We're heading out shortly."

"Here's the stuff you asked for," she said, handing over a small plastic grocery bag. "I did as you asked and bought the items in different markets."

Chasson nodded, pleased she followed his instructions. Purchasing these things in the same store might raise suspicions, although Halloween was only two months away. He looked inside the bag and saw an assortment of colored hair dyes, reading glasses and, of all things, fake mustaches. Now that he had what he asked for, he saw the humor in the request and laughed a bit. It was unlikely that he would ever dye his hair. The idea was to blend in, not stand out. But desperate times often called for desperate measures—and disguises, at the time, seemed to be the best strategy.

"Thank you," he said, reaching out for another embrace. "Please hug Derek for me. We should go. I'll be in touch."

"Okay," Linell said. "Take care of yourself."

Mark also said quick goodbyes, and he and Lee watched the girls as they left the Common.

Returning to their room at the Milner, the duo found Kathleen awake, dressed, and ready to go.

"Where've you been?" she asked.

Chasson was evasive as he mumbled, "Quick errand."

Kathleen knew better than to press for more and began to gather her belongings. The threesome foraged a quick breakfast of muffins and coffee, courtesy of the hotel staff, and stepped outdoors to be greeted by another unseasonably mild, mid-sixties morning, sunny and bright. Kathleen trailed her two companions, stopping briefly to use the house phone in the hotel foyer to call for a taxi, which would take her to East Boston and Logan Airport to pick up a rental car.

It was just after eight o'clock and strangely quiet in the city of more than three million people. Traffic, both motor vehicle and pedestrian, was sparse.

Less than ten minutes passed before the hulking yellow cab rounded the corner from Boylston Street and traveled the block to where its passenger waited curbside.

"It shouldn't take more than an hour," said Kathleen as she grasped the door handle. "I already reserved the car."

"We'll be waiting," Chasson assured her, leaning in for a quick embrace of the woman who was seven years his senior and, as he would learn in their time together, willing to risk everything to be at his side.

Born on January 3, 1942, in South Weymouth, Massachusetts, Kathleen Mary MacDonald was a thirty-five-year-old estranged mother of six children, ranging in age from seven to seventeen. For much of her early life, Kathleen fought a losing battle with drugs and alcohol. In March 1977, her husband, Daniel, of 65 Barnes Avenue, South Weymouth, Massachusetts, filed for divorce and applied for a restraining order, which was granted by the courts. He was seeking to protect the children from what his attorney described as a "drug-addled danger." While his troubled wife sought treatment for substance abuse at the former Glenside Hospital, which was located in the Boston community of Jamaica Plain, Daniel also filed for custody of the children. Kathleen and her attorney, by necessity, didn't put up much of a fight. She wasn't in the frame of mind to care for herself, much less her children.

Upon her April 1 release from Glenside, which in later years became the Arbor Hospital, Kathleen enrolled in a government-funded nursing assistant program coordinated by the Quincy City Hospital. She successfully completed the six weeks of training, earning the certificate, which qualified her to work as a nurse's aide in a nursing home or, in some instances, a hospital setting.

Living with her parents at 15 Williams Avenue in South Weymouth, she arranged to take an apartment at 95 Upland Road, Quincy. She was supposed to move on September 1, 1977. While it seemed that she might be piecing together her fragmented life, Kathleen took a dramatic turn for the worse.

Her troubles began two years earlier, in November 1975, when she answered an advertisement in *The Real Paper*, which was a Boston-based publication featuring alternative news and commentary. The ad that caught Kathleen's eye was a request from Walpole State Prison inmate Leroy Chasson. The habitual offender was seeking one-dollar donations toward a five-hundred-dollar attorney fee. At the time, Chasson was incarcerated for the armed robbery of a Cambridge, Massachusetts pharmacy and, in his quest for an appeal, was accumulating funds toward that end, one dollar at a time.

Without a second thought, the kind-hearted Kathleen promptly tucked a dollar bill inside a nondescript greeting card and dropped it in the mail. Ignoring the possible repercussions, she also provided a return mailing address. Chasson wrote back and before long, their correspondence deepened. Kathleen soon abandoned her bonds of family, replacing them with misguided loyalty for a career criminal.

She paid weekly visits to MCI-Norfolk State Prison, as well as the Middlesex Jail in Billerica when he was moved for pre-release. The relationship between Kathleen MacDonald and Leroy Chasson flourished. Her divorce from husband Daniel was finalized in mid-1977, around the same time Leroy earned parole, paving the way for the couple to unite outside of prison walls. According to police documents, Kathleen stated, "Regardless of what he had done, she was in love with Leroy Chasson."

# TWENTY-FOUR — TROOPER ENCOUNTER

Later that Monday morning, Kathleen MacDonald returned from Logan International Airport in an olive-green Plymouth Duster she had rented at the Avis counter. It certainly wasn't a show car, but the drab color and model better served their purpose. Chasson settled in the front bucket passenger seat while Bray slid in back, claiming the entire rear bench seat.

"You know how to get back to the highway?" Chasson asked as Kathleen tossed the car into drive and pulled away from the curb. She frowned at him wordlessly. He smiled, nodding. It was nearing ten o'clock as they reached an off-ramp near South Station and began to trek north toward New Hampshire. Twenty minutes into the trip, they transitioned to Interstate 95 and before long, crossed the southern border of the Granite State.

It was approaching midday as the trio arrived in Portland, Maine. The trip north had, to that point, covered predominantly highway miles. It was inherently safer, particularly during the daylight hours. More cars on the road, less attention on them from patrols. Not that they really had to be overly concerned. Kathleen MacDonald was unknown to the police; thus, the rental car was not yet on their radar. And even if law enforcement officials were savvy enough to check rental car agencies, there was little to connect Kathleen with the fugitives. There were records of her visits with Chasson in prison but to that point, she was a relative unknown. It was likely the cops had no idea what make or model they were seeking. By that juncture, the police had certainly found the stolen vehicle Chasson had abandoned on Stuart Street in Boston. Whether it was fingerprints or some other method of identification, it wouldn't take long for Boston Police to link the Bel Air to the fleeing pair. Perhaps the cops put the screws to Donald Bains and determined he had stolen the car and subsequently his two accomplices had used it to continue their flight from Somerville. But the vehicle trail would end there.

Rolling slowly through downtown Portland with Kathleen at the wheel, Chasson figured it would make more sense to wait for nightfall before switching over to the country roads of Maine, namely Route 302. In the daylight, bored, meddlesome local cops would be more apt to make a traffic stop, particularly if they spotted a vehicle with Massachusetts license plates.

Chasson and his associates stashed the car in a remote parking lot and sought out an eatery to grab a bite. They settled on an establishment named Carbur's, which was in the Old Port section of Commercial Street and had opened just months before in March 1977.

In the seventies, the Old Port neighborhood was described by locals as a shoreline community that reeked of day-old fish and was crisscrossed with filthy streets that needed a good scrubbing. Today, the district is a vibrant tourist location featuring historic sights and cobblestone streets with scores of restaurants and high-end shops.

Carbur's certainly could not be described as "off the beaten path," but Chasson felt they were far enough away from the Boston-area dragnet to safely show their faces in public. He had been wedged with his companions in a tiny room at the Milner Hotel for days and it felt good to breathe in the fresh sea air of Coastal Maine.

"This place okay?" he asked as they were led by a waitress to a booth near the rear of the restaurant. Both Bray and Kathleen nodded in agreement. Chasson slid across the vinyl seat and scanned the menu, which was filled with humorous quips and oddly named dishes. He grinned as he read the caption pleading with patrons to refrain from stealing the popular, souvenir-like menus.

Their money dwindling after several days of takeout meals in Boston, all three settled on simple, inexpensive cheeseburger plates.

"How much further to Fryeburg?" Bray asked as he sipped from a water glass placed on the table by the waitress.

"About fifty miles," Chasson replied. "I checked a road map at a filling station. Little over an hour, I guess."

"You think we should crash somewhere and head to the antique shop in the morning?" Bray suggested. "It's getting late."

After a moment's thought, Chasson nodded in agreement. "You might have a point there, friend. We'll drive part of the way and find a room."

The weary travelers soon discovered that finding a room proved easier said than done. With the summer tourist season winding down and the Labor Day holiday weekend fast approaching, most of the area lodging was either already booked or rates were bloated beyond what the threesome could afford. It was obvious that motel proprietors and innkeepers were exploiting guests with exorbitant prices.

As they drove north along scenic Route 302, passing through the Maine towns of Windham, North Windham, Raymond, and Casco, with Sebago Lake as a backdrop, Chasson and his consorts encountered a number of small, roadside establishments. As they neared the town of Bridgton and the Pleasant Mountain resort area, they spotted several possibilities that indicated there were vacancies but, in each instance, it was simply a matter of the innkeeper not updating the signboard in a timely manner. Everything was booked solid, they were told, save for a few rooms well above their price range. Despite combining their remaining money, they fell short. Kathleen had topped off the Duster's gas tank and they were down to their last forty dollars. Bray's cash envelope was also depleted.

Frustrated, Leroy suggested that they navigate across the state line into neighboring New Hampshire in hopes they might stumble on something. Passing through Fryeburg at the border, they found that the Granite State was even worse. Here, the vacation crowd had already descended in droves. It was late afternoon, and traffic was heavy along Route 302, which was the most desirable route to reach touristy North Conway and the White Mountains.

Darkness fell as they gave up the search for a room and pulled into a gravel-surfaced rest stop on the outskirts of North Conway. The rental car had been running nonstop since leaving Portland. Kathleen angled into a parking spot and cut the engine.

Settled in the rest area, all three paid a visit to the facility's restrooms, followed by a trip to the vending machines for soda and snacks before they settled in for an uncomfortable night's sleep. They returned to the car and chatted briefly, but fatigue soon gained the upper hand.

Just after two o'clock in the morning, Kathleen was startled awake by blue beacon lights flashing in the rearview mirror. Heart pounding, her breath caught in her throat. She glanced at Leroy, who was already awake. In the gleam of a spotlight bathing the interior of the rental with garish light, she noticed the glint of the brushed black metal of a firearm clutched in his hand. She was aware of the gun. She knew he was carrying it but until this crisis moment, he had been discreet about it, taking great pains not to let her see it. She appreciated the gesture on his part.

The weapon was tightly gripped in his right hand, resting across his lap. Chasson pivoted slightly to get a better look at the patrol car that had pulled up behind them. Mark Bray was stretched out across the wide rear seat, sound asleep and oblivious to the growing peril.

"What should we do?" Kathleen asked, her voice hushed, barely above a whisper.

"We wait—we sit tight," he answered brusquely as he disengaged the safety on the weapon with a muted but ominous clicking sound. "Let the cop make the first move."

The look on his face said it all. Chasson's thin lips were pulled back, baring his clenched teeth. His brow was deeply furrowed and his eyes were narrowed in a menacing squint like an Old West gunslinger bracing for a showdown under the baking sun. It was a disturbing expression and gave Kathleen an icy chill. It was a side of her boyfriend she had not seen before. She fought off a shiver. Deep in the recesses of her mind, she understood that he had already killed, perhaps more than once. He had nothing to lose by shooting an unaware police officer.

"Lee, please try to stay calm," she pleaded. "I'm sure it's routine."

Chasson nodded but the look on his face remained fixed and threatening. He moved his hand lower, slipping the gun alongside his thigh, against the car door, positioning it out of view from anyone standing at the driver's door window. The cop, when he approached them, wouldn't see the weapon until it was too late to do anything about it.

Kathleen began to spin the handle on the driver's door, lowering the window. A cool mountain breeze, laden with the scent of nearby evergreens, wafted through the opening and wicked away a thin layer of nervous perspiration on her forehead. With her free hand, she primped her sleep-tousled hair. In the rear seat, she heard Mark Bray begin to stir. The sound of heavy boots crunching across the loose gravel woke him fully.

"What's going on?" he asked, abruptly sitting upright. He rubbed at an apparent stiff neck. The intermittent blue beacons unveiled the apprehension on his face.

"Shhhh," came her reply. Bray complied and went silent. He remained frozen, statue-like. Chasson, meanwhile, said nothing as he continued to stare at the gun concealed at his side.

"Evening, ma'am," said the New Hampshire state trooper as he bent at the waist to get a look inside the car. Despite the late hour, the young man's uniform was crisp and sharp, with only the top button of his forest green shirt undone, revealing a starched white crewneck t-shirt beneath. To Kathleen, he looked as if he were readying to march in a precision military parade.

"Good evening, officer," she replied, forcing a weak smile. She tried to make it appear genuine, but it was obvious that she was nervous. There was no hiding the slight tremble in her voice. In addition, there was little she could do to hide her unkempt hair and disheveled clothing. "Is there a problem, sir?"

"No, ma'am," he said. "We just make random spot checks in these rest areas to make sure folks are all right. We typically frown on all-night parking."

The trooper turned his attention to the two male occupants in the vehicle, eyeing them suspiciously. Highly trained, he was alerted that something was amiss. Stepping back slightly to minimize his angle, he grasped the handle of his holstered service revolver.

"Evening, gentlemen," the officer said, addressing Chasson and Bray as one. Both men grunted an unintelligible response. Chasson was taut, and like Bray, locked in a forward stare at the windshield. Making eye contact with this prying cop was not on the agenda.

Seeking to diffuse the building tension and potential for hostilities, Kathleen diverted the trooper's attention back to herself.

"We just needed a break," she stressed. "I'd been driving for a while and we were getting tired. We couldn't find a room."

"Where are you coming from?"

"Massachusetts," she said, and added, "Boston. We've been driving all day."

"Where are you heading?" the officer asked.

"North Conway," she answered, again trying to sound convincing but failing. "To see the sights."

"You're not far, I'm sure you could get a room," he suggested.

"Thank you, officer—we'll try again."

The trooper nodded and said, "I'll just need to have a look at your license and registration."

"Certainly," Kathleen agreed.

Chasson, meanwhile, tensed. The familiar adrenaline rush surged through his body, and he broke out in a cold sweat. At first, he thought they might be off the hook. This trooper was just checking their well-being, as he explained. But now, he was asking for Kathleen's identification. What if he also wanted to see something from him or Mark Bray, who continued to remain silent in the rear seat of the Plymouth? Neither man had credentials. There hadn't been enough time to get hold of fake IDs. Chasson had only been out of prison for a month and had not had time to renew his driver's license, not that the Massachusetts Registry would grant a license to a convicted felon. And Mark Bray, a prison escapee? How could they explain a total lack of proof of identity?

Chasson's hand tightened on the gun in a white-knuckled grip. His index finger brushed the trigger. He imagined engaging in a firefight with the law enforcement officer, guns blazing, a hail of bullets, and one or both of them later zipped snugly into black plastic body bags.

Kathleen reached across to the glove box to retrieve the Avis rental agreement she had stashed. Leroy was in a much better position to lend a hand, but he did not dare budge, fearing inadvertently revealing the concealed gun. Kathleen handed the document to the trooper and then began to fish through her purse nervously for her driver's license.

The officer clicked on his flashlight and aimed the beam so he could examine the registration in the darkness of the rest area. Kathleen found the license and held it out to him. He scrutinized both and asked, "Rental?"

She had anticipated the question before it was asked and responded as she snapped her purse closed. "My car is in the shop."

"Uh huh," murmured the lawman, sounding suspicious. "I'll be back in a minute or two."

The trio listened to his retreating footsteps on the loose gravel. When he reached the patrol car, they could hear the door open, then close. The crickets in the nearby brush that edge the parking lot, paused briefly with the interruption, but then resumed their chirping.

Minutes ticked by and no one in the car said a word. The breeze picked up a notch. Winter arrived early in this region and weather highs and lows were often set, particularly at the peak of nearby Mount Washington, where a record wind speed of two hundred and thirty-one miles per hour was charted and had stood for decades.

It was obvious the trooper was running Kathleen MacDonald through his dispatch, seeking warrants. Leroy Chasson still could not understand why he and Mark Bray weren't asked for their identification, but he wasn't complaining. Thankfully, Kathleen was at the wheel. If either he or Mark had been in the driver's seat, the circumstances would have been decidedly more complicated. Granted, days earlier, they had driven to and from Rhode Island in a stolen car but in that instance, a lack of a driver's license was the least of their worries.

"If he orders us out of the car," muttered a menacing Chasson, "I'll shoot him."

Ten minutes passed but it seemed like much longer. The trooper returned and handed Kathleen her documents, stating, "Everything checks out, ma'am."

"Thank you, sir."

"But I'm sorry to say, you can't sleep here."

"We tried to find a room, but everything seems to be booked."

"I can help," the highway patrol officer offered.

"I'm embarrassed to say," she said, "but we're a little short on money."

Nodding that he understood, he said, "Look, I have a few favors owed at some of these motels. Follow me and we'll get you a room."

"Sure," she agreed, glancing at Chasson. He was noticeably more relaxed. They might just escape unscathed. He stashed the gun under the seat and sat back.

Kathleen followed the patrol car. The trooper made his way toward the business district of North Conway. Their first stop was the Red Jacket Mountainside Inn, which was reached via a long, undulating driveway that climbed up a steep slope. Once inside the lobby, the ragged trio listened as the proprietor fumbled through an excuse, explaining to the trooper that there were no rooms available. He eyeballed them with a sour expression. Kathleen sensed the refusal had more to do with the state of their rumpled clothing, which she later described during a police interview as "dirty looking."

Decades later, during the spring of 2022, a substantial portion of the Red Jacket was consumed by fire, forcing an indefinite closure of the popular resort.

"I have another place to try," said the cop as they filed out of the hotel and returned to their respective cars.

The next stop yielded better results. The Eastern Slopes Inn desk clerk eyed them with disdain and argued but their uniformed escort was convincing. Not only did the innkeeper eventually relent and agree to give them a room, but he also accepted their forty dollars as payment. It was obvious the "favor" owed to the trooper was substantial.

"Thank you, officer," said Kathleen.

"You're welcome, ma'am," he said, tipping his wide-brimmed hat in parting. "Enjoy your stay in North Conway."

It was three o'clock in the morning when the travelers' weary heads met with pillows. Sleep came quickly.

\*\*\*

The Quincy Police, acting on an anonymous tip, paid a visit to the Milner Hotel in Boston to question staff members. They had missed Leroy Chasson and his companions by a matter of hours. While Karen McLaughlin, the desk clerk who frequently dealt with the fugitives, was tentatively forthcoming with information, the trip to the hotel failed to yield any substantial leads to the whereabouts of the fugitives.

"Have you seen these individuals?" asked Detective Thomas Casey as he showed Miss McLaughlin mugshots of Chasson and Mark Bray.

"Yes," she answered with a nod. She retrieved the registration book and pointed to Chasson's signature and then pointed at his mugshot. "There was a woman with them too. She was with this guy. They checked in under the names Mr. and Mrs. Walter Travers."

McLaughlin, who Mark Bray had hoped would withhold information from the cops, caved under the threat of further questioning at Quincy Police headquarters. She might have been loyal to her former high school classmate, but she was certainly not a fool. She identified Mark Bray as the couple's companion and added that he had registered as "James Roach" and had been staying at the Milner for some time, as much as a week prior to the other two joining him.

While the Quincy investigators didn't think they would glean anything of use from the registration cards, they asked McLaughlin to produce them. She claimed they were locked in the manager's office and she did not have the key.

"Who's the manager?" Casey asked.

"Richard Smith," she answered. "He lives here in the hotel but he's out today. I don't know when he'll be back."

"We'll wait for him," Casey said, realizing that the manager's deception meant he knew something—perhaps Chasson's whereabouts or his destination.

Smith was known to the Quincy Police. Casey had spoken with him in the past about other cases related to Quincy-based crimes and found him to be uncooperative. Like his clerk McLaughlin, it was obvious that Smith had Quincy ties and people he would try to protect from the cops.

They waited for a brief time but it was obvious Smith had somehow been tipped off that the cops wanted to speak with him—likely by the McLaughlin girl. She had not left their sight while they stood in the small hotel foyer but she had used the phone, so they assumed she had paged Smith with some type of code number. A predetermined signal, perhaps. McLaughlin also refused to grant access to the room that had been occupied by the fugitives.

"That room was cleaned this morning and there is already another guest using it," she explained. "I'd rather not disturb him."

"Here's my card," said Casey as he prepared to leave. "Make sure Smith gives me a call when he returns."

# TWENTY-FIVE—ANTIQUE SHOPPING

It was a warm and overcast mid-morning on Tuesday, August 30, when the three outlaws wheeled out of the parking lot of the Eastern Slopes Inn, which was built in 1926. With Leroy Chasson once again riding shotgun, Mark Bray occupying the rear seat, and Kathleen MacDonald back behind the wheel of the Avis rental car, North Conway was soon in the rearview mirror. The Duster lifted a trail of swirling dust in its wake as they weaved along Route 113 into placid Fryeburg, where most of the two thousand townspeople who made their homes in the New England border town were at work, running errands, or tending to their chores.

Armed with directions provided by the Eastern Slopes innkeeper, along with several sumptuous muffins from the continental breakfast, the trio stopped briefly at a local drug store. Leroy Chasson had woken that morning with a sore throat and was seeking cough syrup. Using their last few dollars, he purchased a small bottle. He drank directly from the bottle, capped it, and tossed the remainder in the glove box. A brief drive later, they crossed the New Hampshire-Maine state line and, soon after, arrived at their destination.

Not far from the White Mountains-fed shores of the churning Saco River, Chipman Ela was busy arranging some of the newly arrived merchandise in his little shop, the Carriage House Antique Store on Smith Street in Fryeburg.

Ela, fifty-four, glanced up from his work as a big green Plymouth sedan turned into his parking lot. He watched intently through a large pane window at the front of his emporium as the driver – a woman, he noted – carefully backed the vehicle into a space in his gravel lot.

The Carriage House had been open for business for several hours that morning but the folks in the car were the first customers of the day. While summer weekends were busy with antique hunters, Tuesdays were typically quiet, and Chipman and his wife usually welcomed only the occasional patron. Ela, a native of Somerville, Massachusetts, was known to have an eye for detail. In 1978, he self-published *The Banjo Timepiece* which, according to the book's subtitle, was "an in-depth study of the weight-driven banjo clock."

Chipman Ela observed the activity on Smith Street and began making mental notes as a pair of men emerged from the vehicle, which had a Massachusetts license plate attached to the rear bumper. One of the men was thin, six feet tall or so, with scruffy blondish hair, a narrow face, and a thick Fu Manchu-style mustache. His companion was several inches shorter with close-cropped, light brown hair parted down the middle. Both were unkempt and bedraggled and neither looked as if they'd bathed in some time.

Ela set to work, cleaning his shelving and displays with a long-handled feather duster, working gingerly around some of the expensive antiques.

"Honey, we have company," Chipman called out to his wife of several decades, who was busy preparing lunch in the kitchen. Conveniently, their tidy home was attached to the store and the kitchen was within shouting distance. "These folks seem to have traveled a distance. Massachusetts, from the looks of things."

He'd received customers visiting from the neighboring state to the south and, over the years, Ela had gotten to know a number of them, some by first name. Many were repeat clients who included his Carriage House in their New England antiquing tours. But he did not recognize these folks. He was on full alert.

Before long, the two men climbed the steps to his porch and entered the store. The woman, oddly enough, remained in the car. This raised the proprietor's suspicions further.

"Good morning," said Ela cheerily, sensing there was something treacherous afoot with this pair. While he remained wary, he understood it was best to keep his mistrust concealed until he could safely summon help.

"Morning," mumbled the taller of the two men. "Nice shop you have here."

"Much obliged," Ela replied, forcing his best smile. "Looking for anything in particular, gentlemen?"

"Just having a look around—gift for my mother," said the dubious customer with the Fu Manchu mustache.

"Certainly. Give me a holler if you have any questions." Chipman placed the duster on a shelf and shuffled toward his wife in the nearby kitchen. She looked up from her meal preparation and offered him a sandwich. He waved her off and in a low tone said, "I'll eat later—I need to make a quick call."

Peering around the corner from the threshold of the kitchen, Ela could see the men were still looking over the merchandise. They were absorbed in an assortment of tabletop antique clocks. When Ela was certain neither of the pair could hear him talking on the phone, he lifted the receiver and dialed. It rang just once.

"Hello?" answered a familiar voice on the other end.

"Deputy, it's Chipman Ela, over at the Carriage House."

"Hey, Chip!" said Oxford County Deputy Sheriff Francis Ontengco. "How've you been, my friend?"

"Very well, thanks for asking," the shop owner replied as he continued to keep tabs on his shady customers. "But we seem to have a situation brewing over here."

He went on to explain there was a pair of unsavory men giving his business a once-over. They hadn't yet said or done anything to indicate mischief but he sensed there was something untoward about their visit. A local reporter later said Ela was alerted by their "mannerisms." Both were in their twenties, he described, and they didn't seem to be the typical rare find or vintage antique enthusiasts. They did, however, seem to have a taste for finer clocks. They hovered in that segment of the store for some time. Most of the patrons who frequented the Carriage House had questions about specific pieces and often interacted with Chipman. Except for their initial greeting, this skulking pair did not attempt to engage the owner or seek information. Clearly, their intentions were dubious.

"Sheriff," he continued, "there is also a woman waiting in the car."

"You caught me stopping by the office for a minute," said Ontengco, who was enjoying an uncommon day off. "But I'll be sure to send someone over."

Without delay, Ontengco, who hailed from nearby Brownfield, Maine, reached out by phone to a law enforcement colleague. "Fred, it's Frank."

"Frank, good to hear from you," said Fryeburg Police Chief Fred Gould.

"I just got off the phone with Chipman Ela over at the antique shop."

"Uh huh."

"He tells me there's a pair of suspicious characters visiting his store," the sheriff explained. "He seems certain they're casing his place."

"I'll head right over there!" Gould said excitedly. As one might imagine, there wasn't much criminal activity to speak of in Fryeburg, especially in an antique shop. He could not recall the last time there was any trouble at the Ela place.

"I'll join you as soon as possible," said Ontengco, who was a retired twenty-year veteran of the NYPD. He worked in the city as a patrolman and homicide detective before settling in Maine and joining the Oxford County Sheriff's Department. "Chipman suggested we wear civilian clothing and pretend to be shoppers."

"Good idea," the police chief agreed. "I'll be there shortly."

Gould quickly changed out of his uniform, climbed into his personal car, which had no official markings to give away his identity, and drove across town to the Carriage House. He decided not to enlist any of his Fryeburg officers as backup—the added manpower might tip off the potential wrongdoers that they'd been made. While he certainly trusted Chipman Ela's assessment of the two men who seemed to be casing his business, an alarm that the shop owner had raised with Deputy Ontengco moments earlier, Gould understood there was no need to manufacture a confrontation. Nevertheless, as he waited for a traffic signal on Main Street, the sheriff drew his service revolver from the holster concealed beneath his suit jacket and ensured it was fully loaded.

It was just after noon as Gould pulled into one of the vacant parking spaces in front of the little antique shop. He glanced to his left, taking note of the Plymouth Duster parked several car lengths away. It was the only car in the small lot. As reported by Chipman Ela, the vehicle had been backed into a spot. To the trained eye of a law enforcement professional, this was an obvious indicator that the operator was preparing for a rapid exit.

Gould glimpsed the woman behind the wheel, who returned his gaze and then quickly turned her head, taking great pains to avoid a prolonged stare. While brief, the encounter added to the chief's gut feeling. But it was entering the store that truly heightened his intuition. The two men glanced up from their browsing to take stock of the new arrival. They eyed him nervously as he moved along the narrow aisles to the far end of the store.

Ela greeted him, "Hey, Fred, been a long time!"

For a moment, Gould braced, half-expecting Ela to inadvertently address him as "Chief" out of longtime habit. Chipman was on the ball, thankfully. Gould also realized that the shop owner had reason to be concerned. This duo was up to no good and the chief's presence in the store was a hindrance to whatever scheme they had in mind.

Chief Gould gradually edged toward the rear of the business, feigning interest in a glass display case standing adjacent to the entrance of the family home.

"Mrs. Ela," the chief greeted the middle-aged woman in a muted tone. Chipman's wife was tidying her cozy kitchen, but her face was pale and drawn. She was justifiably frightened. It was obvious her husband had alerted her to the tense situation gaining momentum in their store. A standoff seemed imminent.

"Yes?" she answered, forcing a smile fraught with fear. The look on her face said it all. This kind of thing just didn't happen in easygoing Fryeburg.

"Ma'am, I'm sorry to ask, but I need you to make a call for me."

"Yes, certainly."

"Please call Deputy Ontengco and tell him I could use his help," he urged. He was confident the two target men were out of earshot but added, "Speak softly—don't let them hear you."

She nodded and without delay, moved to the phone as Sheriff Gould returned to his mock antique browsing. He checked on the two suspects. They did not seem to be paying attention to him. From what he could gather, they had not zeroed in on his deception.

No sooner had Mrs. Ela hung up when Deputy Ontengco arrived. He later explained that after receiving the original distress call from Chipman Ela, he decided to set aside a day of fishing on the nearby Saco River and rushed to the store to provide an assist. As he emerged from his car, the two men were leaving. It was likely the additional customers made them anxious. The deputy observed the pair as they got into the Plymouth and drove off.

The deputy nodded in greeting to Sheriff Gould, who had emerged from the store. He then quickly got back into his car and set out after the suspects. He soon closed the gap, following them as they drove north on Route 113. He got close enough to mentally record the registration number of their Massachusetts license plate without alerting the occupants that they were being tailed. He circled back to rejoin Gould at the antique store.

Deputy Ontengco and Sheriff Gould relocated their personal cars to a nearby parking lot belonging to a branch of the Norway Savings Bank. Both men found it odd that the aspiring culprits had focused so much attention on antiques, which would have to be fenced, when there was a bank across the street. If they were contemplating a crime, why not hold up a bank?

At 1:45 in the afternoon, the two officers made their way inside the branch and asked the manager for permission to use a phone. The sheriff was well known to the bank staff and they were accommodating. While Gould observed the antique store from a window at the front of the bank, Ontengco dialed the South Paris Sheriff's Office and provided the Massachusetts vehicle registration number (D38-455), which he had scribbled on a note page while tailing the suspects.

"Check with the Massachusetts authorities," the deputy ordered, providing brief descriptions of the two men. "And reference the Teletype for recent APBs and wanted persons from their state. We'll be at the Norway Savings Bank when you have something."

"Yes, sir," said Desk Sergeant Ronald Beaudoin. "I'll get right on it."

Gould and Ontengco remained in the bank, eagerly awaiting the response. A call was also placed to Chipman

Ela to let him know that police would be watching his shop and not to be concerned. He was very appreciative.

A bank employee brought the men chairs and hot cups of coffee, and it wasn't long before the phone rang.

"Chief, you were right," Beaudoin said excitedly. "That vehicle is a rental, under Kathleen MacDonald from Weymouth, Massachusetts. And I provided the descriptions. The two guys with her are wanted for a murder in Quincy, Massachusetts. One of them— a Leroy Chasson—is accused of stabbing a man to death."

"Great, very helpful."

"Should we send more help, sir?"

"Just put a few men on alert, in case they're needed," Ontengco replied. "But make sure they keep a safe distance. We don't want to scare these guys off."

The deputy glanced at his colleague and nodded. He didn't have to say a word; Gould could read it on his face. Moments earlier, a wanted killer was an arm's length away, obviously casing the antique store for a robbery. It was likely these fugitives had chosen the Ela place because of its rural location, with the misguided belief that the Fryeburg Police might be less capable than law enforcement from a larger city or town.

"Think they'll be back?" Gould submitted.

"I'm certain of it," Ontengco replied, confidently. "They spent an awful long time in that store. I'm guessing they know exactly what they want. We should get ready."

The two police officers thanked the bank staff for their hospitality and made their way outside. The skies overhead were cloudless and azure, and the afternoon had warmed into the eighties. "A perfect day for fishing or apprehending a murder suspect," Ontengco later commented to reporters.

They got into Sheriff Gould's car, which was oriented in such a way as to supply them an ideal view of the Ela property, and settled in for a stakeout of the Carriage House.

There was small talk between the men—Ontengco could share volumes of war stories from his years with the NYPD—but as the law officers waited anxiously for the return of the criminals, the tension was far too thick to carry on much of a prolonged conversation. Between frequent glimpses of the antiques store across the street, each lawman checked and rechecked his service weapon.

At 2:15, Sheriff Gould glanced up from another look at his revolver and saw the familiar Plymouth sedan lumbering along the street. The vehicle slowed as it neared the Carriage House, angled into the traffic-free street, and backed into a space adjacent to the store's entrance. The MacDonald woman, Gould noted, was again driving. When the car came to a stop, the two males wasted no time exiting and making their way into the shop.

"I'll block her in!" announced the sheriff as he started his car, engaged the shift, and barreled forward, the engine roaring. Both men felt the familiar adrenaline rush, hearts pounding heavily in their chests. Ontengco clenched the armrest, bracing as the sheriff raced at breakneck speed toward the target; Gould pulled in front of the Plymouth Duster, the tires of his vehicle protesting as he came to a sudden, violent stop. He threw the lever into park, flung the door open, and leapt out. Ontengco was also out and sprinting toward the obvious getaway driver, gun drawn. He reached the Plymouth first and pointed the weapon at the woman inside. She frantically whipped her head back-and-forth, seeking an avenue of escape. There was none.

"Get out of the car!" Ontengco hollered, noting that the vehicle was still running. He had the woman point blank through the driver's side window, though she refused to comply with his command, simply shaking her head and mouthing the word, "No."

"Fred, you secure her!" the deputy shouted as he turned and hastened for the store entrance. "I'm going in!"

As he neared the door of the Carriage House, however, one of the two robbers unexpectedly came rushing out, nearly running headlong into the lawman. The perpetrator had obviously heard the commotion outside between the police and his female companion, who was now handcuffed and in Gould's custody.

Ontengco anchored his feet on the gravel surface, lowered into a crouch, and aimed his firearm at the suspect's midsection. "Freeze!" he shouted, pointing his gun at the fleeing man, who was drenched in sweat.

The robbery suspect—one Mark Bray, as he was later identified during police questioning—did not offer any resistance. As ordered, he raised his arms skyward and shuffled across the lot to the rear of the Plymouth. His face had turned a ghostly pale. He looked like he might be sick at any moment. Ontengco seized hold of the man's shirt collar and leaned him over the trunk of the car, splaying Bray's arms over the sun-warmed metal.

"I'm not armed," the con insisted.

"I'll be the judge of that," Ontengco barked as he began to frisk his captive for weapons. He brusquely clamped the youth's wrists in handcuffs. Sheriff Gould, meanwhile, was frisking Kathleen MacDonald. Ontengco's breath caught in his throat when he heard a telltale sound behind him. Shuffling across the loose gravel, not attempting to cloak his approach, was the second suspect: Leroy Chasson had emerged from the antique store. He was grasping Chipman Ela by the wrist. The store owner later told police that he complied because he saw that his captor had brandished a weapon, which he noted was pointed at the deputy. With one hand, Ontengco gripped the back of Bray's neck, holding the man firmly in place over the trunk of the getaway car. With the other, he raised his service revolver and trained it on Chasson.

"For a mercifully brief but exceedingly dangerous time Tuesday," wrote a staff reporter with the *Portland*

*Press Herald*, "an Oxford County Deputy Sheriff and a Massachusetts murder suspect looked over their gun barrels at each other." Chipman Ela, when interviewed by reporters who later converged on Fryeburg, described the scene as a "Mexican standoff."

"Back off!" Chasson screamed at the lawman. "Back the fuck off, cop! Let him go!"

Bray, sensing his criminal accomplice might have the upper hand in this tense impasse, urged him to take deadly action. "Shoot him! Shoot the cop!" he shouted.

But Sheriff Fred Gould had also sighted the criminal. For Chasson, it was simple math—two guns to his one. He could easily take out the deputy, but Sheriff Gould would make him pay.

In the midst of the stalemate, Chipman Ela broke free of Chasson's grip and bolted for the store entrance. The perpetrator spun around and was hot on the man's heels, trailing closely behind. Ela's familiarity with the layout gave him a chance to escape. He sped through his antique shop and quickly withdrew into the depths of his attached home, out of Chasson's sight. Ontengco and Gould, meanwhile, wisely chose not to fire at the fleeing suspect, fearing that a stray bullet might hit either Chipman or his wife, who was hiding inside. Ontengco, who was a crack marksman after a stint in the US Marines and twenty years with the NYPD, was not about to trade the life of an innocent bystander for this outlaw. It would have been reckless.

Leroy Chasson burst through the front door and scampered through the home. Before ascending a staircase to the second floor, he yanked a folded knife from his pocket and tossed it in an unlit fireplace. Upstairs, he found an open window in a bedroom, climbed through, and without pause, clambered from the sill to the soft ground below. He landed awkwardly but was unhurt. He wasn't spotted by the two lawmen at the front of the home; they were busy tending to his companions, both now in custody. He felt a twinge of guilt leaving them behind but that was something he could deal with later. Perhaps he could find the means to break them out of jail.

Sprinting across a wide, grassy meadow, Chasson soon reached a thickly wooded area. He slipped into the strand of trees and paused briefly to catch his breath and size up his situation. Risking a glance back toward the Ela home, Chasson was surprised to see police had not followed. With a grin, he turned and began to make his way into the dense brush, promptly disappearing from view. Twice in less than a week, the killer had successfully eluded the cops.

# TWENTY-SIX—CHASSON CAPTURED

Vacant parking spots in the vicinity of the Androscoggin County Courthouse were at a premium as dusk fell on the city of Auburn, Maine. Police officials from Maine and New Hampshire, along with scores of media types, both print and television, jockeyed for the few available spaces.

The late August sun had descended below the horizon and temperatures lingered in the low eighties, with cooler sixties forecasted after dark. While it was still warm in the medium-sized city of twenty thousand, there were unmistakable signs that autumn was near at hand as the month came to a close. An occasional breeze from the northern mountains rippled along Court Street, where the formidable brick courthouse occupied a full city block at the Turner Street intersection. A stone's throw to the east, the turbulent waters of Great Falls and the Androscoggin River cascaded to their confluence with the mighty Kennebec River sixty miles downstream.

Across the river was the larger Lewiston, Maine, known as the sister city to Auburn and home to Bates College. Peaceful and relatively crime-free in the seventies, Lewiston drew national attention decades later in 2023, when a troubled Army reservist took eighteen lives and then his own in a mass shooting. It was the deadliest shooting in Maine's history.

Curious onlookers craned their necks from adjacent sidewalks, watching as a flotilla of police vehicles arrived and pulled into reserved spaces in front of the courthouse. Emerging from the rear of a Fryeburg patrol car was a blonde woman, just over five feet tall and slightly portly. Even from a distance, observers could see that she was in desperate need of a shower and a change of clothing. Securely handcuffed to chains encircling her waist, Kathleen MacDonald was guided across the wide sidewalk and up the granite staircase to the structure's main entrance. She was escorted by a pair of plainclothes officers, each gripping one of her upper arms as she carefully negotiated the steep concrete flight. As cameras clicked, a murmur could be heard from reporters extending microphones and asking unanswered questions. MacDonald lowered her head and tried to ignore the intrusive throng, which was cordoned off from getting too close to the accused.

The police were aware that this grand entrance was all about the drama of the moment. There was alternate access at the rear of the courthouse, typically used to deliver suspects. It was out of view of the public. But in this instance, because of the newfound notoriety of Fryeburg, officials chose this uncommon opportunity to garner headlines.

Fryeburg, Maine, had no jail to speak of. There wasn't really a need for one. The two suspects had been held under guard in a makeshift lockup at the town's firehouse until they could be transported to more suitable confinement. While Mark Bray faced serious charges, stemming from his early-August escape from MCI-Concord, officials accused Kathleen MacDonald of "hindering in the apprehension of a felon." Under Maine law, her crime was considered a Class B felony, which could result in a ten-year sentence. Her ill-advised relationship with Leroy Chasson had, over a brief span of time, entirely altered her sedate life. She made the leap from existence as a simple housewife and mother of six to felon and soon-to-be prison inmate.

A day earlier, as arrangements were being made to move the two suspects from Fryeburg to Auburn for arraignment, local and state authorities made every effort to apprehend the ringleader on the run.

The search for Leroy Chasson was spearheaded by the Maine State Police with assistance from New Hampshire law enforcement, such as patrolmen from nearby Carroll County and several other agencies. Under the command of Maine State Police Sergeant Bradford Smith, a heavily armed contingent of twenty men fanned out across the sweeping wooded area. Several men patrolled the roadways and established roadblocks, while others set out on foot. Unlike their quarry, police were well-equipped for a dangerous trip through the woods.

After handing over the two perpetrators to officers for transport, Deputy Ontengco and Sheriff Gould left the antique store and joined in the hunt.

The police searching for Chasson were made aware that he was a Maine native. Their cagey prey had grown up sixty miles to the north, in Rumford, and was no stranger to the pitfalls of hiking across treacherous wooded terrain. But he was ill-prepared for the elements and carried no equipment or sustenance police were aware of. He was also armed, which compounded their concern.

In a small town, news travels fast. For the townspeople of Fryeburg, it was obvious a search was underway. A heavy police presence in and around their community was uncommon. Word spread of an attempted robbery at Chipman Ela's Carriage House and helpful citizens were soon on the lookout, some armed with hunting rifles.

Several hours into the search, around 5:30 p.m., a pair of alert citizens placed a telephone call to the command post at the Fryeburg firehouse. They claimed they had seen a man walking along the roadway. When this mysterious individual heard them, he suddenly ducked into the nearby brush, raising their suspicions that he was the person the police were seeking.

Armed with that information and a description, Sheriff Alton Howe arrived at the location shortly thereafter to confirm the sighting. Other officers joined in the search, which was now concentrated in a small, wooded area. While the police set up a perimeter, part-time Deputy Sheriff Donald Laffin took off in his personal aircraft from an airstrip in Sweden, Maine, to aid in the pursuit. In this instance, the authorities were fortunate. It was nearing 6:30 p.m. when the drone of his single-engine Cessna could be heard from the sky above. Darkness was, at most, an hour away. It wasn't long, however, before Laffin spotted the suspect from the air and radioed the ground forces with pinpoint coordinates.

The search party closed in on Chasson, who surrendered without incident. He emerged from behind a large tree, arms raised skyward. Making the arrest were Maine State Police Corporal James Nolan, Maine State Police Trooper Stephen Holt, and New Hampshire State Police Corporal Ray Landry. The lawmen placed Chasson in custody and secured a Colt revolver, stashed in the crotch of his trousers, which was later proven to be stolen. The police loaded him into a patrol car for the trip to join his comrades at the Fryeburg firehouse and later, for arraignment at the Androscoggin Courthouse in Auburn.

On the heels of the drama at the antique store, the four-hour manhunt for the wanted killer came to a rather anticlimactic conclusion.

***

Under cloudless bright blue skies on the morning of Wednesday, August 31, 1977, a detachment of Quincy Police Department patrol vehicles wended their way along

Interstate 95, heading north out of Massachusetts through New Hampshire and into Southern Maine. A half-dozen officers in a trio of vehicles negotiated the one hundred and fifty miles in just under three hours, reaching the Auburn Police headquarters near eleven o'clock.

It was mild, in the mid-seventies, as the police angled into adjacent parking spaces at the rear of the station, gathered their paperwork, and made their way into the stately one hundred and twenty-year-old building. The task force had been sent to collect Leroy Chasson, chief suspect in the murder of twenty-year-old Paul Melody at Quincy's Pageant Field a week earlier, and Mark Bray, an escapee from MCI-Concord, where he had been serving an eighteen-year sentence for armed robbery.

"Such was the respect for the two male suspects," Oxford County Sheriff Alton Howe remarked during an interview with a *Press Herald* reporter, "that six officers were sent to Maine Wednesday morning to take them back to Massachusetts."

The six officers Howe spoke about were Quincy Detectives Robert MacDonald, Robert Perchard, and Thomas Healy. They were joined by Massachusetts State Police Detective Robert Masuret and a pair of troopers for added security. Based on an earlier agreement made with the Maine authorities, rendition papers were completed, and the three detainees were taken into custody and transported to Quincy. The warrants filed for Leroy Chasson were No. 74082, 74083, and 74084, and were primarily for homicide. Along with charges for his escape in early August, Mark Bray was also considered an accomplice after the fact for the murder committed by his former cellmate.

Kathleen MacDonald, an accessory in the flight from the Milner Hotel in Boston as well as an accomplice in her boyfriend's botched robbery attempt at the Carriage House was, at first, ordered detained by Maine officials pending a hearing in mid-September. Permission was granted, however, for detectives to transport her to Quincy headquarters for interrogation.

"We met with District Attorney Thomas Delahanty, who informed us that her arraignment was being continued until September 12, 1977," wrote Quincy Police Detective Thomas Casey in a report later delivered to Captain Tighe. "He said that she was free to go with us voluntarily."

Filing into a small conference room buried deep in the courthouse, Kathleen took a seat opposite Quincy Detective Thomas Healey, who prepared a yellow legal pad for notetaking. Miranda Rights had already been recited by the arresting officers in Fryeburg but to be certain Kathleen MacDonald fully understood, she received them once again from the Quincy officials.

"We informed her that after she left Maine, she would not be under arrest," Healey wrote. "We explained that she did not have to come with us and was free to leave at any time."

On two earlier occasions, prior to the arrival of the Quincy Police representatives, Kathleen MacDonald reached out to her attorney, Lory Rosenberg, whose office was in Cambridge, Massachusetts. Rosenberg—who, decades later, would launch a firm specializing in immigration law—agreed it was acceptable for her client to return to Quincy.

"I'm willing to go with you," Kathleen said, according to Healey's written report. But she was unwavering when it came to questioning about the robbery attempt at the antique store. On the advice of her attorney, and her boyfriend, she would not speak about it.

When Leroy Chasson was handed over to the Auburn Police following his capture and arrest in the woods of Fryeburg, he was allowed to speak with both Kathleen and Mark Bray. Space in the jail was limited and, for a time, the trio was held in a shared cell. It later became obvious to officials that Kathleen had been coached by her boyfriend in matters that could be damaging to her case, including her role in the robbery attempt. If there was anyone who knew the inner workings of the law, it was Leroy Chasson. He was well-educated in that respect.

The trip from the Auburn lockup to similar accommodations at the Quincy Police headquarters was uneventful. Kathleen MacDonald, as expected, said very little as the procession of law enforcement vehicles drove south into Massachusetts. Her escorts preferred it that way. Until they could get her settled in the interview room at headquarters with a spinning cassette recorder in front of her, they'd rather she kept silent.

The morning of August 31, 1977, was rapidly slipping away as the Quincy detectives guided their detainee into the Sea Street headquarters. Thankfully, there was no media presence; word that Leroy Chasson and his accomplices would be transported from Maine back to Quincy was kept under wraps. There was no doubt that news agencies for television and newspapers would learn the suspects had been relocated soon enough but until word leaked out, the Quincy Police were able to sidestep another media circus and focus on the all-important interviews.

When Kathleen MacDonald was processed, there were several items in her possession. Maine authorities examined them but let her keep her property on her person. Quincy Police, on the other hand, collected the articles for safekeeping. Along with a book of poems and a blank passport application, eight photographs were taken from Kathleen—three of family members and five of Leroy Chasson. When later asked about the passport application, she declined to comment.

Kathleen took a seat in the interview room, where a steady stream of witnesses had filed through, one at a time, for a week. She was fed and made comfortable, at least as much as the rigid steel chair would allow.

Tired and haggard, she asked her interviewers where Leroy was brought. "Is he still in Maine or is he here in Quincy?"

Detective Casey, who was joined by Officer William Donnelly and Detective Barbara DiNatale, did not see a need to withhold that information. "Mr. Chasson is being temporarily held at the Dedham Jail, per order of Judge Albert L. Kramer," said Casey with a glance at the paperwork on the table in front of him. "Mr. Bray will soon be returned to MCI-Concord."

She lowered her gaze, obviously disheartened, and nodded.

As the interview commenced, Casey cut to the chase with questions about the events of August 23, 1977: the night of Paul Melody's murder.

"Between eight and nine p.m., he called me at home," Kathleen recalled, according to the interview report later delivered by Casey to Tighe. "He said he was at home, in Somerville. The conversation was general."

"When did you learn about the incident?"

"The next day. Wednesday," she replied. "I came home from work at about 6:30 p.m. and was reading about the Melody murder in the *Patriot Ledger*. I saw that Lee was being sought for murder."

Casey asked Kathleen when she next heard from Chasson, who said that it wasn't until Thursday at ten o'clock at night, two full days after the incident. He called her at home—at her parents' place. He would not say where he was. "He was crying," she shared hesitantly. "He told me that something awful had happened. There was a fight, that people came at him, and that someone got stabbed."

Casey noted in his report that Kathleen MacDonald sensed Chasson wanted to talk more about it, to get it off his chest, but she stopped him, explaining she knew what happened because she had read about it in the paper.

"He said he was leaving and that he wanted to see me one more time," she shared, adding that they planned to meet on Friday, August 26, at five o'clock in the evening. He told her to wait next to the fruit stand near the MBTA Park Street Station in Boston.

"Who met you at the fruit stand?"

"Mark Bray," she replied, stating that she had never seen him before but knew about him because Lee had mentioned they were in prison together. "He came up to me and kept motioning with his head for me to go with him. I figured that Lee had described me. We walked a short distance to where Lee was waiting."

Casey documented that Kathleen MacDonald and Bray spoke little but nothing was said about the murder in Quincy. "He was very quiet and had little to say," she recalled.

According to the report, Kathleen recounted how she reunited with Leroy Chasson. They walked around Boston Common for hours, had something to eat, and as evening fell, retired to the Milner Hotel, where the three of them shared a room.

"What do you know about their plans to make a run for the border—to escape to Canada?" he asked.

"Yes, Canada," she acknowledged with a nod. "I was planning to return home after I was sure that Lee was safe and that he would not be caught by the police."

Detective Casey shifted back to more significant questions: namely, the murder of Paul Melody.

Kathleen MacDonald remained forthcoming. "Lee talked about the murder a great deal," she began. "He said he went to Quincy to punch out a guy who gave Mark Bray some trouble. Lee punched the guy in the jaw and he fell backwards. He said that people came at him and someone had a knife."

Foley was silent, engrossed in his notetaking. Kathleen took a sip of her coffee, leaned back, and collected herself before continuing. The more she spoke about the murder, the more her emotions consumed her.

"Lee told me he took the knife away from this person," she said as her bloodshot eyes welled up with tears. "Then the killing began."

## TWENTY-SEVEN — BRAY QUESTIONED

Before delivering Mark Bray to resume his sentence at the Massachusetts Correctional Institute-Concord, where he faced the unpleasant prospect of a stay in solitary confinement, detectives diverted the prison escapee to Quincy Police headquarters for a highly anticipated interrogation session.

It was late morning, August 31, and unbeknownst to Bray, Chasson's companion Kathleen had wrapped up her visit with Quincy investigators and departed for her parents' home in Weymouth. Her attorney, Lory Rosenberg, drove her to the oceanfront South Shore community. Kathleen would eventually return to Maine to face felony charges. In Quincy, she had left a number of questions unanswered, but Rosenberg had arrived to bring Detective Casey's interview to a rapid conclusion. It was within her client's legal rights. Kathleen was not under arrest, at least not in Quincy's jurisdiction, and was free to do as she pleased. Attorney Rosenberg thought it was better to separate her from the probing detectives before she said too much.

On hand to question Mark Bray was Lieutenant Neil MacDonald who, in the previous week, had spent more time wedged in the interview room than he had spent at home. In this instance, he didn't mind. He was chomping at the bit to speak with Bray—and immediately following, with murder suspect Leroy Chasson. Lieutenant MacDonald was joined by Captain Tighe and Detective Healey.

"Good morning, Mark," the lieutenant greeted his suspect.

The response was lukewarm. "Morning," Bray mumbled. A look of distaste was fixed on his unshaven face. He stared at the interviewer across the surface of the brushed steel table, gleaming beneath overhead fluorescent lights.

MacDonald loosened his tie and drew a deep breath. Glancing at his notes, he ventured ahead. "So, Mark... can I call you Mark?"

"Uh huh."

"Okay, then, Mark. Before we ask you any questions, we have to advise you of your rights," MacDonald announced, diligently checking to ensure the cassette recorder was functional. He then read the Miranda warning, which was printed on a small square card and slid it across the table with a pen. Bray, who was understandably weary after a sleepless night in a dingy Maine lockup, gathered the card, signed it without hesitation, and slid it back.

"Mark, would you verify your date of birth?"

"November 24, 1955."

"That would make you twenty-one."

"Twenty-two in a few months," the suspect volunteered with a nod.

"Okay," the lieutenant said as he penciled a quick notation on the yellow tablet in front of him. Introductions dispensed with, MacDonald went directly to the crux of his questioning and said, "You understand this interview is part of a murder investigation?"

"Yeah."

"Mark, where are you from?"

"Quincy," Bray answered. "584 Hancock Street."

"Are you an escapee from Concord, Mark?" MacDonald asked without any sugarcoating. He was all business and was not wasting any time attempting to placate the suspect.

"Yeah."

"When did you escape?"

"I'm not sure of the date," the wrongdoer answered, shrugging his shoulders. "I think it was the first week of August."

"A week ago, did you go to a party in Chelsea?"

"Yes."

"Who was with you?"

"Leroy Chasson and Donald Bains."

"Who did the driving?"

"Donald Bains."

"Did he have a stolen car?"

Bray had been straight through the first several questions but in this instance, he chose to answer untruthfully. He had a recent history of lying to the police. During his booking in Auburn, Maine, for instance, Bray identified himself as Michael J. Bray, who was his younger brother who didn't have a criminal record.

"I'm not sure," he said, turning his gaze away from the prying eyes of the lieutenant and his colleagues.

"Are you currently dating anyone?"

"No."

"Do you know Patricia Landon?"

"Yes," Bray replied, his expression making it known that he was baffled by this line of questioning. "I've known her for a long time."

"Was she at the party?"

"No."

"Sometime during the party, did Leroy and Bryan Fitzgerald leave?"

"Yeah."

"Where did they go?" MacDonald asked.

"They left to get beer."

"What time did they return?"

"No idea," answered Bray, a touch of belligerence now in his tone. "I guess it was 11:30 or midnight."

The lieutenant shifted to a series of questions about Chasson's condition when he returned to the party, primarily what type and color of shirt he was wearing and whether Bray noticed bloodstains on it. He answered that he wasn't sure about the shirt and didn't recall seeing any blood. MacDonald asked Bray if he'd joined Chasson in the bathroom while he tried to rinse the shirt. The suspect answered that he did not enter the bathroom, claiming he waited in the hallway. *More dishonesty*, the lieutenant noted. Several earlier witnesses, each of who had attended the house party and had unobstructed views of Chasson, agreed that blood was clearly visible on the shirt and that Bray did, in fact, go into the bathroom to help eliminate incriminating evidence.

"Did you learn they went to the park that night?" MacDonald continued.

"Yes."

"What did they tell you about that?"

"They had an encounter with Racette."

"What did that consist of?"

"Words, between Lee and Racette," Bray replied. "Lee punched Racette, and a couple of kids jumped on Lee. One of them had a knife."

The lieutenant paused briefly, glaring at the youth. The earlier deceit—referencing Bains and the stolen car and whether Bray had seen bloodstains on his friend's shirt—could be classified as simple falsehoods. But to suggest that the knife did not belong to Chasson was an outright lie. All the earlier witness statements indicated that the perpetrator wielded the blade. The knife was one vital piece of evidence that MacDonald would sorely like to get his hands on.

"What did Lee tell you then?" the lieutenant asked.

"He just scuffled," Bray answered. "Lee took the knife and I'm not really sure; people were cut."

"What beef was there between Lee and Racette?"

"They never liked each other. They never have."

"Did you hire Lee to go after Racette?"

"No."

A number of interviews had revealed the fight was over a paltry sum—fifty dollars, according to the consensus of witnesses. MacDonald sought verification of the amount from Bray, who obviously had firsthand knowledge of the debt.

"Did Racette rip you off while you were at the Concord Reformatory?"

"Yes," Bray replied bitterly.

"Was it over heroin?"

"It was over money."

"How much?" MacDonald asked.

"Fifty."

Bray went on to answer a series of questions related to the aftermath of the stabbings when Leroy Chasson returned to the Chelsea party with Bryan Fitzgerald. He mentioned how Donald Bains drove them to Lee's apartment in Somerville, the brief encounter with Patricia Landon, the one-night stay in a Rhode Island motel, and a few details about the Milner Hotel.

"You knew that Chasson was wanted for murder?"

"Yeah, but that was just for questioning," Bray stressed. "A suspect sought for questioning. I didn't learn he was wanted for murder until he was arrested in Maine."

"Did you and Lee plan an antique robbery in Maine?"

Mark Bray smirked and sarcastically replied, "No, we were in Maine for a holiday."

The suspect's attitude grated on the investigator but he did his best to ignore it. Retaliating would only ruffle feathers. As much as it appealed to him, he didn't want to descend into a battle of wits with this youth and lose control of the interview. It was obvious Bray had been down the legal road a time or two and was well-versed in the approach to police or attorney questioning.

"Was Kathleen MacDonald in on the robbery?"

"There was no robbery," the alleged perpetrator insisted. "She was outside in the car. I was just discussing something with the owner. I went outside for a minute and suddenly, a cop was yelling, 'Don't move!' Someone told those Maine cops there was going to be an antique robbery."

"Would it surprise you if I told you that I called them?" said MacDonald, who received a phone call from an informant days earlier disclosing that Chasson and Bray intended to rob a business in Oxford County, Maine. While the caller admitted to being a friend of Bray, he was unable to provide specifics or narrow down the location. He did claim that Chasson and Bray had attempted to drum up interest in an antique robbery in Maine, which MacDonald felt added plausibility to the caller's anonymous tip.

"No, it wouldn't surprise me," the arrogant miscreant chafed. "Who called you and told you that?"

"Let me ask the questions."

Bray glared icily at the lieutenant across from him but his sullen expression soon returned and he slumped in the chair once again.

MacDonald ignored the gesture and continued with the questioning without pause. He asked Mark if he was aware that Chasson was carrying a gun. Bray nodded but didn't elaborate. He also denied—lied, actually—when asked if he and his companions were planning to leave the country—to flee to Canada.

Bray was surprisingly forthcoming with details about his assorted travels during the three days he and his two companions were on the run in Boston. He explained that his mother had sent money for living expenses. She was acting as a go-between with her son's attorney, conveying information and advice. It was from his supportive mother that Bray learned that he would be charged as an accessory after the fact. "I was preparing to turn myself in," he claimed.

"Well, if that's the case, you were going in the wrong direction. To Maine," MacDonald said snidely.

Bray shrugged and countered, "From what I heard from people in Quincy, I thought I would be shot on sight if I showed up in town. People weren't happy with me."

The interviewer reverted to an earlier question, seeking to implicate others. There was a lengthy list of people who allegedly lent a helping hand to the fugitives. "Was Patricia Landon involved in hiding you guys out? Or Linell Travers?"

"No." Mark chose not to say anything about the brief get-together he and Leroy had with the two girls in Boston Common to accept delivery of the assorted disguise materials. It was a meaningless event, at least in his opinion, and contributed nothing to the getaway attempt. As it turned out, he and Lee chose not to use the supplies. Leroy Chasson, it seemed, was far too vain to alter his hair color. Besides, the idea was to blend in, not stand out.

The interview of Mark Bray continued into the afternoon. Lieutenant MacDonald repeated a number of the key questions, foraging for inconsistencies in the suspect's answers. Obviously, most important was drawing out information about the murder of Paul Melody. While Bray was not a witness to the murder, he did spend a week on the run with the alleged perpetrator. The lieutenant was certain the two men had discussed the killing. He sought to glean additional evidence from Bray before he was returned to MCI-Concord to serve out his original sentence, plus added time for escape.

"So, again, did Linell or Patricia hide you out?"

"No."

"More or less, you and Chasson were on the run," MacDonald stated.

"I've been on the run since I escaped from Concord."

"Did Donald Bains hide you out?"

"No," the suspect answered. "We stayed in motels, places where people didn't know us."

That, too, was inaccurate. Karen McLaughlin, the desk clerk at the Milner Hotel, knew him from high school but MacDonald chose to set her aside for the time being. Better to stay on track with this witness. Bray was talking, even though he didn't have to. He was heading back to jail whether he answered questions or not.

"And the guns?"

"Gun," Bray corrected, insistent that the only gun he was aware of was Chasson's Colt revolver, which the arresting Maine and New Hampshire State Troopers found stuffed in his pants.

"What about the knife?" MacDonald asked. "What happened to the murder weapon?"

"I have no idea,"

"All right, Mark, we'll wrap up this interview," the lieutenant announced. "One of the officers will arrange to transport you back to Concord."

MacDonald would have spent more time questioning Mark Bray, but he figured he'd catch a catnap before the next subject, who was slated to occupy the chair after lunch. Leroy Chasson would, at long last, face questioning for the murder of Paul Melody.

# TWENTY-EIGHT—CHASSON'S TURN

"Leroy, before I ask you any questions, I have to advise you of your rights," Lieutenant Neil MacDonald said, holding the familiar document in his hand for the alleged perpetrator to see. "I'm going to read from this Miranda Warning Card."

Chasson, who looked every bit the part of someone who had been stewing in a dingy jail cell, nodded once. He was in desperate need of a shower and a change of clothing. His t-shirt and blue jeans were tattered and stained, mostly from his failed flight from the authorities in the Fryeburg woods. He was looking forward to getting through this round of questioning and relocating to an actual prison or jail where he could get cleaned up and settle in. He listened intently as the lieutenant explained his rights.

It was just after two o'clock in the afternoon as MacDonald began to read off the small card. "You have the right to remain silent. Anything you say can and will be used against you in a court of law."

Chasson glanced at the cassette tape recorder on the table in front of him and made a mental note about his right to remain silent.

"You have the right to talk to a lawyer for advice before we ask you any questions and to have him with you during questioning," the lieutenant droned as he checked the recorder. All the previous interview recordings had earlier been handed off to the department clerks to transcribe. While each was of value in this developing case, the discussion taking place with Chasson was of utmost significance. "If you cannot afford a lawyer, one will be appointed for you before questioning if you wish. If you decide to answer questions now without a lawyer present, you will still have the right to stop questioning at any time until you talk to a lawyer." Chasson had decided to forgo a lawyer, at least at this early stage in the proceedings. He felt he was savvy enough to match wits with a police detective.

"Do you understand what I have read to you? Having these rights in mind, do you wish to talk to me now?"

Chasson nodded his agreement, said, "Yes" for the sake of the spinning recorder, and signed the Miranda Card as requested.

"Okay, would you identify yourself?" MacDonald began, glancing at his two colleagues, John Perchard and Thomas Healy. Both men were prepared to take notes.

In response, the suspect said nothing about his preference for Lee as opposed to Leroy. He was far too exhausted to drag out this inquest over petty details. "I'm Leroy Chasson."

"On August 23, 1977, which would have been a Tuesday night, were you at a party in Chelsea?"

"Yes."

"And at some time, did you leave the party and go to Quincy?"

"Yes."

"Why did you go to Quincy?"

"I wanted to see Racette," Chasson said, pausing to take a sip of water that had been provided for him. As he picked up the Styrofoam cup, the handcuffs attached to his wrists jingled like a pocket full of loose change. The interviewers had considered his penchant for escape attempts and felt it was safer for all involved if the alleged perpetrator remained in cuffs during the interview. "I intended to have a fistfight with him. I wanted to just beat on him but there were about ten other kids there, so I talked with Kevin for about ten minutes, and I left."

Despite the troublesome content of Chasson's statement, that he planned to rough up a man in the park, his honesty was refreshing. With many of the interview candidates to that point in the probe, MacDonald often had to work around twisted truths and outright lies. Leroy Chasson was straight to the point.

"I have a note here," said MacDonald, holding up a document, "that reads that you first approached Joey Marnell to ask if he was Racette."

"Yeah."

"Didn't you know Racette from jail?"

"Uh huh, but I wanted to be sure. It had been a long time since I'd last seen him. It had been a couple of years."

"What did you and Kevin Racette talk about?" the lieutenant asked.

"Oh, small talk."

"Then you left?"

"Yes."

MacDonald was aware that Chasson had actually paid two visits to the park and Racette. During the initial visit—which, according to witnesses, lasted no more than ten or fifteen minutes—a brief conversation took place between the two men. He then left with Bryan Fitzgerald. They stopped for a bite at a nearby greasy spoon but instead of continuing to Chelsea, Chasson insisted they go back to Pageant Field. There was no indication from Fitzgerald during his interview that he tried to talk his unwelcome companion out of returning. Fitzgerald did question his motive but all Chasson said was that he had unfinished business with Racette.

"When you returned, did you ask Kevin to get you three bags of heroin?"

At this, Chasson paused briefly, obviously searching for an answer. He scanned the room, growing annoyed. The lieutenant waited patiently, preparing himself to respond to some form of falsehood. "I just did that to get him away from the other kids," was his reply. "Before I did, I had told Rocky…"

MacDonald interrupted and said, "You mean Bryan Fitzgerald?"

"Yeah, Bryan," Chasson amended. "I told him if he knew any of the other kids, to keep them away. When I got Racette aside, I just punched him in the face, and as he went back, a bunch of kids came running over—about six or seven. One had a knife."

MacDonald had been wondering what Chasson might say about the knife. The answer sounded contrived. But the lieutenant, not wanting to lose the suspect, allowed Chasson to continue along the path and wait for him to stumble.

"Could you describe the one with the knife?"

"I can't describe him," he dodged, which was no surprise to his interviewer. "It was dark. You know, only one streetlight."

"What happened then?"

"The first kid I grabbed was the kid with the knife," Chasson recalled. "There were other kids jumping on my back, but I got the knife away from the kid and I started slashing. I didn't know who else had a knife there."

"How many people did you slash?"

"I don't know how many people got slashed, but I know the kid got Rocky too."

Leroy was obviously referring to the minor wound Bryan Fitzgerald received to his fingers but that was either confusion on the part of this suspect or a fabrication. As MacDonald understood it, Fitzgerald sustained the laceration when he interfered as Chasson continued his attack near the picnic tables.

"What hand did you hold the knife in?"

"My right hand," he replied, "but I beat Racette with my left."

"Could you describe the knife?"

"I can't describe it except it had a big handle."

"What was the beef between you and Kevin Racette?"

"It was a personal beef from when we were in Concord," Chasson answered. "I was missing some of the things from my cell."

"Lee, wasn't the beef because of Mark Bray? A debt owed to him?"

"No," Chasson lied.

"How did you get out of Pageant Field after the fight?"

"We got into Rocky's car," he said, reverting again to Fitzgerald's popular nickname. "Rocky was driving. We went directly to Chelsea."

"Didn't you stop at Rocky's house?"

"No."

Another outright lie.

MacDonald had been furnished with the report from two patrolmen who had paid a visit to Bryan Fitzgerald's home and spoke with his mother. According to the officers, she had initially resisted. But under duress, during a second visit to her home, she finally yielded useful information. Mrs. Fitzgerald verified that her son had, in fact, made a quick stop at the house and that a man fitting Chasson's description was at his side. That man, she reported, was wearing a bloodstained blue shirt and seemed jumpy.

"Was there blood on your shirt, Leroy?"

"Yeah, my shirt was soaked with blood," he admitted with a tentative nod. He slouched forward in his chair and crossed his legs at the ankles.

"What did you do with the shirt?"

Thinking back to the night at the Rhode Island motel and how he tied the incriminating shirt around a rock and sank it in a nearby stream, he responded, "I threw it away in Somerville."

"Where in Somerville?"

"In a dumpster at a Dunkin Donuts."

"Which Dunkin Donuts was that?"

Leroy answered without delay so the lieutenant would not suspect he was lying. "Inman Square, Somerville."

"What did you do with the knife?"

"I threw it out of the car, no idea where, but it wasn't long after we left the park," the murder suspect declared.

An exhaustive search of Pageant Field was launched soon after the stabbings took place. The surrounding wooded areas were thoroughly canvassed by a small army of Quincy Police, with assistance from the Massachusetts State Police. There were several subsequent visits by the authorities to search other areas in and around Merrymount Park. Officials also paid close attention to properties along the route that Bryan Fitzgerald claimed to have driven in their withdrawal from the scene of the crime.

They repeated visual inspections, as well as deployed metal detectors to scan the grass frontage. Homeowners curiously watched the police at work and when it was explained to them what was being sought, agreed to keep an eye out for the evidence. The officials scoured roadside brush and arranged for the Quincy Department of Public Works to pull up a number of heavy iron catch basin covers to search the murky waters below. If he was telling the truth, Chasson revealed that he had tossed the knife out of the moving car, possibly along the Southern Artery, but the hunt failed to turn up anything.

Lieutenant MacDonald moved on to other topics, intending to circle back with further scrutiny of the possible murder weapon location. Chasson had lied about how he came to possess the knife and he was also lying about where he disposed of it.

"Did you have a conversation with Rocky on the way back to Chelsea?"

"Yeah, I told Rocky to make up an alibi."

"On the way back to Chelsea, did you tell Rocky and, I quote, 'that you were glad I got that fucking Racette.'"

"Yeah," answered Chasson with a sinister grin. He certainly wasn't trying to hide the fact that he was one deranged individual. "But I wasn't really satisfied because I only got one shot at him. If I went there with a plan to stab anybody, I would've stabbed Racette."

MacDonald again tried to grasp what would drive a man to foster such hatred. From what he could gather, this was Mark Bray's fight. Kevin Racette had stolen money from Bray, not Chasson, and an inconsequential amount at that. Leroy Chasson was little more than Bray's errand boy, yet he spoke of killing Racette with such maliciousness and outright disregard for human life. It was difficult to wrap one's head around.

"Did you know Paul Melody?"

"No."

"When did you learn Paul Melody had died?"

"The following morning."

"How did you learn this?"

"Newspaper," Chasson answered matter-of-factly. There was no discomfort in his voice, no regret whatsoever. It was as if he were in the middle of a meaningless discussion as opposed to answering questions about the brutal homicide of a twenty-year-old. There was not a trace of remorse in Chasson. There was ice water in this ruthless man's veins, MacDonald felt.

"Did you go back to the party?"

"Yes."

"When you got back to the party, did you go in the bathroom and rinse off your shirt?"

"No, just washed my hands."

"Did you leave the party with anyone?" the lieutenant asked.

"Yes."

"With whom?"

"Mark Bray and a guy named Mike."

MacDonald paused at this point, caught slightly off guard by the answer. Mark Bray and other witnesses had said the third man was Donald Bains and described him. But Chasson claimed their driver was someone named "Mike." The lieutenant assumed it was just a matter of his suspect attempting to protect Bains, who had been thoroughly questioned by the state police at the Somerville apartment.

"What was Mike's last name?" he asked.

"I don't know," Chasson lied without batting an eye. "Mike picked up Mark and me and drove us to the party and he also drove us to Somerville."

"How did you get in touch with Mike?"

"I don't remember."

"Did you go to 87 Bartlett Street in Somerville?"

"Yes."

"Who was present at the apartment?"

"My fiancée, Linell, and my son."

"Is that Linell Travers?"

"Yes."

MacDonald had a great deal of questions related to Leroy's girlfriend, or fiancée, as she was described. If this woman were, in fact, engaged to Leroy Chasson, how would the perpetrator explain his relationship with Kathleen MacDonald when it came time to exchange wedding vows? Not that the lieutenant really cared about Leroy's sordid love life. He just wanted to determine if this woman, Linell Travers, provided aid while he was hiding out in Boston.

"What time did you arrive in Somerville?"

"I'm not sure of the time," Chasson answered. "Linell and my son were asleep, and we didn't wake them."

"Was the car you were riding in stolen?" MacDonald asked, fully aware that Donald Bains had helped himself to the vehicle in Quincy and attached stolen plates. The Boston Police had found it abandoned in the theatre district, and it was currently impounded with the BPD.

Sticking with the falsehood about the third man, Chasson said, "I don't know, Mike drove us."

It was obvious to the lieutenant that Leroy was doing his best to protect Donald Bains from imprisonment. Bains was interviewed at length by both Somerville and State Police at Linell Travers' apartment but at the time was not arrested. He would later face time behind bars when it was found that he had stolen a car and helped Chasson.

"When Mark and you left Somerville, where did you spend the night?"

"At the Milner Hotel in Boston," answered Leroy, unaware that Mark Bray had been asked the same question and answered truthfully about the one night they spent in Rhode Island. It was something he and Mark failed to corroborate between them while jailed together in Auburn, Maine.

"What did you do then?" the lieutenant continued.

"Well, in the morning, we got the paper to see what happened at Pageant Field," Chasson disclosed. "Mark and I read the paper at the HoJo's in Dorchester while we had breakfast."

"And after that?"

"I called my house and spoke with Linell," he said. "She said the police were there several times."

"Did you tell her you planned to leave the state?"

"Yes."

"When did you actually leave the state?"

"A couple days ago. Monday."

"This past Monday, August 29?"

"Yes."

"Did you and Mark plan a robbery in Maine?"

An exasperated Chasson suddenly drew a deep breath and exhaled audibly. His face darkened with fury. He sat upright and steely-eyed, scowled at the lieutenant, stating through clenched teeth, "At this point, I want to stop the questioning."

MacDonald paused long enough to absorb the sudden change of heart on the part of his suspect. He was exercising his constitutional right to remain silent and not respond to questions. It was disappointing for the investigators.

"All right, Lee."

"Look," Chasson added, placing his palms flat on the table, "with my criminal record, nobody's going to believe anything I have to say, so why bother? We're wasting our time here."

Despite the explanation, MacDonald could not grasp the meaning behind the sudden reversal on the part of Leroy Chasson. Throughout the interview, he had been composed and cooperative. While at times he wasn't fully truthful, at least he was answering questions. But something about the botched robbery in Fryeburg ticked him off. Perhaps he was upset because it hadn't gone to plan and he was caught red-handed. While he was attempting to rationalize the murder charges and construct a plea of self-defense, as farfetched as that might be, he had little excuse for the robbery attempt. Simply put, the failure embarrassed him.

The lieutenant reached across the table, positioning the cassette recorder closer so he could make a statement of his own. He spoke into the built-in microphone. "It is 3:05 p.m. on the afternoon of August 31, 1977. The questioning has ceased at the request of our subject, Leroy Chasson."

The murder suspect did not stop talking at that moment, however. "What happens now?" he asked.

MacDonald explained that he would be brought to the booking room, then photographed, fingerprinted, and transported to court, where an attorney would be appointed.

"Is Hayward okay?" Leroy asked, suddenly getting a little choked up.

The lieutenant found it odd that the suspect would ask about Hayward, who was seriously wounded during the melee, but not make mention of the Melody boy, who perished.

"He's okay," MacDonald replied. "He was stabbed twice in the kidney area but pulled through."

"Good," said Chasson. "Thank God."

In hindsight, the lieutenant was disappointed that the interview ended so abruptly. He was hoping to ask a few more questions about the knife. He was certain he could persuade Chasson into furnishing the location of this vital piece of evidence but, at that stage of the investigation, was not afforded the opportunity.

\*\*\*

On September 2, 1977, two days after the three suspects were shuttled from Auburn, Maine, to Quincy for questioning; the alleged murder weapon was recovered in Fryeburg at the scene of the attempted robbery.

A Teletype had been sent by the Quincy Police to their counterparts in Maine, requesting they keep a watchful eye for the weapon, which was described as a folding Buck knife. Investigators believed that Leroy Chasson had kept the knife in his possession since the night of the murder. From what the detectives could gather, he tried to dispose of the incriminating weapon in Fryeburg while fleeing the antique store.

A response from the Maine authorities stated, "Our department has located a knife in the residence attached to the antique shop that Chasson tried to rob. Have reason to believe that it might be Chasson's as the owner of the place claims that he has never seen this knife before. Please advise if this is anything you might be interested in."

"I called the Sheriff's Department, Oxford, Maine, and spoke with a Deputy Carman," wrote Quincy Detective Perchard in a report filed with Captain Tighe. "He stated that the knife is in the custody of Deputy Sheriff Francis Ontengco. They will retain custody of the knife until they hear further from us. They were advised to be careful regarding possible prints and to preserve continuity."

Several days later, on September 6, Quincy Police representatives were dispatched to the residence of Deputy Ontengco. Lieutenant James Fay and Officer Ralph Hood were tasked with making the drive north to the tiny town of Brownfield, Maine, home to fewer than eight hundred people. Ontengco resided on Main Route 5, which was on the doorstep of the New Hampshire state line.

According to Perchard's report, "Deputy Ontengco proceeded to turn over a white cardboard box which was sealed with tape and upon which, both top and bottom, there appeared several written lines."

"When I was given the box, I wrote on it to document the date and time of the exchange, as well as the names of the people who came in contact with it," Ontengco said to the Quincy officers, explaining the meaning behind the writing on the box. "It has been secured under lock and key until now."

Hood and Fay shared their appreciation for the diligence of the Fryeburg Police Department, not only for the capture of Leroy Chasson but for the preservation of vital evidence. It was believed by some that the knife would never be found. There were countless opportunities for Chasson to ditch the weapon in Quincy, Boston, New Hampshire, Maine, and numerous points in between. It was surprising he held on to it for as long as he did.

The officers who took possession of the white box protected it as if it were a fragile trinket destined for a museum. Fay, who rode shotgun for the trip back to Massachusetts, gripped it like it was a Fort Knox gold brick.

"Mr. Ela, the owner of the antique shop, found it in his fireplace," Ontengco explained. "He knew well enough not to touch it and called police."

When Lieutenant Fay and Officer Wood arrived at Quincy Police headquarters, the box was handed over to the detective bureau. The seal was broken and the box opened. The report attached to the evidence reads as follows:

THE PACKAGE WAS FOUND TO CONTAIN A JACKKNIFE TYPE KNIFE WHICH HAD BRASS-APPEARING ENDS AND A WOOD-APPEARING CENTER FOR HANDLES. THE WOOD-APPEARING SUBSTANCE WAS DARK BROWN IN COLOR. THE KNIFE CONSISTED OF ONE BLADE WHICH WAS 3-3/4 INCHES LONG AND WAS SECURED WITHIN THE HANDLE OF THE KNIFE BY A LOCKING DEVICE WHICH PRESSURE HAD TO BE ASSERTED BEFORE THE BLADE COULD BE EXTENDED. THE HANDLE OF THIS KNIFE WAS ABOUT FIVE INCHES IN LENGTH. THE BLADE AT THE WIDEST POINT WAS ABOUT SEVEN-EIGHTHS OF AN INCH. THE HANDLE AND THE BLADE OF THE KNIFE WERE PROCESSED FOR LATENT FINGERPRINTS BY FAY AND SOME IMPRESSIONS WERE LIFTED AND PRESERVED. THE KNIFE IS SECURED IN OFFICE OF CAPTAIN OF DETECTIVES.

# TWENTY-NINE—MURDER TRIAL

In February 1978, a historic winter storm ravaged the Eastern seaboard, specifically New England and New York. In its wake, the surprise Nor'easter dumped more than two feet of heavy snow on the region in a brief span of time, killed more than one hundred in its path, including many who asphyxiated in stranded cars trying to stay warm, and became forever known as the Blizzard of '78. Decades later, those who endured mountains of snow, power outages, the weeklong closure of businesses, schools, and roadways still speak of the catastrophic storm in reverent terms. "Where were you during the Blizzard of '78?" is a question often asked of those old enough to remember the once-in-a-lifetime weather event.

A storm of a different type gathered over Dedham, Massachusetts four months later, despite a bright shining sun, light breezes, and prevailing temperatures in the mid-seventies. Surrounded by a heavily armored detachment of local and state police, Leroy Chasson arrived at the Norfolk County Superior Courthouse in Dedham to stand trial for the murder of Quincy youth Paul Melody.

Since his arraignment at the Quincy District Court, which took place soon after his interview with Quincy Lieutenant Neil MacDonald, Leroy Chasson had been housed at the Dedham Jail. The facility was a decrepit, two-story stone structure located on residential Village

Avenue, several blocks from Dedham Square. Built in 1817 and expanded in 1851, the jail was converted to upscale condominiums when the newly constructed Norfolk County Correctional Center, situated on the median of Route 128, began receiving inmates in 1992.

Unless the homeowners residing on the site of the original Dedham Jail are history buffs, it is unlikely they're aware that a pair of executions took place in the rotunda of the original mid-nineteenth-century building, a matter of feet from where they rest their heads each night.

In mid-June of 1875, James Henry Costley, of Hanover, Massachusetts, met with a noose for the murder of two women, including his housekeeper and a former love interest, Julia Hawkes. To this day, the beam that was pressed into service to string up Costley remains in storage in a Norfolk County warehouse.

Earlier, in 1862, George C. Hersey was hanged in the Dedham gallows for poisoning to death Betsey Frances Terrell of Weymouth, Massachusetts. According to several newspaper accounts, tickets were sold to an audience of three hundred who sought to be on hand to view the execution. Each paid a hefty sum of ten dollars (or three hundred dollars in today's money) to witness the murderer's grisly punishment.

"The prisoner was brought in from his cell at 9-1/2 o'clock, looking haggard and appearing extremely weak, and had to be supported by officers in ascending the scaffold," detailed an account published in the August 8, 1862, edition of the *Boston Transcript* newspaper. "He was encased in a long, black gown and the black cap was drawn over his face, when the Sheriff touched the fatal spring, and in a moment, the unfortunate criminal was launched into eternity. There was no struggling, but the contractions of the muscles continued for about five minutes. The body hung for half an hour when the examining physicians declared it to be perfectly lifeless. The deceased was twenty-nine years of age."

Leroy Chasson was twenty-nine years of age when his trial got underway on May 18, 1978. The jury pool for the trial numbered one hundred and seven candidates, from which fourteen were selected. The Commonwealth and the defense challenged and dismissed twenty-eight combined potential jurors.

Transported by state car the brief half mile from the Dedham Jail to the High Street courthouse, which was an imposing Greek-Revival structure built in 1820, Chasson was ushered through a rear entrance to a basement lockup of the cavernous building to await the proceedings. Fifty years earlier, wrongly accused murder suspects Nicola Sacco and Bartolomeo Vanzetti sat in the very same holding cell awaiting their capital trial that would, at its conclusion, lead to their executions in the electric chair.

Over a span of three weeks, ending with sentencing on May 31, 1978, Leroy Chasson was ferried each morning from his dank, dismal cell to the defendant's table. At one point near the end of the murder trial, he chose to take the stand in his own defense, a strategy that often has more pitfalls than benefits. In Chasson's instance, as a precursor to his agreement to testify, his extensive criminal record would be read aloud in the courtroom, planting a seed in the minds of the jurors. In addition, he surrendered his Fifth Amendment protections. Chasson would have no choice but to answer questions from the prosecution and there would be little recourse if hostile attorneys vilified him on the stand.

"The Fifth Amendment guarantees any person accused of a crime the right not to take the witness stand in their own trial," wrote Connor Roe, Summer Associate, in her legal blog. "If the defendant should choose to exercise that right, the judge will remind the jury that not taking the stand is not an admission of guilt. However, often in the minds of jurors and spectators, this is an admission of guilt."

Leroy Chasson was of the belief that the Commonwealth lacked sufficient evidence to substantiate a charge of murder in the first degree and felt he could convince the jury that he stabbed Paul Melody and Robert Hayward in self-defense. Understandably, Chasson's defense attorney, Alan Caplan of Cambridge, did not fully agree with his client's strategy but was unable to change the bull-headed defendant's mind.

Norfolk County Assistant District Attorney Robert Banks, tasked with sending Leroy Chasson to prison for the rest of his years, eyed the defendant like a ravenous wolf preparing to dine on a captive rodent. In his mind, the State's case against Chasson would be open and shut. The preponderance of evidence was in the prosecution's favor.

"Self-defense, is it?" Banks began.

"Yes," Chasson acknowledged with a nod.

"Would you explain to this Court how stabbing these two men, one fatally, could be interpreted as self-defense?"

"I did not have a knife with me when I joined the group at Pageant Field that night," the accused said resolutely. "Someone else brought a knife and when it dropped to the ground, I picked it up and started to run."

Of course, Banks took this opportunity to remind the Court that testimony from eight earlier witnesses to the deadly melee stated that Chasson did not run but rather remained in place near the baseball backstop long enough to allegedly stab two men and threaten several others.

"I did lash out with the knife, but I was not aware of striking anyone with it," Chasson explained. "I was pounded and kicked all over my body. I saw flashes and I heard something metallic drop to the ground. I grabbed it and told them to stay away from me. I was scared."

"Pounded and kicked," Banks mimicked sarcastically, repeating the comment for effect. "Wasn't it strange that there was not a single scratch or bruise on you when you were later apprehended? And you weren't aware of striking anyone with the knife?"

Earlier testimony from State Pathologist George Katsis pointed to the fatal blow as a "classic thrust, right out and straight to the heart." He indicated that the Buck knife believed to be used in the attack was three-and-three-quarter inches in length, while the depth of the wound was of equal depth. In addition, Katsis mentioned the certificate of death, which was completed by Dr. Samuel Solomon and read, "Stab wound left chest penetrating left ventricle heart leading to sanguination."

Banks strode to the evidence table and picked up Exhibit A. He held up, for all to see, a folding-type Buck knife retrieved by the Fryeburg, Maine Police in the home of Chipman Ela. Wrapped in plastic, the apparent murder weapon was partially coated with gray dust from the ash in the fireplace, where Chasson threw it as he escaped from authorities. The forensic lab technicians had taken great care to leave the evidence as it was found as they lifted a set of Chasson's fingerprints from the false wooden handle.

Attorney Banks identified the Buck knife for the benefit of Judge James McGuire, the eight-man-four-woman jury panel, and the court reporter. He asked the defendant if he recognized it.

"Yes," he said. "It belongs to Mark Bray."

"It doesn't belong to you?"

"No," Chasson answered, shaking his head. "It was not in my possession before or during the incident at Pageant Field."

"But you had it while you were in Fryeburg, Maine?"

"Yes."

"Why did you toss it in the fireplace in the Maine home?"

"I didn't need it anymore."

"Is that because you now had a gun?" Banks speculated aloud, emphasizing the word "*gun*" for the benefit of the jury.

"Yes, that's part of the reason," Chasson admitted. "But I'm also not familiar with knives. I've only handled them a few times, including when I was in the Boy Scouts."

"Mr. Chasson, why did you go to the park on the night in question, August 23, 1977?" Banks asked.

"A friend of mine was owed money," Chasson answered. In this instance, his reply was consistent with prior witness statements. To a person, all who were aware had said the amount was fifty dollars. But when asked who was due the money, he veered away from earlier testimony. He said he went to Pageant Field to help Bryan Fitzgerald, the man who drove him there. "The person who owed the money was big in stature. Everyone was afraid of him, so I went along to back up Fitzgerald."

The prosecutor was quick to point out that Bryan Fitzgerald, at six-foot-six, didn't need "back-up" services from the likes of Leroy Chasson, which drew subdued laughter from the gallery. It was obvious that Chasson had altered his story to protect his close friend and robbery accomplice, Mark Bray. Attorney Banks referenced his notes and earlier interviews conducted by Quincy Police Lieutenant Neil MacDonald and corrected Chasson.

"You meant to say it was Mark Bray who was owed the money in question, am I right?"

"Yes," Leroy conceded, admitting his error. "It was Mark who was owed the money."

"What first happened when you reached the park?" Banks asked.

Chasson launched into the oft-repeated description of the events that took place from his viewpoint. Animated, he gestured with his hands as he recounted how Fitzgerald had driven him to Quincy and Pageant Field only to leave almost immediately to pick up a bite to eat. They returned to the park a brief time later, leading to the confrontation with Kevin Racette. "I recognized Racette. I asked him for three bags."

"Three bags?"

"Heroin," Chasson clarified. "Three bags of heroin."

"And when he refused?"

"I struck him to the ground and then everyone started to jump on me," he described. "They had broken bottles."

Earlier, defense attorney Caplan stressed to the jury that his client had the right to protect himself when Kevin Racette's friends charged at him like a pack of savage wolves, bent on retribution. "Chasson saw the flash of a knife, picked it up and began lashing out with it, trying to keep people back," Caplan said.

On the final day of the three-week trial, the opposing attorneys presented their closing arguments. Defense attorney Caplan railed on for an hour, ranting endlessly about the lack of evidence and claiming that the prosecution's witnesses were part of a longtime, close-knit group who echoed each other's testimony and fabricated a "litany of lies and contradictions."

"The government has built its case on bits, pieces, and snatches of statements that might support a guilty finding," Caplan emphasized.

To prop up the self-defense front, Caplan explained that Leroy Chasson did, in fact, go after Kevin Racette with violence on his mind, but intended to do battle with his fists, "one on one." It wasn't until Racette's friends joined the fray that his client resorted to whatever means possible to protect himself. In this instance, it was a knife dropped by one of the assailants.

"He had good reason to fear for his life and had the right to defend himself," Caplan insisted.

His opponent, District Attorney Banks, only required twenty minutes to deliver his rebuttal. It was far more impactful than that of his adversary.

In a captivating demonstration, Banks stood before the jury and proceeded to propel an imaginary knife into an equally imaginary stabbing victim. Banks lunged once, driving his arm forward with a modicum of force, and then a second time, with far more ferocity. His riveting theatrics drew the desired effect as a horror-struck member of the jury gasped aloud. In the silence of the standing-room only courtroom gallery, her emotional reaction was even more pronounced. The gallery itself, bursting with family members and reporters, observed with rapt attention, their eyes fixated on the skillful attorney as he refuted the defense for Leroy Chasson.

"He used that knife twice, first an inch-and-one-half deep," said Banks, midway through his closing argument. "The second time, he buried it into the heart of Paul Melody. To the hilt and beyond," the attorney stressed, again driving a simulated knife forward.

***

The jury deliberated for four hours on May 31 and wrapped up with forty-five additional minutes on June 1. They came back with a unanimous verdict of "GUILTY." There were those on hand for the one-sided trial that were surprised it took as long as it did to convict Leroy Chasson of first-degree murder. It was a slam-shut case for attorney Banks and his prosecution team.

For the murder of young Paul Melody, Chasson received a sentence of life without possibility of parole. Not that it mattered but Judge McGuire handed the defendant a concurrent sentence of seven to ten years for the attack on Robert Hayward who, along with eight other witnesses, testified in the three-week trial.

Eighteen months after his conviction and sentencing, Leroy Chasson filed an appeal, citing what he believed was an absolute failure on the part of the prosecution in bringing sufficient evidence for a charge of first-degree murder.

The appeal was argued by the Massachusetts Supreme Judicial Court on December 2, 1980, by District Attorney Charles J. Hely. Not only did Chasson and his attorney, Robert L. Shetetoff, contend that self-defense was not carefully considered by the original judge, but also claimed abuses took place during the May 1978 trial.

In his appeal, Chasson sought a lesser charge, based on the premise that Judge McGuire "abused his discretion in permitting the victim's mother to testify even though none of her testimony was essential to the Commonwealth's case." He and Shetetoff felt that she had swayed the jury. But reading over the transcripts, the Supreme Court was confident Judge McGuire effectively controlled Mrs. Melody's statement, as well as the questioning that ensued.

Through Shetetoff, Chasson also sought clarification regarding an allowance made for District Attorney Banks who, according to the defendant, acted improperly in the trial. Supposedly, Banks cited certain advanced testimony from a witness who never materialized. The comments of this mystery witness were included in Banks' opening statement and according to Chasson, the prosecutor failed to produce this individual for cross-examination by the defense.

The principal part of Chasson's appeal, however, dealt with the murder weapon. He claimed that he did not bring a knife to Pageant Field but rather picked one up off the ground and used it in self-defense against his attackers. Chasson also claimed that he had thrown the knife out of the moving car as he and Bryan Fitzgerald sped from the park. But the Quincy Police scoured the park and surrounding area, conducting full-scale searches on three separate occasions without any findings. The knife was found a week after the stabbings in the Maine home of Chipman Ela, from which the defendant launched an escape.

Once the folding Buck knife was established as the murder weapon and it was determined that Leroy Chasson did, in fact, bring it with him to Pageant Field, the question of premeditation was brought to bear in the case. In the decision to uphold Chasson's conviction and life sentence, which was decided on March 18, 1981, the Justices wrote:

THE DEFENDANT TESTIFIED THAT HE SOUGHT OUT RACETTE TO "PUNCH HIM OUT" BECAUSE RACETTE HAD "RIPPED OFF" A CLOSE FRIEND OF THE DEFENDANT WHILE IN PRISON. THE DEFENDANT CALCULATINGLY ATTACKED ONE PERSON, KNIFED TWO INNOCENT BYSTANDERS AGAINST WHOM HE HAD NO GRIEVANCE, DID NOT SURRENDER TO THE POLICE AS A PERSON WHO ACTED IN SELF-DEFENSE MIGHT BE EXPECTED TO DO, AND FLED THE JURISDICTION. THE CONVICTION OF MURDER IN THE FIRST DEGREE SHOULD STAND.

\*\*\*

Ever loyal to his friend Leroy Chasson, Mark Bray was evasive during questioning in the original 1978 trial. When prosecuting attorney Banks accused Bray of being complicit in the death of Paul Melody, Bray admitted that he did, in fact, mention that an amount of money was owed to him for a prison drug deal. Bray claimed he asked Leroy to deliver a *message* to Racette but never suggested that the Pageant Field assailant take it as far as he did.

Following the trial, Mark Bray was not returned to MCI-Concord as he had hoped. Instead, because of his earlier escape, the twenty-two-year-old was eventually turned over to the dreaded Walpole State Prison. His stay was brief, and he was released on October 25, 1978, just months after his friend Leroy Chasson arrived to begin a life sentence.

Later in life, Mark Bray's second act was inspirational, indeed. He began his "fresh start" in the mid-eighties, relocating to Sterling Heights, Michigan, which is a medium-sized city situated on the shores of Lake St. Clair, thirty minutes north of Detroit. Raising two boys, Bray succeeded in his career in a brand-new technology known as the Internet.

Cancer claimed Mark Bray a day before Christmas 2014. He was fifty-nine. In his death notice, the Bray family said that his "loyalty to family and friends never wavered and you always knew exactly where you stood with him."

# THIRTY—IN WAITING

The hulking locomotive and a half-dozen trailing passenger cars rounded a slight bend in the track before screeching to a grinding, steel-on-steel halt into the station. The quiet of the slumbering neighborhood flanking the Norwood Central Depot was splintered by the arriving MBTA train bound for South Station in Boston. The engine belched gray diesel exhaust as the train idled, discharging several passengers while a number of others boarded for the thirty-minute trip into the city.

A few riders peered through expansive panel windows, observing the activity on the wide platform and inside the station. Many of the disinterested patrons who rode the T, as the Massachusetts Bay Transportation Authority was known to locals, sipped coffees and barely glanced up from their morning papers.

It was September 6, 1982—Labor Day Monday—and for most, a day off from work. But instead of flipping their pillows to the cooler side, a number of hardy commuters chose to make their way into the city for work. As the train waited, these ambitious folks left their cars and scurried across the near-empty parking lot.

It was a warm, pleasant summer morning and promised to heat up into the balmy mid-eighties as the day wore on. While Memorial Day in May marked the official start of summer for New Englanders, Labor Day signaled the end of the season. With the chill of autumn lurking just weeks away, the holiday forecast was a welcome one, even for those heading to work.

The conductor guided the newly arriving passengers up the metal staircase and into the hollow of the train, offering obligatory greetings as they entered. Once the riders safely reached their seats, he signaled the engineer operating the locomotive and before long, the train lurched forward, continuing north to Boston.

Directly across traffic-free Central Street and occupying several blocks in a mixed-use segment of the town, the sprawling Norwood Hospital campus cast pale shadows over the train station and the surrounding neighborhood with its blend of residential homes and businesses. Save for a few early opening storefronts, such as the Mug n' Muffin Café, the nearby Norwood town center was hushed.

Norwood Hospital, established in 1919, had been one of the largest employers in the community, which boasted a population of thirty thousand. But a year after celebrating a century of providing top-notch medical care for a dozen surrounding towns, the town of Norwood suffered a monumental rainstorm and subsequent flooding, featuring five inches of rainfall in less than three hours. Subsequently, the hospital lost power and staff were forced to relocate ninety patients to alternate facilities. The catastrophic flooding in the hospital was captured on film and later broadcast nationally on the Weather Channel. The damage proved irreparable and the buildings were eventually demolished.

Three decades earlier, however, Norwood Hospital was thriving. Just after eight o'clock on the morning of Labor Day 1982, most of the medical staff tasked with the holiday shift had long since settled in for the anticipated inflow of patients, both scheduled and emergent. Scores of physicians were absent, marking the unofficial end of the vacation season by enjoying the three-day weekend at their summer homes on Cape Cod or up in New Hampshire and Maine. The patient appointment docket, by necessity, was limited.

In a tiny, cramped office adjacent to the main emergency room entryway, hospital security director Al "Sarge" Hemphill absently thumbed through a tattered magazine. He paused to finish off the remnants of his lukewarm morning coffee as he watched with interest as the commuter train pulled out of Norwood Central Station.

"Right on time," he murmured under his breath, glancing at the train and then the glowing digital clock on his desk. It was 8:10 a.m.

The sixty-five-year-old Hemphill, who was born and raised in Tylertown, Mississippi, began to rise from his creaky chair, intent on refilling his mug in the department kitchenette, when something caught his eye. In a parking lot reserved exclusively for hospital staff transportation and physicians' personal vehicles, a car he didn't recognize was maneuvering into one of the spaces. It was a blue Chevrolet Malibu, which certainly did not belong to any of the doctors of whom he was aware. Stereotypes aside, they were partial to BMW or Mercedes. While his body was aging, Hemphill's eyesight was as sharp as it was when he served in the Marines decades earlier. From his vantage point less than one hundred feet away, Hemphill could see the vehicle had a Massachusetts license tag. Typically, the lot would be crammed by this time of the morning, but there were a number of vacant spots due to the holiday.

Hemphill, who had been in the security business for more than twenty years after retiring from the Marines, watched keenly as the Chevrolet came to a stop. The brake lights glowed crimson for a moment and then went out. The driver remained in the car. Sarge, as he was known by many of his friends and colleagues because of his military background, wondered if the occupant was having a medical emergency. It would not be the first time a patient in crisis had made the ill-advised decision to drive themselves to the hospital. Over the years, since he accepted the retirement job with Norwood Hospital, the astute security guard had witnessed scores of people who parked in this lot seeking the emergency room and life-saving aid for themselves.

He made up his mind to approach the Malibu and investigate when the driver's door opened suddenly and a woman emerged. He was briefly distracted as the automatic sliding doors leading into the department parted with a whooshing sound. The warm morning air filled the vestibule and ruffled the pages of the magazines stacked on a shelf in the security office.

"Good morning, Al, my friend," the man said jovially as he hastened past Hemphill and into the parking lot.

"Morning, Dr. Wulf," the security guard replied.

Dr. Wulf was always quick with a smile; that is, when he slowed down long enough to share a greeting. A prolific distance runner and road racer, Wulf was always darting about at a rapid pace with his trademark long, loping stride, whether rushing off to see a patient or dashing through his daily dosage of mileage on nearby Norwood streets.

No sooner had the automatic doors closed after Wulf passed through when they slid open again as the driver of the Chevrolet approached, triggering the sensor. She was making her way into the emergency room. She strode forward with purpose, not saying a word as Hemphill observed. He sensed she was trying to avoid making eye contact with him.

"Morning, ma'am," he uttered, politely tipping his head.

"Good morning," she replied with a strained smile.

Hemphill noted that she was blonde, in her late thirties, perhaps forty, and heavyset.

Just ahead, the emergency room was coming to life. Sheet-covered empty stretchers lined the brightly lit corridor. Several staff members, an hour into their shifts, flitted about preparing for the day ahead. To the right of the entrance, a pair of bored receptionists shuffled papers and attached blank documents to clipboards in anticipation of arriving patients. Adjacent to their cubicles, an empty waiting room beckoned. A wall-mounted television droned in the background, broadcasting a morning news program. Sunlight beamed through windows overlooking the parking lot, warming the interior space.

"Will you be long?" Hemphill asked the woman as she tried to hurry past the uniformed security officer.

"Excuse me?"

"Your car, ma'am," he said, clarifying his question as he gestured toward the Chevrolet.

"Oh, I'm so sorry," she replied. "Should I move it?"

Hemphill, trained to recognize facial expressions, noted that this woman looked extremely uncomfortable. He sensed that there were places she would much rather be than standing in the entryway of an emergency room, chatting with a security guard. He considered asking if she was all right but refrained. It was not an appropriate question.

"No, it's okay to leave it where it is," he said. "Holiday. There are plenty of spaces available."

He noticed her bag had slipped from her shoulder. It was large, heavier than the typical woman's pocketbook. "Can I help you with that?" the security officer offered, pointing to the heavy tote.

"No!" she shouted tersely.

Taken aback by her sharp response, Hemphill withheld comment. His suspicions, however, were raised. The longtime security officer noticed the woman's forehead was glistening with perspiration. She looked anxious and her complexion was blanched. Her eyes darted back-and-forth, avoiding his gaze. Hemphill's instincts were on full alert as he sensed something was not right with this woman. She was acting shady.

"No, no, thank you," she said softly with a smile. She was obviously trying to temper her outburst. And yet she continued to clutch the handle of her bag with a white-knuckled grip—a "death grip," as Sarge later described to the authorities.

"Have a nice day," he said as he watched her make her way across the threshold and into the emergency room ahead.

She visibly inhaled, drawing a deep breath, and replied, "Thank you."

Hemphill observed as she turned right, toward the reception desk and the waiting room beyond. When she slipped from view, he shook off the unease and turned to retrieve his empty coffee mug.

***

Nine miles to the south of Norwood Hospital, as the population of the Walpole State Prison settled in for breakfast, Leroy James Chasson began to stab himself with a ballpoint pen he had acquired. Once, twice, and a third time, he drove the rudimentary weapon into his abdomen. The pain was excruciating. With the macabre task accomplished, Chasson stood and with great difficulty, started to painfully lurch toward the mess hall, leaving a trail of blood in his wake.

# THIRTY-ONE — PRISONER BLOODSHED

Leaning against the interior cinderblock wall, which stretched as far as the eye could see, MCI-Walpole Corrections Officer Paul Reynolds was monitoring the chow line of the sprawling prison mess hall from the corridor. This section of the twenty-six-year-old facility was in the depths of the East Wing, which to officers and inmates was known as the "Max End." Inside the expansive cafeteria, scores of inmates were consuming the first of their daily "three squares," as meals were better known in the institution. The morning's menu featured soupy scrambled eggs and something resembling strips of bacon. Visually, the food was repulsive, barely fit for human consumption. Still, with little choice, the men shoveled the unsavory fare into their mouths and often bartered for more.

"I couldn't eat that shit," declared Officer Tommy Oliveira, who had drawn mess hall duty with Reynolds. He kept his voice muted so the men couldn't hear him disparaging their meal. It wouldn't sit well with the residents.

"Me neither," his colleague replied, wrinkling his nose as if he just caught a whiff of something rancid. "If it were me, I'd buy food from the canteen."

"Sure," Oliveira replied. "Canned tuna. Breakfast of Champions."

Reynolds chuckled. He opened the top button of his light blue uniform shirt. Beneath, he wore a crewneck white t-shirt. It was early September and summer had yet to release its grip on the New England region. Certain areas of the prison always seemed warmer than others, including the corridor where he and Oliveira stood opposite the barbershop and mess hall. The industrial-strength ovens in the nearby kitchen were certainly guilty of adding heat; it was as much as ten degrees warmer than the residential tiers. The supplemental heat was welcomed by prisoners and guards in the depths of winter but not at this time of year. Still early in the morning, temperatures had soared well into the eighties where the two officers stood. Reynolds wiped the back of a hand across his sweat-soaked forehead and took a deep breath.

"Double-time today," stated Oliveira, referring to the additional pay for working the Labor Day holiday.

Reynolds nodded and grinned. He was grateful for the extra money but still regretted accepting the assignment. Many of his coworkers were enjoying the final official summer weekend of 1982 with their families at the beach or up north in New Hampshire. There were a million places he would rather be than standing guard in this dark, dank home to more than five hundred hardened criminals. Fishing for blues at the Cape Cod Canal or hunting in the Gilbert Hills Forest in Foxborough. In hindsight, he would have relinquished the double pay for either pursuit.

The rising heat did not bode well for the mood of the institution's occupants. It had been a long, hot, and humid summer, and the prisoners, for good reason, were looking forward to the cooler conditions of the New England autumn and winter. Many of the communal areas and the tiers were often unbearable, more so for those locked up in maximum security Ten Block, which housed sixty highly volatile inmates. These men were allowed only one hour of daily outdoor exercise and that took place bottled up inside of individual chain-link cages.

Trying to put a positive spin on the dreaded Ten Block, James Bender (acting commissioner from 2003 to 2007) described the tiers as "a special management unit which houses inmates who violate house rules." An anonymous corrections officer was far less eloquent when he termed Ten Block as "an awful place to work where the residents frequently spit on you or fling all sorts of human waste at you."

During the seventies, MCI-Walpole was a seething powder keg, rife with violence and frequent uprisings. Some of the revolts were small in scale, while others spiraled to full-blown riots. Corrections personnel, at the time, were poorly equipped to handle these incidents. "It was before they supplied us with helmets or vests or shields to protect ourselves," recalled Reynolds. "We couldn't go home when something happened. At Walpole, they sometimes locked the gates with the guard inside. We'd be standing there looking at a locked door while they went through the roster for the incoming shift."

In later years, the prison established a highly trained commando-type unit that was often called upon to put down disturbances. These men would arrive decked out in head-to-toe combat gear, their heads shielded by thick black metal helmets, prepared to dish out controlled violence to restore order. Some of their equipment would have to be destroyed after such an operation. The rampaging prisoners were known to pelt the invaders with human waste.

There were also a number of in-house killings. At one time, the murder rate at Walpole State Prison climbed to one of the highest in the nation. Noteworthy inmate homicides in a particularly violent 1973 included that of Albert DeSalvo, who was better known as the Boston Strangler. DeSalvo was accused of raping and strangling to death thirteen women between the ages of nineteen and eighty-five during the tumultuous early sixties. Ten years into his life sentence at Walpole, the forty-year-old DeSalvo was stabbed to death in the infirmary. His murder remains unsolved.

Situated in a small bedroom community nestled midway between Boston and Providence, MCI-Walpole was described by many as one of the most dangerous prisons on the East Coast, rivaling New York's Attica and Sing Sing, among others. It later became MCI-Cedar Junction at the insistence of the townspeople who sought to separate the name of their community from the institution.

Drug-fueled assaults were commonplace, from simple stabbings with crudely fashioned shanks to more elaborate attacks. Talwin was routinely smuggled into the penitentiary by family and friends and transferred during physical contact visits, making it the narcotic of choice by inmates during the seventies and eighties.

The dog days of summer were particularly treacherous for the prison population and corrections officers alike. When temperatures soared, tempers flared.

One hot, steamy July afternoon in 1981, for instance, a troublesome prisoner was invited to join a pickup basketball game in the recreation yard near the front of the prison. Without warning, several ballplayers grabbed the man, two of them clutching his upper torso while a third firmly grasped the victim's legs at the ankles. This took place in full view of a nearby observation turret but before guards could respond, the ruthless assailants broke into a sprint and slammed their struggling target into the unyielding steel of the basketball stanchion, across his thighs. The brazen ambush shattered both the man's femurs, the largest bones in the human body. Witnesses in the yard later described the fractures as a sickening, splintering sound that reverberated off nearby prison walls—it was something they would not soon forget. But the sounds of the breaking bones, later compared to snapping dead tree branches in two, were not as terrifying as compared to the man's blood-curdling screams of agony as he was transported to Boston's Brigham and Women's Hospital. The shrieks grew more pronounced as the ambulance rattled headlong over the trolley tracks on South Huntington Avenue in Jamaica Plain, the route of choice to the former Peter Bent Brigham emergency department.

Self-inflicted injuries were also common. Inmates would hurt themselves to earn a few days on the outside, even if it meant surgery. While most common-sense people would prefer avoiding hospitalization, for inmates, it provided a welcome respite to the drudgery of incarceration, no matter how brief.

Despondent prisoners were known to swallow assorted shrapnel, such as fragments of razor blades or crushed light bulbs. These desperate men would wrap the jagged shards with duct or electrical tape in an often-futile attempt to fend off internal lacerations. Once at the hospital, x-rays would soon reveal the immediate need for surgery.

One intrepid individual got hold of a three-colored pen, which were extensively used by medical staff to mark patient charts and inserted the ink cartridges into his penis. Corrections officers found him standing at the center of his cell, his white underwear drenched in blood. According to a witness, the man was happily grinning because, despite the pain and trauma of self-mutilation, he would soon be on his way to a hospital stay.

Another inmate, a child molester marked for death, took matters into his own hands. Wrapping himself in bed sheets, he knelt on the floor of his cell and lit the cloth ablaze. The ambulance that transported him to the hospital, where he perished from head-to-toe third-degree burns, was removed from service for several weeks due to the revolting stench of burnt hair and flesh.

Many of the guards who worked stints at MCI-Walpole have similar tales to share, including Reynolds.

"On my first day on the job in 1978, there were two murders by ten o'clock in the morning," recalled the powerfully built officer. "I was only nineteen, but you grow up fast in this place. They once called Walpole Prison the Wild West."

At twenty-three, with four years under his belt, Reynolds was already considered to be a seasoned veteran of the Massachusetts Department of Correction. Long hours, high stress levels, and deplorable working conditions weren't a recipe for long-lasting careers. Burnout drove scores of officers to seek management jobs or assignments in minimum security facilities that were less taxing on the mind and body, such as a pre-release center or the forestry camps.

Reynolds glanced at his wristwatch. Breakfast was, thankfully, winding down without incident. Many of the convicts were diligently scraping their trays with plastic utensils, gathering the final bites. Little went to waste. As he observed the activity through the double doors, Reynolds noticed unexpected motion to his left at the end of the long corridor. Across the distance, it looked as if a man was slowly heading in their direction. Stooped over and gripping his midsection, he was clearly in some distress. Oliveira had seen it too.

"I'll check it out," Reynolds said to his partner in a hushed tone as he began to make his way toward the unknown figure. "Radio for some backup down here."

Oliveira nodded and prepared his portable radio. He hurriedly moved to the mess hall entrance. Until his partner determined the extent of the situation, he could not allow the inmates to exit. Most of the men were accustomed to the prison routine and it took little to trigger a disturbance.

Reynolds, meanwhile, broke into a full run. As he closed the gap, he recognized the man. He was well-known to prison officials; it was Leroy Chasson and he was in obvious pain. As Reynolds drew closer, he saw that the inmate was hunched over, clutching his gut with both hands. Chasson groaned and dropped heavily to his knees. His face was chalk white and glistening with sweat. His abdomen, Reynolds noticed, was blood-soaked. Some of it began to pool on the floor.

"Jesus!" Reynolds gasped. "What the fuck happened?"

"S-stabbed," was the labored reply as Chasson's chest heaved. He panted, fighting for a breath. It was a strain for him to speak. "S-someone… stuck… me! I need help!"

Wary of Chasson's tendency to commit violent attacks against officers, Reynolds remained ever vigilant as he crouched to render aid to the cagey inmate. The lighting in this segment of the corridor was dim, but there was enough for the cautious guard to see a moderate amount of blood seeping between the victim's fingers as he clutched his midsection.

As Oliveira arrived at his side, Reynolds instructed, "Tommy, help me get him to the hospital."

Each officer clutched one of Chasson's upper arms and carefully guided him to his feet. Once upright, the bleeding seemed to intensify, flowing freely. Reynolds looked at the inmate's face, pale and drawn. He also noticed a moderate amount of blood trickling from the man's mouth, running down his chin. Reynolds had enough medical know-how to understand this development might indicate internal bleeding. Chasson glanced at the guard and recognized concern.

"I don't wanna die," Chasson whimpered. He began to weep as the two prison guards half-dragged him along the corridor toward medical help. Thankfully, it was a short distance.

"C'mon, let's move," urged Reynolds as they shuffled along the corridor, leaving behind a trail of blood. The warmth of the morning made the effort more challenging. Both Reynolds and Oliveira were soon drenched in sweat from the strain. Chasson, although on his feet, was dead weight. It took ten minutes to reach the prison infirmary, which, thankfully, was air-conditioned.

The Walpole prison infirmary was a small, cramped room, not much larger than the scores of six-by-nine cells occupied by some of the worst criminals known to Massachusetts. Just outside the open door of the tiny clinic, a small cellblock held some of Walpole's sick and infirm. Most of their illnesses or injuries were minor in nature. Had they needed more advanced care, nearby Norfolk State Prison was better equipped in that respect, complete with a fully staffed hospital ward. And there was always MCI-Shirley, sixty miles to the north, with its Health Services Unit, offering progressive medical treatment—at least by prison standards.

The commotion of Chasson's arrival stirred a number of the occupants of the adjacent block. Each of the cell doors was equipped with a one-foot square window-like cutout with a pair of horizontal bars. The prisoners kept in this segment of the facility were able to scrutinize the comings and goings to the infirmary by way of small handheld mirrors positioned at an angle through the narrow gap between the vertical bars. The sight of these resourceful men, with extended arms gripping mirrors and surveying every move in the narrow corridor, was a bit unnerving. It also raised a question about the glass itself and the potential for the owner to render a weapon. It was explained that only inmates who were proven non-risk were allowed to possess the item.

Taking great care, Reynolds and Oliveira guided Leroy Chasson onto the surface of the narrow gurney positioned in the center of the room. The wounded inmate was still cognizant of his surroundings, but barely, it seemed. He writhed in pain, which made Reynolds uncomfortable. Chasson was a reprehensible inmate and had tried to harm officers over the years, but nonetheless, did not deserve this suffering.

Dr. Ira Cohen, a balding, diminutive man in his late sixties, moved to the patient, who was now stretched out flat on his back along the full length of the metal gurney, which had seen scores of dying or dead prisoners over the years. Leroy Chasson, at first glance, seemed destined to join them. "He ain't gonna make it," Cohen casually remarked, oblivious to the fact that his patient was conscious and could hear his every word.

The doctor turned his back on Chasson briefly as he retrieved a box of latex gloves from a wall cabinet. Reynolds looked on, unsure if Leroy was meant to hear the malicious remark. Dr. Cohen had certainly exhibited questionable bedside manner in the past.

It was a known fact in the corrections industry that many prison-based physicians, while possessing perfectly legal credentials, were often derelict in their patient care. Unable to find work in a standard hospital environment for one reason or another, these men and women were often employed by private agencies and remained on the periphery of the medical community. Armed with the knowledge that inmates had little recourse in the event of negligent treatment, many of these borderline caregivers were reckless and irresponsible. There were lawsuits filed by inmates, of course, but most became mired in the court system.

Cohen pulled two blue gloves from the box and slipped them over his hands, one by one, with an audible snap at the wrist. The added drama was for effect, clearly not necessary. He then offered the box to Reynolds and Oliveira. Both men declined but did move to a nearby sink and took a turn washing the dried blood from their hands. Reynolds found a small brush and vigorously scrubbed beneath his fingernails. Of all the risks that working in the prison system held, disease was one that corrections officers feared most. Hepatitis C was rampant in most jails, in addition to tuberculosis and HIV/AIDS.

"I don't think he'll make it," Cohen repeated as he disengaged Leroy's hands from his abdomen and began to peel back the victim's blood-soaked shirt. He was a bit rough with the treatment and Chasson winced in pain.

Cohen removed the cloth material, which was stuck like adhesive to the skin. The doctor then leaned in closer to scrutinize the wounds. His examination took several minutes. He introduced a penlight for a better assessment. Beneath the harsh overhead fluorescents, it was a garish sight. But without the shirt to obscure his view, Cohen's meticulous probing soon brought into question the extent of the trauma. Cohen verbalized his preliminary findings, stating aloud for the two observing guards.

"Hmmm," he mused as he pushed his eyeglasses back on his nose. Taking a second look and shaking his head, he said, "Not quite as bad as I first thought. There are three puncture wounds and they don't seem very deep after all. And the bleeding has all but subsided."

It was at this point in the examination that Reynolds began to suspect something was amiss. Was this a case of Chasson earning his just reward or was there something else behind the alleged stabbing? Were the injuries rendered by an angry inmate seeking revenge against Chasson? That scenario was assumed when he and Oliveira came across the stabbing victim in the corridor, clutching his abdomen. And he did claim that he was stabbed. It was a frequent occurrence in the tense prison. But what about the blood that mysteriously flowed from his mouth? Dr. Cohen did not suspect internal bleeding. There seemed to be no logical explanation. It just didn't add up.

"Dr. Cohen, what about all the blood?" Reynolds questioned, verbalizing his thoughts. "He was bleeding like a stuck pig when we first found him."

In response, the doctor said, "Abdominal wounds, even those that are superficial, tend to bleed extensively."

"Should we get him to a hospital?" Oliveira interjected. With that comment, Chasson stirred and mumbled something unintelligible. Reynolds was not certain, but it sounded like the prisoner uttered the words, "Yes, hospital."

Dr. Cohen nodded and said, "It would be a good idea to have him checked at the emergency room, just in case the implement penetrated any internal organs."

Closely eyeing Chasson for even the slightest indication of trickery, Reynolds circled the gurney and reached for the house phone, mounted on the wall over the sink. Lifting the receiver to his ear, he dialed "0" on the phone.

"Yeah?" answered a male voice from the control center.

"Reynolds here," he said. "We need an ambulance for an inmate in the infirmary. If they ask, tell them we have a thirty-three-year-old stabbing victim."

"Got it," the officer said as he lifted the receiver on his desk phone, pressed the button for an outside line, and began to dial.

# THIRTY-TWO — AMBULANCE RESPONSE

The phone rang shrilly in the tiny office, startling veteran Dispatcher Patty Barry, who was nestled in the worn-out vinyl-covered office chair. Like most of the furniture scattered haphazardly throughout the cramped space, the chair had seen far better days. It squealed in protest as she leaned forward and lifted the telephone receiver from its cradle before it could ring a second time.

Through sleepy eyes, the exhausted dispatcher glanced at the digital clock mounted on the wall of the dingy office she had called home for the last fourteen hours, now approaching fifteen. She was wrapping up her overnight Sunday shift. The glaring red numbers indicated it was just past eight o'clock in the morning and her relief was an hour late for his shift. Labor Day 1982 was well underway and she was still at work when she should have been having a nice breakfast at a local café—or, better yet, home in bed.

As she answered the phone, Barry gazed through the large plate glass window which overlooked Main Street in Brockton. The seedy downtown district was just coming to life.

Dubbed as the City of Champions because of natives Rocky Marciano and Marvin Hagler, both accomplished professional boxers, Brockton was once known as the country's largest producer of shoes and leather goods. In the late nineteenth century, the city was chosen by noted inventor Thomas Edison as the testing site for the first centralized use of electricity. Edison oversaw the 1884 installation of this experimental power source in assorted buildings, including a firehouse and the city's high school.

As the 1980s commenced, Brockton had become a city stricken with poverty and a crime rate ninety-six percent higher than any other Massachusetts city or town. Statistics provided by the FBI showed that a resident of Brockton had a one-in-forty-four chance of becoming a victim of crime during the decade.

Cradling the phone receiver between her shoulder and tilting her head to free her hands, Dispatcher Barry readied a notepad and pen.

"Norfolk-Bristol Ambulance," she said, stating the oft-used greeting. "This line is recorded."

"Morning," gruffly greeted the man on the other end. "Walpole Prison."

*Great, a prison call*, Patty Barry thought as she scribbled on the yellow legal pad. *Just what I need to deal with at the end of this never-ending shift.*

"How can I help you?" she asked, feigning politeness.

"We need an ambulance for an injured inmate," the caller said. Nonchalantly, he added, "Stab wound, I believe."

"Sure, I'll have someone on the way."

"Have them pull in front of the vehicle trap, okay?"

"I'll let them know," she agreed, wishing she could tell this guy that she was fully aware of prison protocol. After a decade dispatching ambulances, this was not her first rodeo.

"Thanks, ma'am."

In the garage behind her, Patty Barry heard muted voices. The day shift was going through their morning routine, stocking the ambulances, ensuring each vehicle was packed with the necessary medical supplies. Labor Day was a work-free holiday for some but in Brockton, the sick and injured seldom took a day off, especially if the summer weather of recent weeks persisted. Hot weather always brought out the worst in people.

When the phone rang in the dispatch office, the emergency medical technicians and paramedics braced, listening as a group. A call before breakfast wasn't something any of them wanted. They were relieved to learn, as they intently listened to Patty's side of the brief conversation, that the call was for the crew out of the Norwood base. Breakfast was still a possibility.

Norfolk-Bristol Ambulance was a company that got its start in the mid-seventies when former Boston firefighter Robert Zammito Sr. parlayed a small investment in a pair of Cadillac-style ambulances. By 1981, the fledgling firm provided three full-time ambulances for 911 responses in Brockton, as well as a bustling transfer-based service out of Norwood. The Norwood staff handled mostly routine hospital and nursing home trips for tests and specialized treatment. But the Norwood crews also dealt with a fair share of emergency transports due to a lucrative contract signed with the Commonwealth of Massachusetts to provide emergency medical services for both the Norfolk and Walpole State Prisons. In the brief span of only twenty years, Norfolk-Bristol Ambulance grew to become one of the largest private medical transportation providers in Greater Boston. In the mid-nineties, the firm was acquired by American Medical Response, a national interest.

Dispatcher Barry disengaged the call and prepared to make another, pulling the phone closer to the edge of the desk. She pressed the speaker button and tapped the speed-dial key, sending out a message to a pre-programmed number. She listened for the rapid beeping sound. Satisfied the pager signal had been successfully sent, she repeated the sequence for a second number.

"Hey, PB, need a coffee?" asked a voice behind her. She turned to see one of the medics, who had addressed her by her popular nickname, standing at the threshold of the dispatch office.

"Sure, I could use one."

"Okay," he said. "We just have to drop off some paperwork at Station 2 and then we'll swing by Dunkin' Donuts."

"Thanks," she said as the phone rang again. She knew who the caller was and skipped the formal greeting. "Yeah?"

"Good morning to you, too."

She sighed, glancing wearily at the clock again. "Sorry, Paul, long night."

"What do we have?" Paul Kilroy asked.

"Stabbing," Patty replied. "Walpole."

"Bobby call yet?" asked the longtime EMT who, along with his brother Robert, was part of a small group of inaugural employees who joined the ambulance service in the late seventies. The brothers later owned and managed an auto parts business in West Roxbury but, in an ironic twist, Paul later embarked on a new career as a corrections officer at Essex County Jail in Middleton, Massachusetts.

As she prepared to answer his question, the button for the second phone line began flashing. "He's calling now."

"Tell him to meet me at the Walpole firehouse," Paul said. His trip from Dedham was a brief twenty minutes, less time if he lit up the ambulance to skirt traffic and signal lights. His partner, meanwhile, would have a shorter drive—less than ten minutes from Foxboro, which bordered Walpole.

"Will do, Paul," she said. "I'll let him know."

Paul Kilroy was one of the two Norwood-based EMTs who had agreed to cover the Labor Day holiday weekend. His partner, Bobby Zammito Jr., was the son of the owner of Norfolk-Bristol Ambulance. Because nights and weekends were generally quiet in the Norwood operation, the area was typically covered on-call as opposed to basing personnel out of the station around the clock. Each EMT tasked with this coverage was assigned an ambulance and remained at home. In this instance, both lived with their respective parents: Kilroy in Dedham and Zammito in Foxboro. When a request for an ambulance was received and dispatched, the two would rendezvous at a predetermined site, park and lock one of the vehicles, then continue to their call destination.

Dispatcher Barry pressed the blinking button on the phone console, connecting her to Zammito while, at the same time, disengaging from Kilroy. "Hi, Bobby."

"Hey, Patty."

"There's a stabbing at Walpole," she said. "Paul said he'd meet you at the Walpole fire station."

"On my way, thanks."

Patty logged the times of her two conversations on a run card, adding notes about the request. Her task complete, she leaned back in her chair and closed her eyes against the encroaching fatigue. Between running errands the day before and the double shift that would hopefully soon be wrapping up, she hadn't slept in more than twenty-four hours. It was common for her to take on extra hours, but it did not make it any easier.

The morning was progressing as sunlight, brightening downtown Brockton, streamed through the expansive windowpane. Rising from her chair for a stretch, Patty stifled a yawn, wondering which would arrive first—her shift relief or her promised cup of coffee. As it turned out, both occurred at the same time. The phone rang; it was her relief dispatcher, calling to apologize for his tardiness. He said he would arrive shortly. As she hung up, her coffee was delivered, not a moment too soon.

***

EMT Paul Kilroy nosed the ambulance into a vacant parking spot at the rear of the Walpole firehouse. He had parked in this same lot two months earlier to observe the town's Independence fireworks display, which is launched annually over Memorial Pond. His partner Bobby Zammito had arrived minutes earlier, as expected, and was waiting in the idling ambulance, a white van-like vehicle with orange striping and bold blue lettering depicting the company name. Kilroy grabbed his bottle of Pepsi from the cup holder and quietly closed the door. The Walpole Fire Department was accommodating, allowing them to park the spare ambulance on the property. He didn't want to change that by waking any of the guys who were sleeping in beyond their morning shift change.

"Hey, Bobby," he said cheerily, greeting his weekend partner as he climbed into Ambulance 12, settling into the passenger seat and fastening his seatbelt.

"Morning," Zammito said as he flipped the toggle switch to ON to light the red-and-white strobes mounted above. He guided the ambulance toward Main Street, also known as Route 1A, and turned left. He accelerated toward Walpole Prison, only several miles to the south.

The duo drove in relative silence. Paul sensed his partner wasn't pleased about the call. While none of the workforce out of the Norwood station relished prison calls, risking their necks in those dirty, dangerous places, Bobby Zammito had further reason to be perturbed about the holiday morning wake-up call.

"Regretting working for Dan?" Paul asked.

"I could have said no," Bobby replied with a shrug of his broad shoulders. He had reluctantly agreed to cover the Labor Day weekend for colleague Daniel Greene[1], who was seeking time off to take his girlfriend Mary to Montreal for a getaway weekend. "He couldn't find anyone else."

---

1. Name has been changed

Paul nodded knowingly. They had all made similar sacrifices to help each other out in a pinch at one time or another.

Zammito flipped the switch to extinguish the flashing red-and-white lights. There hadn't been a need to deploy the siren during any part of the brief trip. The sparsely populated roadway between the Walpole business district and the prison was traffic-free. He turned right into the driveway and slowly rolled toward the ominous structure, surrounded by imposing eighteen-foot white walls topped with electrified barbed wire. Driving to the right side of the facility, which faced out to Route 1A, Bobby came to a stop in front of a huge steel door large enough to accommodate a delivery panel truck—or, in this instance, an ambulance.

An unseen sentry, stationed in the observation turret spaced strategically atop the wall, threw a switch and the immense door began to slide open on tracks. Once open, Zammito slowly eased forward into what was known as the vehicle trap—an apt description. Inside the cavernous space, with both doors closed, the vehicles' occupants were indeed trapped. They were surrounded by steep walls on all four sides, and like rats in a cage, observed by the guards in the turret above.

Two blue-uniformed guards emerged from a door at the base of the observation belfry. As the EMTs remained seated, their vehicle was thoroughly inspected, top to bottom. One of the guards opened the rear door, climbed into the patient compartment, and saluted. "Happy Labor Day, gentlemen!"

"Hey, officer," Kilroy returned respectfully, taking a swig of his ever-present Pepsi. He was one of those uncommon types who could drink the beverage throughout the day, early morning included. It was his substitute for coffee.

The officer in the module began to confiscate items from the interior cabinets that could be fashioned into a weapon by an inmate. He was well practiced on where to look and what to take, including screwdrivers and a hammer from the toolbox, road flares, and a crowbar. His sidekick, meanwhile, was examining beneath the rig with a telescoping mirror.

A metal bucket soon appeared, lowered on a rope from the turret above. The two guards on the ground deposited the goods inside the pail along with the officer's firearms, which were understandably not allowed inside the walls.

Soon, the interior steel door began to slide open. One of the two inspecting guards returned to his post above the wall while the other joined the EMTs, taking his place in the patient chamber in the ambulance.

Bobby Zammito rolled the ambulance forward slightly, coming to a stop in front of a gate secured with a heavy chain. The guard leapt out and unlocked the enclosure, allowing the ambulance crew to edge beyond the gate. He then closed the gate, padlocked the chain, and clambered back into the ambulance.

As the trio made their way to the rear of the prison, this well-orchestrated series of steps was repeated at two additional gates, including one directly adjacent to Ten Block, where restless inmates paced back-and-forth in individual exterior cages. It was the only means available to keep dangerous men separated from one another while they took part in their daily exercise allotment. These prisoners, many of them vicious killers and rapists, were known to "shoot" the ambulance crew with imaginary rifles or simply flip them the bird while the guard was busy with the padlocks on the gate. The gestures were occasionally returned to the chagrin of the escorting guard. "Please don't provoke these guys," he would plead. "My job is tough enough."

The final stop of the prolonged stop-and-go trek across the MCI-Walpole grounds was the infirmary, which represented a troublesome design flaw. Two decades earlier, when the facility was first constructed, little consideration was placed on the considerable amount of time it would take to reach an inmate in need of medical intervention.

For instance, fifteen minutes had already elapsed since the emergency personnel arrived for Leroy Chasson. And it would be a matching fifteen or more to reverse direction, driving back through the series of gates to the vehicle trap. In this instance, Chasson's injuries may or may not be life-threatening but there have been those inmates over the years who were in dire need of treatment only available in a hospital setting. The time-consuming exit from MCI-Walpole often contributed to fatal outcomes.

\*\*\*

Months earlier, in the summer of 1982, Bobby Zammito was driving Ambulance No. 1 while his partner, Daniel Greene, performed CPR on an unresponsive sixty-year-old Walpole inmate. As the duo recalled, it was an oppressive ninety-degree July afternoon. No sooner had they driven out of the vehicle trap and embarked for the hospital when the vehicle's air conditioning system failed. If it weren't for the protracted exit through the prison grounds, the patient might already have been in the capable hands of the Norwood ER staff.

Zammito glanced in the rearview mirror, through the narrow passageway that connected the cab with the patient compartment. He observed that his unfortunate partner was already drenched in sweat. Greene's uniform shirt, usually light blue in color, was darkened with sweat as the temperature exceeded one hundred in the unventilated, oven-like rear compartment. That, coupled with the exertion of performing CPR, made for unbearable conditions.

"You okay back there?" Bobby shouted over the din of the straining motor and the screaming siren. He already knew the answer.

"I've had better days!" his partner hollered in response as he anchored his leg for balance against the carriage of the stretcher in the speeding vehicle. "Fucking hot back here!"

The corrections officer on board chimed in. He was hanging on for dear life as the unchecked interior humidity turned the squad bench slick with dampness. He clutched futilely at the vinyl surface as the ambulance rounded a bend in the road. "I wouldn't try so hard," the guard said, who was also soaked to the skin with perspiration.

Greene, sweating buckets as he pumped on the prisoner's chest, tried to catch his breath and said, "What, what are... you... t-talking... about?" His words were gasped in rhythm with each compression.

"This asshole raped and killed a child," the guard declared, gesturing toward the unconscious inmate, who was fully cyanotic. "Just let the piece of shit die."

"Can't... do... that," Greene replied exhaustedly as he pumped the man's chest. He shook his head. Droplets of sweat fell to the floor when he did so. "But you... could... help me."

"Sure, man. What should I do?"

"Sit in that chair." Greene nodded toward the jump seat positioned behind the inmate's head. As Bobby raced the ambulance along, the guard did as he was told, moving quickly across the damp, slippery floor and sitting heavily in the seat. A laboring Greene briefly ceased chest compressions and retrieved the demand valve from the cabinet containing oxygen paraphernalia. He applied the firm rubber mask to the patient's face and cracked the flow meter. In the center of the mask was a bright red button.

"Put your hands around it, like this," Greene instructed as he demonstrated. He glanced through the passageway and the windshield, gauging the roadway ahead. Thankfully, they were closing in on the Walpole-Norwood town line. The traffic pattern was crowded ahead and Bobby Zammito was forced to slow. Vehicles in their path were sluggish to pull over, despite the screaming siren. It had grown even warmer in the compartment if that was at all possible.

"Okay," the guard said. "What next?"

"Every time I pump his chest five times," the rescuer said, "press this red button once to ventilate him."

"Sure, will do."

Greene resumed the chest compressions, counting aloud while his newly trained assistant supplied the artificial respirations. At times, the guard was overly rambunctious and depressed the button far too long, over-expanding the man's chest and forcing air deep into his stomach.

"This is pretty intense," he said, smirking as he pushed it again before the EMT had reached the count of five.

"Just a quick blast," Greene insisted, wiping the sweat off his brow with a towel he had retrieved from a supply cabinet earlier. "I don't need the guy vomiting in this heat."

Before long, the grueling ride came to an end. Bobby Zammito guided the ambulance into the Norwood ER parking lot and backed into a vacant space. As hospital staff rushed out to greet them and claim the patient, Greene sought out a pair of fresh towels to dry off. It was a fruitless exercise; he was soaked. He tossed a towel to the officer and said, "Thanks for the assist."

"Anytime, man. He's going to die, right?"

"He was already dead when we loaded him at the prison."

# THIRTY-THREE—CHASSON TRANSPORT

After the burdensome trip across the prison grounds and through several chain-link gates, Bobby Zammito rounded the final left turn at the rear of the jail. He deftly backed the ambulance into a narrow parking space alongside the structure, which was painted the same white as the exterior walls of the massive institution. A half-length metal fire escape-type staircase attached to the side of the building led to a steel door. A small aluminum sign attached above the entrance read "INFIRMARY" in large block letters. Bobby killed the motor and pocketed the keys, which was the policy of the ambulance service as well as the prison. He was not certain how an inmate in a commandeered ambulance would make it past the succession of gates and, subsequently, the steel trap vehicle portal, but it was not his place to question guidelines.

To his left, several wooden tables were scattered over a small grassy area in the shadow of the prison walls. This pleasant oasis was reserved for the fortunate few who, through good behavior, earned the privilege of entertaining loved ones outdoors. As the tale is told, one of the young toddlers who regularly paid visits with his mother was conceived beneath one of the tables. The corrections officers, in the interest of reducing the potential for uprisings, were known to turn their heads and allow inmates to blow off steam. At MCI-Norfolk, the sister state prison two miles to the north, women visitors were often processed through security with heavy winter coats draped over their arms in the middle of summer. The coats, according to a guard who wished to remain unnamed, were used to shield themselves from prying eyes during sexual interludes in the full-contact visiting room. Wads of crumpled Kleenex tissue were left behind, evidence of these romantic trysts. Again, lenient guards would look the other way.

Positioned at the head of the empty stretcher, Zammito led the way up the narrow staircase, taking great care not to catch the sole of his boots on the steel grating. Kilroy followed, hoisting the tail end of the gurney. A guard at the top of the flight of stairs held the door as they entered.

The stretcher, built by the Ferno Corporation, weighed seventy-five pounds unoccupied and was rated for up to four hundred pounds patient-loaded. There were few EMTs who wanted to substantiate that back-breaking fact, however.

"I never get used to this," Kilroy said as he glanced at the long row of prison cells to his left. On both sides of the narrow corridor, inmates were watching their every move with handheld mirrors extended through the barred windows of their individual cell doors. These men were housed here for one illness or another. They were not acute enough to require in-depth medical care in a hospital environment, nor were they well enough to remain mixed with the general population.

Entering the MCI-Walpole infirmary, the emergency personnel gazed at the man on the gurney in the center of the room. He was shirtless with a large, twelve-inch-square gauze pad affixed to the left side of his abdomen. Littering the floor were bloodstained bandages. Obviously, the staff had swapped bandages at some time during his assessment.

A pair of corrections officers stood idle. A man wearing a white lab coat, obviously the house doctor, leaned against a counter and jotted notes on a legal pad.

"Good morning, gentlemen," said one of the guards, who later identified himself as Officer Paul Reynolds. "Meet Leroy Chasson."

Hearing his name, the patient stirred but said nothing. Kilroy asked, "What do we have?"

At this, the doctor turned and said, "He has three puncture wounds in his left abdomen. We've controlled the bleeding but he needs further evaluation. We're not sure if there is any internal damage. There was some bleeding from his mouth."

"Vital signs?" Kilroy asked.

"All within normal limits," the physician mumbled, leading the attending EMT to suspect the doctor hadn't bothered to check them. Not that it mattered. He would take a set of signs during the trip to Norwood Hospital.

"All right, let's get him packaged."

\*\*\*

Thankfully, Chasson was a lightweight, a little more than one-seventy. Any EMT or paramedic who had been in the business for any length of time would have tales to tell about giants of humanity who physically challenged the personnel tasked with moving them to a hospital. Or down a flight of stairs, for that matter. A common witticism shared by first responders is that for every floor in a walk-up apartment building, the standard was to simply add a hundred pounds to the patient's weight. Third floor, three hundred pounds. Fourth, four hundred. And so on. The more stairs involved, the heavier the infirm.

Stories abound in EMS when it comes to treating and transporting morbidly obese patients. In the mid-seventies, for example, the Norwood Fire Department was summoned to a home on Dean Street for a man complaining of difficulty breathing. *No wonder* was the consensus of the arriving team when they entered the small Cape-style residence to find a massive nine-hundred-pound man gasping for air. The medics promptly applied oxygen to ease his distress and then brainstormed about the predicament they faced. Not only did the ambulance lack the capacity to transport this behemoth of a man, but the patient had not left his home in years. His girth increased exponentially as he consumed take-out deliveries three or more times each day. He would not fit through conventional door frames, firefighters discovered. The rescuers had no other choice but to deploy a chainsaw to cut a wider opening.

Once outdoors, it was verified that he was also too large to fit into the narrow patient compartment of their standard-issue van-style ambulance. After a brief conference, fire officials contacted a local towing firm, which dispatched a flatbed vehicle to transport the man to the hospital. The trip was brief but highly embarrassing as curious onlookers gawked at the giant man, who was harnessed beneath a large green tarp. Adding insult to injury for the man, the Norwood Hospital staff directed fire personnel to deliver him to the receiving dock at the rear of the building. Requiring a pre-admission weight, the freight scale was the only available means to acquire an accurate measure of the colossal patient.

\*\*\*

Leroy Chasson had been thin all his life, more so after several years in the joint, where eating was somewhat of a challenge. Time to time, the kitchen help was known to dish out retribution toward a foe by adding substances unknown to the recipient. Restaurant goers often suspected similar tidings from angry chefs or waitstaff unseen in the backrooms, but within the depths of a prison kitchen, the possibilities increase tenfold.

Some inmates skipped meals as a result while others never visited the mess hall out of fear of tainted food. Former MCI-Norfolk inmate Rocco Balliro, for instance, claimed he ate nothing but canned goods purchased from the institution's canteen. His sustenance was tuna fish and beef stew exclusively. The most frequently used implement in his cell was a can opener.

As Bobby Zammito and Paul Kilroy readied their stretcher, Reynolds prepared the waist chains that would encircle Chasson and attach to a pair of handcuffs. Dr. Cohen heard the chains jingling and said, "No, there's no need for those in his case."

Reynolds looked quizzically at Cohen and asked, "How do you want me to hook him up?"

"Just the leg irons," the physician ordered, with the added explanation of, "Wrapping the chains around his abdomen might aggravate the wounds. We don't want him to start bleeding again."

Officer Reynolds was hesitant but soon nodded in agreement. *Doctors' orders*, he thought, even though the instruction was clearly against Walpole prison policy, which required all inmates leaving the institution to be shackled, chained, and cuffed—without exception.

Once the leg irons were attached to the Chasson's ankles with a small chain stretched between, the EMTs paralleled their stretcher alongside the hospital gurney. In a well-practiced maneuver, they guided their patient across the narrow gap. Chasson groaned in pain at the sudden jolt. "Sorry about that, man," Kilroy said as he covered the victim's shirtless upper body with a thin sheet and secured him with several wide safety straps.

The crew guided the stretcher out of the infirmary and into the corridor, where they were met by a crescendo of clanging sounds from the adjacent cellblock. The observers were slamming the metal edges of their various mirrors against the steel doors of their individual cells. It raised quite a commotion. There were also assorted catcalls directed toward the patient. Some were calling for his death. The pugnacious Leroy Chasson, it seemed, was not a favorite amongst his peers, who taunted him until he was out the door and out of sight.

The EMTs negotiated the half-flight staircase, carefully balancing their patient. Reynolds and Oliveira lent a helping hand. Loading Chasson into the ambulance, Kilroy climbed in after him and secured the stretcher to the wall mount.

Reynolds clambered in after the EMT and took his position on the squad bench, facing the inmate, who mumbled something unintelligible. "What's that, Leroy?" he asked.

"I said, 'I'm gonna get him,'" Chasson repeated more clearly, venom in his voice. "I'm gonna get the fuckin' guy who did this to me."

The officer asked Leroy who it was that shanked him but there was no response. He suddenly clammed up, saying nothing further.

After traversing the MCI-Walpole grounds and passing through the three gates, with Reynolds dealing with unlocking-relocking duties, Zammito pulled into the gaping vehicle trap, which the men in the turret above had opened on his approach. Once the massive door slammed closed behind them, a guard emerged from the doorway at the base of the observation tower. He was carrying the equipment confiscated earlier for safety. While Kilroy stashed everything in the toolbox, another guard re-examined the vehicle undercarriage with a mirror before signaling a thumbs up to his colleagues perched above.

The exterior door slid open and Zammito rolled the ambulance slightly forward enough to allow the corrections officers to close and secure it behind him.

Meeting the ambulance was Oliveira and a third guard, Jesse Motta. Reynolds had volunteered to ride in the ambulance and remained inside with Chasson. Idling nearby was the state transport car, a familiar navy-blue Ford Crown Victoria with a blue beacon mounted on the roof and Massachusetts Department of Correction decals affixed to both front doors. Motta, who was the only officer of the three who was armed, got behind the wheel. Oliveira joined him on the passenger side, buckling in. Zammito flipped the switch for the light bar. The flashing strobes reflected off the exterior prison walls, visible even in the daylight. As the EMT piloted the ambulance along the driveway and onto Route 1A north, Motta settled in behind him.

Typically, Walpole inmates were accompanied by two men—one in the ambulance patient compartment and the other driving what was known as the chase car, trailing the ambulance. But because of Chasson's troublesome history, officials were taking no chances and detailed three officers for the nine-mile jaunt.

Zammito, driving Norfolk-Bristol Ambulance 12, which he considered his personal favorite among the growing fleet, began the brief trek to Norwood. Clearing a residential area, he accelerated through a barren stretch of roadway that featured several side-by-side scrapyards stacked high with wrecked vehicles. Upon reaching Walpole Center, he found little traffic. Many of the businesses were closed in observance of the holiday. But in the interest of added safety, he gave the siren several quick yelps to safely bypass red traffic lights as well as to forewarn motorists emerging from intersecting streets ahead.

Kilroy, meanwhile, continued to render treatment to Chasson. There wasn't much he had to do. He pushed aside the covering sheet and checked the bandages on the patient's abdomen. There was a small amount of residual blood oozing through the layers of cotton gauze but nothing to raise concern.

Nearing nine o'clock, the sun-splashed morning was rapidly warming. As the hot and humid summer began its fade toward autumn, early September featured some of New

England's finest open-window weather. But in the confined patient area, with no ventilation to speak of, the conditions quickly grew sultry. Kilroy gave the air conditioner knob a spin to change the stale air before turning his full attention to Chasson.

"I'm going to give you some oxygen, okay?" he informed his patient. Reynolds gripped the edge of the vinyl squad bench and looked on with curiosity. Chasson accepted the oxygen with a nod.

Kilroy stood upright which, for the unskilled, amounted to a precarious task in a speeding ambulance. He reached into a supply cabinet along the sidewall, exercising great care not to lose his balance and take a spill on top of his stretcher-bound patient. Thankfully, most of the trip from Walpole Prison to Norwood Hospital was a smooth straightaway along Route 1A. There were few turns involved. Donning a pair of disposable gloves, he removed a pale green nasal cannula from protective plastic, plugged the prongs into Chasson's nostrils, and looped the pliable tubing around the patient's ears. Leroy compliantly turned his head to the right, then left, to give access. Kilroy muttered his thanks and then re-adjusted the nasal prongs when he noticed they were not sitting properly due to Chasson's thick Fu Manchu-style mustache. Satisfied with the application, he twisted the knob of the onboard oxygen to the standard flow of two liters per minute and affixed the tubing to begin delivery. Oxygen in place, he returned to the squad bench, retrieved his paperwork clipboard, and scribbled a notation on the attached run sheet.

As Kilroy labored, Reynolds turned to glance through the rear windows, observing his two colleagues in the chase car as they maintained contact with the ambulance. Understanding the prisoner and his inclination for raising hell, Reynolds wished he had a weapon. Leroy Chasson had frequently been a problem inmate during his five years of incarceration, assaulting his convicted brothers and corrections officers with equal ferocity. The .38-revolver in Motta's possession did Reynolds little good if something should arise. But he was also aware of the inherent risk of carrying a firearm in the ambulance; it could have been highly perilous. Some convicts were too unpredictable, including Chasson. A struggle for control of a gun in such a confined space held dire ramifications.

"I'm going to take a quick blood pressure," Kilroy informed his patient, who promptly presented his left arm. Wrapping the vinyl cuff around Chasson's bicep, the longtime EMT began to squeeze the bulb, inflating the instrument. Over the years, he had become quite adept at manipulating the device one-handed, using his free hand to stabilize himself against the vehicle's motion.

As he listened with a stethoscope and watched the gauge descend, he found the reading to be within normal limits, just as Cohen had said. The patient's pulse was slightly elevated, which was to be expected, but there was something else afoot. Kilroy noticed Chasson seemed to be growing increasingly jittery as they drew near their destination. At the outset of the transport, he was calm—eyes closed, breathing normally. He was as relaxed as someone taking a sightseeing ride in the countryside. But with arrival at Norwood Hospital minutes away, a sheen of perspiration suddenly appeared on the man's forehead and his eyes began darting anxiously about.

Reynolds saw it too, and for the second time since he encountered the injured Leroy Chasson in the corridor near the prison mess hall, he sensed that something was not right. Earlier, in the infirmary, suspicion had taken hold when Dr. Cohen stated aloud that the victim's abdominal punctures didn't seem as life-threatening as he first suspected. His initial diagnosis was "doom and gloom," and he insisted Chasson was knocking on death's door. But once Cohen removed the blood-soaked clothing and examined the wounds, he upgraded his prognosis to stable. From that moment on, Reynolds was on high alert and seldom took his eyes off the inmate.

"Good ol' Dr. Cohen—a prison doctor," Reynolds later said sarcastically. "That was his diagnosis. He repeatedly stated that Leroy wasn't going to make it. But the whole thing just didn't pass the smell test."

Before long, Zammito turned right onto Chapel Street in Norwood. They reached the home stretch, a mile from the hospital. Kilroy noted the patient's vital signs on his run sheet, which he would share with the ER staff on arrival. The pressure and pulse were normal, as Dr. Cohen had earlier claimed, which was peculiar. Blood loss tends to trigger a drop in blood pressure, known as hypotension. The nagging question was, how much blood had Chasson lost? If the amount was significant, then why were the inmate's vital signs stable? Disconcerting, certainly.

"His pressure didn't back up what we were told about the amount of bleeding," Kilroy said when he later recalled the transport. "It didn't add up."

Zammito pulled up to the apron, cut a wide turn, and began backing into a parking spot designated by "AMBULANCE ONLY" signage.

The steady beeping sound of the back-up alarm alerted hospital staff to their arrival. Minutes earlier, they had been made aware of the inmate's approach because Bobby had radioed ahead with a brief condition report and ETA. In the case of sick or injured prisoners from Walpole or Norfolk, the ER staff insisted on advance notification to prepare a space isolated from other patients. Many of these folks already suffered from frayed nerves due to whatever malady brought them to the hospital; the sight of uniformed personnel, firearms, and a prisoner did little for their fragile state of mind. In Chasson's instance, the head nurse had selected the trauma room separated from the main treatment area.

Climbing down from the cab, Zammito circled the vehicle. When he reached the rear of the ambulance, Kilroy had already thrown open the dual doors, stepped out, and was preparing to release the stretcher once his partner took a side. The two corrections officers who had followed in the chase car, Oliviera and Motta, joined their colleague Reynolds, the EMTs, Chasson, and a new arrival. Norwood Hospital security guard Al Hemphill emerged from his office to greet the group.

"Good morning, gentlemen," said Hemphill as he observed the crew unloading their patient.

"Morning, Sarge," Kilroy greeted, addressing the man by his better-known nickname.

The EMTs gently lowered the stretcher to the ground and then raised the apparatus to its maximum height, waist-high, and began wheeling Leroy Chasson toward the entrance. As the electronic sensor triggered the doors, a warm breeze followed the seven men into the ER beyond.

\*\*\*

Had someone needed to visit the ladies' room located in the rear corridor of the ER waiting area, they would have found the door locked for quite some time. There were alternative restrooms to be found in the main lobby, a short walk to the front of Norwood Hospital. Inside the locked restroom, a woman busied herself with an odd task; she began to change her clothing, from a simple summer dress to a nurse's uniform she had stashed in her large canvas tote bag. She placed the near-empty tote on top of an infant changing table.

Once she had donned the two-piece outfit, white pants and matching tunic, the woman slipped on a pair of white tennis shoes and tied the laces. Taking a deep breath and closing her eyes tight against mounting stress, she spun the cold-water faucet on the sink, cupped her hands for a few sips, and then splashed a small amount on her face. She pulled a length from the paper towel dispenser installed above the sink and dabbed herself dry. Gathering her discarded clothing and shoes, she stuffed the items in her satchel. After a brief pause to gather her wits, the woman reached into the bag and pulled out a white hand towel. Digging deep into the large tote once again, she withdrew a large black handgun. The weapon was a .45 automatic with a full magazine. The brushed metal of the barrel glinted menacingly beneath the overhead fluorescent lighting of the restroom. Gripping the firearm in her right hand, she draped the towel across her arm, concealing it from view. With her free hand, she grasped the handle of the bag and stashed it behind a trash can in the corner.

Standing in front of the mirror, she adjusted the towel on her arm to ensure the gun was not in view. Approaching the door, she turned a small knob to disengage the lock. Drawing one last deep breath in a futile effort to ease increasing dread, Mrs. Kathleen Chasson grasped the knob, pulled the door open, and stepped into the ER waiting room beyond.

# THIRTY-FOUR—BRAZEN ESCAPE

An ER staff member intercepted the entourage as they passed through the sliding doors and crossed the first threshold into the department. "Take him into the Code Room," the no-nonsense charge nurse instructed sternly, pointing to an open doorway to her immediate left. Like many of her colleagues in the Norwood ER, there was little joy in treating inmates because of the communicable diseases that were rampant in correctional institutions. Among others, the staff was on alert for HIV, hepatitis, and of course, tuberculosis. They did everything in their power to avoid bringing an ailment home to their families.

Paul Kilroy pulled the stretcher into the spacious suite as Bobby Zammito trailed, guiding his end. The EMTs turned their patient so the man's head was at the proper end and then paralleled him with the wider hospital bed. A nurse and a male aide joined them for the delicate transfer from one stretcher to the other. It was smooth and gentle, but like he had at the infirmary, Chasson grimaced in pain as they slid him across.

Kilroy had detached the oxygen as they exited the ambulance. Normally, the patient would be connected to a portable tank for the interim so there was no interruption to the delivery of oxygen, but two liters was a trivial amount and it was only a matter of minutes before Chasson was fastened to the in-house hospital feed.

The Code Room was typically reserved for high-risk patients: victims of cardiac arrest, chest pain, acute respiratory distress, and trauma patients from motor vehicle accidents topped the list. When not occupied with a more pressing case, prison inmates claimed the space.

Additional personnel steadily streamed into the room. A radiology technician stood by, preparing to take a portable x-ray, if needed. A staff nurse was tapping Chasson's arm for an IV to replace lost fluids and infuse medications. The male nursing assistant, who had assisted with the move, was busy checking vitals. Kilroy slipped him a segment of notepaper, which listed the vitals he collected in the ambulance. It was important to watch for changes across periods of time, which were often indicative of internal bleeding.

Dr. Carol Hoffman, the ER staff physician, removed Chasson's bloodstained bandages with a pair of forceps and examined the patient's abdomen. A nurse gently wiped the area with an antiseptic-soaked gauze pad, removing the dried blood to give the doctor a better view.

From across the room, Kilroy, who remained in the room with his partner Zammito to assist, assessed the stabbing trauma from a distance. The damage amounted to little more than three small puncture wounds in a triangular pattern, each no larger than a dime. He wondered if the description of the bleeding was exaggerated by corrections witnesses and Dr. Cohen at the prison. It seemed, upon closer inspection, that the wounds were only superficial. It later occurred to the experienced EMT that the injury, located on the left side of Chasson's abdomen, was in a position indicative of a self-inflicted wound for a right-handed man.

Just outside the busy Code Room, security officer Hemphill stood watch over the evolving scene. All was in order. After a moment, he broke away and made his way back to his office to await arriving ambulances and oversee the parking lot. He didn't notice an additional nurse as she hurried past, a white towel draped over her arm. It was not out of the ordinary. Had he caught a better look as they crossed paths, he might have recognized the woman.

Meanwhile, the trio of guards who had escorted the prisoner had scattered. Motta, still the sole guard in possession of a firearm, made his way into the depths of the ER in search of a phone. It was his responsibility to telephone the shift commander, Leo Bissonette, in the prison control room and provide an update on their status. In hindsight, all agreed it would have made more sense for the armed Motta to remain near the inmate and dispatch one of his colleagues to place the call.

Oliveira remained in the Code Room and quietly observed the ER staff buzzing around Leroy Chasson in a hectic but highly orchestrated treatment approach. They were all business. Oliveira, close to the entrance, pressed tightly against the vacant wall space to stay out of their way. Reynolds, meanwhile, had a pressing need.

"Tommy, I gotta take a quick piss," he said in a hushed tone, poking his head into the room to inform his colleague. Oliveira just nodded as Reynolds trotted off to complete his business.

Both Kilroy and Zammito stepped back from the bustle, finding a segment along the wall near Oliveira. Medical staff came and went, most of whom were recognizable to the EMT partners. At one point, however, a nurse entered the room who did not look at all familiar to Kilroy.

"I remember looking at her and I'm like, I knew all the nurses," he later said. "At least I thought I did."

Questioning himself, he figured she was an agency nurse. It was, after all, a holiday and hospitals like Norwood often filled staff vacancies with temporary per diem workers. But it wasn't so much this nurse's likeness that stirred his curiosity but rather her mannerisms. She stood just inside the doorway and was holding her arm upright at a ninety-degree angle across her midsection. He later described it as something a waiter in an upscale restaurant might do—

draping a towel over an outwardly positioned arm, as if she were awaiting a spilled drink.

Zammito, who was standing next to Kilroy, lightly jabbed his elbow into his partner's ribs, trying to gain his attention. Without warning, a shirtless Leroy Chasson had sat bolt upright on the stretcher. The abrupt motion triggered slight bleeding from his three abdominal punctures. An aide grasped the patient's shoulders and tried to guide him to a supine position, flat on his back. But Chasson would have none of it. He straight-armed the aide, effortlessly shoving him aside. With the other hand, he tore off the thin blanket that covered his lower extremities, revealing the irons clamped to his ankles. He pivoted his legs over the edge of the stretcher; his legs dangled and the chain binding the iron shackles attached to his ankles jangled like a metal chime twisting in the wind.

The ER aide again tried to gain control of the rebellious patient but to no avail. Chasson wrestled free and yanked the IV from his arm, touching off more bleeding. It ran down the length of his forearm in a trickling stream. He also ripped off the cardiac leads that had been fastened to his chest, prompting a loud whistling alarm from the device mounted on the wall. Detached from the patient, the monitor indicated a flat line. But Leroy Chasson was far from dead.

Oliveira reacted and began to move toward the prisoner but abruptly froze in his tracks. All activity in the trauma room came to an instantaneous standstill. No one said a word. Nobody moved. The proverbial "you could hear a pin drop" was an apt description.

All eyes in the room now turned to the mysterious nurse, who had now discarded the white towel and was pointing a deadly .45-caliber automatic at the six people in the room. Her face was blanched and she broke out in a sweat. The perspiration coated her forehead and glistened beneath the harsh overhead lights. Her upper body was taut with emotional strain. Tendons stood out prominently in her neck. Understandably, this menacing woman dressed in a nurse's uniform and holding the hospital staff at bay was apprehensive and highly charged. But beneath it all, she was also remarkably unwavering. She held the gun with a white-knuckled grip, but even under the strain, she was steady and unflinching.

"Everybody against the wall," was all she said. It was all she had to say.

An hour or so earlier, as he left his Dedham home, Paul Kilroy was debating where he and his partner could grab a quick breakfast on a pleasant holiday morning but now, instead, he was staring down the barrel of what he thought was the end of his life. Bobby Zammito was still fixated on Chasson's struggle to free himself from the myriad of tubes and wires attached to his body when his partner tapped him on the hip to gain his attention. As Zammito turned his head, Kilroy gestured toward the woman leveling a gun at them and said in a muted tone, "Bobby, we're dead."

It was at that moment that Corrections Officer Paul Reynolds returned from the restroom, still drying his hands with a paper towel. He stepped across the threshold into the trauma room and stopped suddenly mid-stride.

"As I walked into the room, I see all the doctors and nurses and Oliveira are backing up against the wall," Reynolds recalled. "I see a nurse to my right has a gun—a .45—and she's pointing it right at me. Literally, she takes a step toward me. I looked at her and then at Leroy. He's sitting up on the gurney and he's ripping the IVs out of his arm. I just turned and walked out of the room and made my way around the corner toward the waiting room."

Decades later, Reynolds agreed that Kathleen Chasson could have easily shot him in the back as he retreated. From that range, it was unlikely she would have missed. "I guess it was an involuntary response, walking out of that room like I did," he explained.

Chasson leapt from the stretcher and stood amidst the medical debris that littered the trauma room floor. Beneath his feet, which were clad in a pair of blood-spattered white sneakers, was a collection of discarded gauze bandages, IV tubing, and the oxygen nasal cannula Paul Kilroy had attached earlier in the ambulance. Chasson gathered his button-down shirt from the foot of the stretcher and hastily put it on. He didn't take the time to button it.

Wordlessly, the phony nurse began to move toward her husband, who stood less than ten feet away. As she moved in his direction, she continued to train the weapon on her trembling captives, who remained statue-like against the wall, entirely motionless. Reaching her husband's side, she handed over the gun. He clutched the grip, relishing the weight in his palm.

The hostages, including two nurses, a doctor, the EMTs, and Officer Oliveira, remained in the Code Room. It made little sense to give chase to an armed murderer who would not hesitate to take another life. Before filtering out of the claustrophobic room, they waited until they were certain it was safe to do so.

Officer Reynolds, meanwhile, reached the waiting room and began shouting at the two staff members sitting in the registration cubicles, as well as a smattering of patients watching the television while waiting to see a doctor. In the investigation that followed the dramatic event, witnesses claimed they had seen Kathleen Chasson earlier, sitting in the waiting room, casually flipping through a magazine. She then made her way to the ladies' room in a nearby corridor.

"Everybody down!" Reynolds called out, vigorously waving his arms to gain their attention. "Everybody get down! Person with a gun!"

As people dove to the carpeted floor and sought cover behind the waiting room furnishings, Reynolds had no idea the gun was now in the hands of killer Leroy Chasson, who was the real threat.

Reynolds turned to one of the two receptionists, who was already hiding, cowering beneath her desk. She trembled violently.

"I need a phone!" he clamored. "I have to call the police!"

At that, she rose to a half-crouch, reached for the telephone sitting on the corner of her desk, and handed the officer the receiver. The terrified woman then dialed 9 for an external call and quickly pressed the three buttons for 911. She then ducked back under the desk.

"Norwood Police," said a voice on the other end.

"Walpole inmate escaping from the hospital!" Reynolds exclaimed breathlessly. His heart slammed violently in his chest. "Guns involved!"

The distraught corrections officer did not wait for a response from the dispatcher. He assumed his frantic alert would draw the desired response, and police—an army of them would soon be on the way. Dropping the phone receiver on a nearby counter, Reynolds dashed in the direction of a corridor situated to the rear of the department. It was a separate egress for those trying to reach the hospital's front lobby without passing through the ER itself. It was then that Reynolds spotted Officer Motta on a distant phone, still talking with prison officials.

Meanwhile, the Chassons, Leroy, thirty-three, and his wife, Kathleen, forty, were hurrying out of the Code Room. The hostages who were left behind breathed a welcome sigh of relief. Corrections Officer Oliveira paused for a moment, then made his way toward the ER exit, intent on joining his colleagues in the ambulance lot. Paul Kilroy and Bobby Zammito, along with Dr. Hoffman and the nursing staff, turned to their right as they hurriedly left the room, heading for safety.

"After Leroy left with her, we ran out of the room," Kilroy recalled. "We ran toward the front side of the building, not the rear, where everything was happening."

Urban legend, perhaps, but in parting, the witnesses in the trauma room recalled hearing the cocky Leroy Chasson utter the phrase that headlined many newspaper stories following the bold daylight escape. "Sorry, people," he was heard to say, "but I gotta go."

Leroy and Kathleen Chasson, the convicted killer and his accomplice, bolted for the ER exit. Blood steadily streaming from his mid-section and arm, it was slow going for Leroy. He left a trail of red in his wake. More troublesome, however, were the restrictive bindings attached to his ankles. There was little slack in the chain connecting the manacles, slowing his pace. The best he could manage was an awkward shuffle across the tile surface.

Kathleen led the way, a step or two ahead of Leroy. Reaching the getaway car before her lumbering spouse would allow her to open his door and start the vehicle.

Security officer Hemphill had not heard the commotion in the waiting room as Reynolds shouted warnings, but as Kathleen Chasson activated the electronic sliding doors and rushed past his office, he rose from his chair. Now he now recognized her—she was the mysterious woman he had spoken with about parking the Malibu in the reserved lot. She was wearing a nurse's uniform, sparking his curiosity. But he didn't have time to put a lot of thought into it because seconds after she exited, a man shuffled after her. He was bound at the ankles and was brandishing a gun.

With no means to leave the tiny security office without being spotted, Hemphill stepped into the shadows, pressing into a space beside a filing cabinet. The inmate, who was dripping blood, ambled past without a second glance. Either he did not see the security guard or did not care. Either way, Hemphill was relieved as the electronic doors parted and Chasson exited the hospital.

Back in the waiting area, Reynolds began shouting for Motta. "Jesse, c'mere!" he yelled, trying to gain the man's attention. Motta, not responding to the urgent plea, raised his index finger to indicate he would be just a minute.

"Hang up that fucking phone and get over here!" Reynolds screamed across the hundred feet that separated them. Motta, hearing that, dropped the receiver in the cradle and began to run toward his panic-stricken colleague. Reaching Reynolds, he was informed that Chasson was armed with a handgun and had just escaped. As the two men raced for the exit, Motta drew his weapon.

Hemphill, unarmed, joined the duo in pursuit of Leroy Chasson and his wife. As Reynolds and Motta burst through the sliding doors and into the parking lot beyond, Chasson turned, leveled his weapon, and fired. Motta countered, squeezing the trigger of his .38 revolver repeatedly. Two of his rounds struck the bumper of a nearby vehicle and windshield of a Mercedes owned by a hospital surgeon. Chasson's slugs slammed into the side of the building, embedding in the brick and concrete walls of the structure.

Days later, after the yellow caution tape was removed from the crime scene, the bullet holes in the hospital walls became something of a tourist attraction. Observers marveled at the dramatic gunfight that had taken place. Many snapped photographs to authenticate the memorable event.

Reynolds, adrenaline coursing through his body, sought refuge from a hail of lead. In a moment of cognizance, he recognized that Motta was wielding a five-shot firearm and was rapidly expending the ammunition. In later discussions under more sedate conditions, it suggested the infamous line uttered by Clint Eastwood in *Dirty Harry*, the popular 1971 crime movie. "Did I fire six shots or only five?" But unlike the classic showdown featuring the fictional Inspector Harry Callahan, the scene unfolding before Officer Reynolds was not taking place with actors with guns armed with blanks on a movie set. It was all too real.

"Jesse, don't fire the last round!" he exhorted frantically. "Don't fire again!"

"Why the hell not?!"

"What if he fucking comes back?" Reynolds shouted in response.

Motta heeded the sage advice and stopped shooting. As the two prison guards and Hemphill helplessly observed from across the parking lot, Chasson reached the Malibu and climbed in. His wife was already in the car and had started it, nervously revving the engine. Leroy slammed the passenger door closed as she backed out of the space. She threw the shift lever into drive and tore out of the lot, tires screeching in protest. She turned left onto Linden Street, which passed behind the adjacent Norwood Post Office and intersected with Guild Street. Reynolds quickly sprinted to the edge of the parking lot. Linden Street was less than a hundred yards in length. He was hoping to see whether they turned left or right on Guild Street but the vehicle was already out of sight. Twenty seconds later, by his estimate, the first of several Norwood patrol cars appeared. It was soon followed by more, as law enforcement flooded the hospital lot, as well as the streets in the vicinity. Before long, it seemed as if the entire Norwood Police force had converged on the hospital.

"I have to give the cops credit," Reynolds later commented. "They showed up pretty damn quick."

The first arriving police cruiser came to a hard stop. The parking lot reeked of pungent, burnt tire rubber, still lingering in the wake of the Chassons' escape and now the patrol car. The solo officer behind the wheel spotted the trio of prison guards, accompanied by a hospital security representative, who looked visibly shaken.

In later interviews, it was revealed that Hemphill came within inches of taking a bullet to the head. According to a number of witness accounts, Chasson fired his weapon several times, nearly hitting Hemphill. The offending slug was found lodged in the concrete of a nearby wall. The former Marine later explained that he had flopped on top of a hospital staffer's car, which saved his life. He added that the car was not supposed to be parked where it was, which was a welcome twist of fate.

"The bullet passed so close that the damn ear rang for three hours," an animated Hemphill recounted for *Lowell Sun* staff reporter Kristopher Pisarik, who visited the security officer's home a week after the Labor Day dramatics.

When a Norwood police detective took ballistics measurements, based on where the security guard took refuge and where the .45-caliber bullet impacted the concrete wall, the bullet was found to have passed less than two inches from Hemphill's head.

"What the hell?" said the hardened security guard, who had worked at Norwood Hospital for eleven years. "It didn't really faze me. You gotta stay cool and not lose your head."

When asked why he ran after Chasson, Hemphill said he misunderstood what was taking place. As the event unfolded, he mistakenly thought the woman (who was running several strides ahead of the "hopping," shackled inmate) was in some sort of trouble. "I thought she was running away from him. My first thought was that he had kidnapped a hostage to make his getaway," he later explained.

During his visit to Hemphill's tidy home in Billerica, a community thirty miles west of Boston, the *Lowell Sun* reporter also spoke with Phyllis, Hemphill's wife. When asked about his "brush with death," she said that her devil-may-care husband had cheated death many times in his illustrious thirty-year military career, including during a tour of duty in World War II.

"The chief is very lucky," Phyllis shared as she displayed Hemphill's assortment of medals, which included a Silver Star and two Purple Hearts. "He has lived a charmed life."

According to accounts, Norwood Police Sergeant William Travers was the first to arrive at the scene of the escape. Reynolds was standing at the edge of the street while Motta raced to the prison staff car in search of ammunition. Motta also faced the dreaded task of notifying the prison. Returning the nearly spent .38-caliber revolver to the holster attached to his belt, he turned to re-enter the ER. While Reynolds stood in the parking lot as the Norwood cops began arriving, Motta sought out a phone to report the escape. A dead Chasson would have been easier to disclose, but alive and now on the run would not be taken lightly by prison command.

Leroy Chasson proved that escape from notorious Walpole State Prison was, in fact, possible. Certainly, taking flight from within the confines of the eighteen-foot walls was a tall task, indeed. But his escape method left corrections officials red-faced and alert for future attempts by other industrious inmates.

Spotting Reynolds standing in the parking lot, Sergeant Travers hollered through the open window of his cruiser, "Which way?!"

Reynolds pointed west down Linden Street.

"C'mon, let's go!" the sergeant shouted, urging Reynolds to join him. The corrections officer, his heart still slamming in his chest, hurriedly circled the blue-and-white car, opened the passenger door, and leapt in. He was barely settled in the seat when Travers gunned the accelerator and sped out of the lot, adding another cloud of noxious smoke to the spectacle as the tires spun.

"Here, take this," said the grizzled veteran cop as he handed over a 12-gauge shotgun that had been mounted in a dashboard bracket. Reynolds gripped the weapon tightly as the duo began the search for the blue Chevrolet Malibu. They raced up and down streets in the general area of the hospital. Assuming the Chassons might have ditched the vehicle, Reynolds checked driveways and parking lots as they sped along Central, Broadway, and Nahatan Streets. Travers and Reynolds searched the sprawling commuter rail lot adjacent to the hospital, the town lot behind the Norwood Cinema, and a small parking area that abutted Day Street. They made a pass-through Norwood Center along the Washington Street commercial district. It was nearing nine-thirty and traffic was light. Many of the businesses were closed in observance of the Labor Day holiday. There was no sign of the Chevrolet.

Reynolds did not express his thoughts to the sergeant as they canvassed area streets, but he realized their haphazard hunt was a pointless exercise. While only minutes had passed since the escape, there had been ample time for Chasson and his wife to reach Route 1, which would connect the fleeing pair to Route 128 or Interstate 95. If they had, in fact, reached the highway system, the escapees were as good as gone.

Back at Norwood Hospital, Boston media agencies began to arrive in droves, their satellite-topped vehicles claiming every available space in the vicinity. WCVB Channel 5, based in Needham, was first to reach the scene. Others parked in the mostly vacant MBTA lot a block away and walked to the scene. The medical staff, particularly those who were firsthand witnesses in the Code Room, were soon under siege by inquisitive reporters seeking to be the first to break the news.

EMT Paul Kilroy recalled being instructed by a police officer not to answer questions. "The Norwood cop was first to question us," he said. "I don't recall his name but he was a heavyset guy. He told us not to say anything to anybody." Rebellious to the core, Kilroy ignored the command. "We talked with reporters from Channel 7," he recalled with a laugh.

Tips began to roll in to police agencies, both in Norwood and the Massachusetts State Police, who almost immediately issued a nationwide bulletin describing the Chasson couple as "extremely dangerous."

"He was serving a life sentence," said a state police spokesman. "He has nothing to lose."

Norfolk County District Attorney William C. Delahunt, whose office took the lead in the probe, said to reporter Ed Copp of the *Daily Transcript*, "I consider him one of the most dangerous individuals we have dealt with since I have been DA."

Delahunt ordered his staff to reach out to witnesses and jury members from Chasson's 1978 trial and conviction. Learning of the escape, some were fearful that the murderer, with nothing to lose, would seek them out in a vendetta. Delahunt's people tried to ease their minds and offered protection to those fearing retribution for the guilty verdict. "This was nothing on the spur of the moment," State Trooper Joseph Flaherty told reporters. "It appears it was well-planned."

Corrections Officer Paul Reynolds had to agree. From the moment he first spotted Leroy Chasson in the corridor at MCI-Walpole clutching his midsection in distress, he suspected something was amiss. "It was obviously a well-crafted ploy," Reynolds acknowledged, stating he regretted heeding the orders from Dr. Cohen at the prison infirmary. "Leroy Chasson might still be in our custody if I hadn't listened to Dr. Cohen and fully chained the inmate as required. Instead, he got away."

Reynolds also spoke briefly about the abundance of blood found on the corridor floor. He suspected that Chasson somehow got his hands on fake blood capsules, a popular Halloween ruse which creates the realistic illusion of blood when the ingredients mix with saliva.

"That was an afterthought," Reynolds recalled. "I saw the wounds; he was spitting up blood, but we never found out if he had used a blood pill. The immediate thought was that he had been stabbed. Initially, we thought it was a con stuck by another con."

Many would agree that convicted killer Leroy Chasson and his wife Kathleen had pulled off what would later be described as one of the most notable prison escapes in Walpole State Prison history.

Several years earlier, in 1979, a Walpole inmate by the name of Kenneth R. Wightman, who was serving a sentence for armed robbery and the attempted murder of a pair of Boston Police detectives, had managed to conceal himself beneath the wheel-well recess of a station wagon belonging to a visiting chaplain. The Houdini-like escape was short-lived, however. The escapee was recaptured within hours.

Leroy and Kathleen Chasson would not suffer a similar fate. In the aftermath of their daring flight for freedom, some would compare the couple to the infamous Bonnie and Clyde. The resourceful Chassons would manage to evade the authorities for the next seven years.

# THIRTY-FIVE—THE AFTERMATH

It wasn't long before the getaway car turned up—a little more than twenty minutes—but it proved sufficient for Leroy Chasson and his wife to switch into an alternate vehicle and flee. The blue Chevrolet Malibu was found abandoned in a parking lot belonging to a Stop & Shop supermarket situated on the corner of Railroad Avenue and Central Street, several blocks northeast of the scene of the brazen daylight escape.

Police later fixed on a likely route from the hospital to the popular supermarket. They concluded Chasson followed Central Street, skirted the Town Common, and crossed the intersection at Nahatan Street before reaching the entrance to the Stop & Shop. There would have been only a single traffic light in their path, adjacent to the Norwood Town Hall, which was a Gothic-inspired structure many thought resembled a church. There are stained-glass windows in the one hundred and seventy-foot granite tower that depict Norwood's patriot Aaron Guild, who was said to leave his plow and oxen standing in the fields while he rushed off to join the Revolutionary fight in Lexington, Massachusetts.

The Chevy, which was registered in Kathleen's name, would remain impounded at the Norwood Police Station and closely examined for evidence. There was hope that the couple had left something behind—an invoice or incriminating receipts which might lead law enforcement to their destination. It was a long shot but detectives had little else to go on. Leads to that point in the investigation were scarce. The police also knew that the longer the Chassons remained at large, the more difficult it would be to make an arrest.

Detectives did find a large pair of bolt cutters discarded on the passenger side floorboards of the Malibu. Later visits to area hardware stores revealed the tool had been rented by a woman and, according to the proprietor, was perfectly capable of shredding the shackles binding Chasson's ankles. Shards of iron and chain fragments were found embedded in the carpeting covering the floorboards. Most of the metal was missing, which meant that the escapee took it with him and disposed of the debris elsewhere. The remnants of the leg irons were never recovered.

Also discovered was a patchwork of drying blood stains, both on the passenger seat of the Chevy, as well as the grips of the bolt cutters. The blood obviously belonged to Leroy. At first, the Norwood Police thought the convicted killer might have been hit with a bullet fired by Walpole Corrections Officer Jesse Motta during the shootout. But all the slugs at the hospital were accounted for. Each was pried loose from walls and parked vehicles and later identified via ballistics. The police gathered that the small amount of blood left on the seat came from either the escapee's self-inflicted abdominal wounds or his forearm from having violently yanked out the IV that had been inserted by hospital staff. Or it was a combination of the two. There was also discarded packaging from gauze pads, likely supplied by an astute Kathleen to stem her husband's bleeding wounds.

As the investigation progressed, the police surmised a third party had delivered a second car. It turned out that the detectives who handled the inquiry were spot-on in their assumption.

Decades after the escape, a well-informed source came forward with answers under the condition that he remain anonymous. This individual stated that a friend of the Chassons left a second getaway car in the supermarket parking lot. This person precisely timed the vehicle delivery with the escape taking place mere blocks away. The car, with a full tank of fuel, was left running. The source of this information would only describe it as a "sedan." Not only did this mysterious accomplice provide transportation, a change of clothing for both Leroy and his wife, and provisions for a few days' travel, he also left an envelope stuffed with cash. The amount is unknown, but it would prove to be enough to pay for motel rooms and meals as they began their journey.

The anonymous informant was also well-versed in the route the Chassons took to reach their final hideaway. First on the agenda was an overnight stop in Seabrook, New Hampshire, a short drive from Portsmouth and less than an hour's drive from Norwood Hospital. After exchanging vehicles and gaining their bearings, within minutes, Leroy and Kathleen were on their way north on Interstate 95.

In conjunction with the Massachusetts State Police and the FBI, the Norwood Police launched an intensive search for the fugitives. Interviews were conducted with witnesses who were on hand at the hospital, as well as area business owners who might have seen unusual activity at the Stop & Shop. There was hope that someone could offer a description of the accomplice. While Norwood was a relative ghost town on Labor Day, some of the businesses were open to customers. But the supermarket was off the beaten path, a block south of Washington Street, the main thoroughfare. There was a pair of popular drinking establishments within shouting distance of the Stop & Shop—the Shamrock Pub and the Irish Heaven—but the police found neither was serving patrons at that early hour and could not provide eyewitnesses.

At the outset, investigators held on to the belief that the pair had remained in the general Norwood area. State police suggested they might have made their way to Boston, which would open further avenues to shake off their pursuers. Armed with photographs, officials canvassed airlines, trains, bus lines, and car rental agencies. The effort failed to yield workable leads.

Police were aware that Kathleen Chasson maintained an apartment in nearby Walpole at 167 South Street. It was a brief drive to MCI-Walpole, and it was likely she rented it so she would be close for frequent visits to the prison. She also had roots in the coastal community of Weymouth, around a twenty-mile drive, where her parents lived. She had stayed with them for a time after her release from the Glenside Hospital in Jamaica Plain. Was the couple staying close by or trying to put a safe distance between themselves and the authorities? It was thought, mistakenly as it turned out, that the Chassons lacked the financial means to reach a remote location and therefore, had no choice but to remain in familiar territory.

Subsequent visits to Kathleen's South Street apartment yielded little evidence as to their whereabouts. There was an assortment of children's toys strewn about the backyard and in one of the bedrooms. A few abandoned personal items left behind were claimed by police. Neighbors were interviewed at length by both local detectives and the Massachusetts State Police. Don Moscatelli, who lived nearby, was asked to review a number of photographs of the getaway car. He verified that Mrs. Chasson's blue Chevrolet Malibu was seen parked in the driveway.

Neighbor Christine Zajac told *Daily Transcript* staff reporter Michelle Chambers that Mrs. Chasson kept to herself. She said that children also lived in the apartment and claimed one of the kids would often play with her family's dog. "She was just another rental," said Zajac, who lived across the street from the white, two-family clapboard house. It was, she noted, the only apartment of its kind on a street which was made up of middle-class, single-family homes. "I didn't really know her."

Other neighbors had similar accounts of the mysterious woman who lived quietly among them for a year and a half under the alias Karen Ryan.

It was learned that Kathleen Chasson worked the graveyard shift at the nearby Wrentham State School, which was a state-run facility providing long-term housing and care for developmentally disabled people, much like the Fernald School in Waltham, where Mark Bray carried out his walk-away escape during a work detail. Walpole Police Sergeant Joseph Betro was told by Zajac that the suspect was often seen in a nurse's uniform. "I used to see her when I left for work in the morning," the neighbor shared with reporter Chambers. "She must have worked the night shift."

Wrentham State School Superintendent Francis Kelly confirmed with Betro that Mrs. Chasson did work the graveyard shift and did so under the name Karen Ryan. It wasn't until investigators visited that Kelly learned Kathleen was using a false name. She was an attendant, he said, working with "retarded people" since July 1981. The superintendent described her as an average worker and said she was a "quiet person."

Kathleen's landlord, who chose not to reveal his identity to probing reporters, told police that she was a divorced mother of six. He explained that he rented the apartment to only Kathleen Chasson, but she later took in a woman named "Ellen," who was also married to a Walpole Prison convict. Both women had married their respective inmate spouses in the prison chapel. It was likely that she struck up a friendship with Ellen during one of her frequent visits to the jail. Investigators spoke at length with the roommate, who worked at the VFW Hospital in West Roxbury, but she had little to offer.

Police found that of the six children under the care of Kathleen's ex-husband, Daniel MacDonald, a few were living in Colorado with one of the older siblings. Only one, a preteen boy, remained in Massachusetts with his mother.

Mrs. Chasson, who the landlord described as five-foot-two-inches tall and an "overweight" one hundred and sixty pounds, was asked to vacate the apartment by the first of September. He had already rented the space to a new tenant. When asked by the police, he claimed to have no knowledge as to where Kathleen stayed during the five days leading up to the Labor Day escape. She did not leave a forwarding address.

In the immediate fallout of Leroy Chasson's flight from state custody and the subsequent parking lot shootout, there was a great deal of finger-pointing. A convicted killer was now on the loose. Norwood Hospital staff and patients in nearby rooms had been placed in harm's way as indiscriminate gunfire was exchanged between the fleeing inmate and one of his pursuers, Officer Motta. Small chunks of concrete and brick had been gouged from exterior walls by impacting bullets, and a pair of hapless physicians would need to arrange for repairs to their respective vehicles.

While tight-lipped prison officials, led by Massachusetts Department of Correction Commissioner Michael Fair, ultimately accepted responsibility and assured hospital executives that measures would be taken to prevent further incidents of this nature, Norwood Hospital's Chief Administrator David Buchmueller earned approval from the president of trustees and hospital attorneys to establish a revised policy. According to *The Daily News Transcript*, a Norwood-based newspaper, drastic—some would say, illegal—steps were taken to thwart a recurrence but the hospital was willing to face the repercussions as well as a lawsuit from the Commonwealth of Massachusetts and the Massachusetts Department of Correction.

"Norwood Hospital will no longer treat prisoners as patients, even those seriously injured," *Transcript* staff reporter Tom Bowman later wrote. "Buchmueller's decision on Monday night came less than twelve hours after Leroy Chasson, 33, a convicted murder[er] from Walpole Prison escaped from Norwood Hospital with his gun-toting wife disguised as a nurse."

Marjorie Clapprood, the hospital information director who later served as a Massachusetts state representative, spoke at length to reporters. "She stopped at the front desk at about 8:30," Clapprood stated, adding that Mrs. Chasson asked the ER receptionist if there was any word about her son. She was told there was no such patient when she provided a name, which was obviously false. "She told the receptionist that she would wait in the ER for her son and then sat on one of the blue couches, often gazing out the window and reading magazines."

Clapprood, who also worked for a time as a talk-show host with Boston's WRKO, offered a brief description of the female perpetrator, stating that she was "in her forties and overweight. She was also familiar with the layout of the department."

As information director, Clapprood was tasked with outlining the updated hospital policy, which had been hastily prepared by administrator Buchmueller and his attorneys. One of the stringent measures put in place by Norwood Hospital was to simply deny the acceptance of inmates from either of the two area prisons, Walpole and Norfolk, and the Dedham Jail. This measure was phased in to curtail similar future escape attempts and protect hospital staff and patients. A monthly rotation was established, cycling through four Boston-based medical facilities: Brigham and Women's, Massachusetts General, Beth Israel, and Tufts Medical Center. All would share the burden in turn, each accepting sick or injured inmates for a month at a time.

"These large-scale medical facilities have the means to handle patients of this nature," said a hospital spokesman at the time. "Particularly, city hospitals and medical centers have sufficient security sources to effectively cope with prison inmates."

While Buchmueller was unable to cite similar violent incidents from the past, he did recall what was described by reporters as a "suspicious event." "About five years ago, two men came into the hospital looking for a prisoner from MCI-Walpole who had been admitted," he recounted. "Both looked suspicious and were apprehended by police."

It wasn't long before the questionable policy was put to the test. Prison staff cars and ambulances would arrive, patient-loaded, and wait in the Norwood Hospital Emergency Room receiving lot. Physicians and support staff would saunter out to the idling vehicle and perform a rapid evaluation and stabilization of the patient. Security officers would emerge and stand guard at the department entrance, armed with orders not to allow an inmate or prison personnel to pass. Often, the Norwood Police Department would dispatch a patrol car and the officer would stand at the ready, supplementing the corrections officers, one of whom would position himself adjacent to the ambulance with his gun drawn. Often, the EMS crew would spend mere minutes before being waved on to Boston.

On a warm, late-September morning only two weeks after the Chasson debacle, a Norfolk-Bristol ambulance arrived patient-loaded from MCI-Walpole. The inmate, in his fifties, had complained to prison staff that he was experiencing chest pain. He did, in fact, have a history of a heart attack and, by all indications, seemed to be having another. An ambulance was summoned to the prison and the man was transported to Norwood Hospital.

ER staff was alerted and, after a moment, a physician and a nurse emerged, a Lifepak 5 monitor/defibrillator in hand. They approached the vehicle as the gun-wielding officer opened the rear doors for them.

"What do you have?" questioned the doctor as he and his white-uniformed assistant climbed into the back of the ambulance. He was noticeably miffed, obviously displeased with this bizarre method of patient care. Inmate or not, the man deserved the best of care as far as he was concerned.

The escort, who drew the short straw to ride in the ambulance, checked and rechecked the security of the inmate's abdominal chain, handcuffs, and legs shackles. Content that the man was trussed up like a roped calf in a rodeo, the guard then moved to the vacant jump seat behind the patient's head.

The EMT slid forward on the squad bench to make way for the additional medical staff. "Chest pain," he responded as he twisted the air conditioning knob to add cool air to the cramped patient compartment. The space was designed for two, not five. Autumn had arrived in New England, but warm, short-sleeved weather persisted, and it quickly grew stifling inside the vehicle. "He's fifty years old with known cardiac history. Vital signs are within normal limits."

The ER doctor unbuttoned the man's shirt to expose his chest. He accepted a four-by-four square of gauze from the nurse and wiped dry the damp skin as the inmate looked on with interest. The physician then applied the leads and initiated an EKG. He pulled the green-tinted oxygen mask away from the prisoner's face and asked, "How's the pain on a scale of one to ten?"

"Five," was the answer.

"Better or worse than it was at the prison?"

"Same," the inmate mumbled.

The doctor tore the narrow strip of paper off the Lifepak 5 and glanced briefly at the printout, mumbling, "Normal sinus rhythm. He's stable."

He glanced at the EMT and asked, "Which facility is next on the rotation?"

"The Brigham."

"Okay, guys," the doctor said. "I'm clearing this gentleman to continue to the Brigham. Administer five liters of oxygen and monitor signs. Remain aware of alternate hospitals along your route in case his condition worsens, and you must divert. I'll call ahead to the Brigham and Women's and notify their staff." He was obviously reluctant. You could hear the concern in his tone. What he was doing, following the risky hospital policy, went against everything he valued as a physician.

"Got it, doctor," the EMT said as he checked the oxygen flow, ensuring it was set at five as ordered. The hospital staff exited the vehicle, and the corrections officer resumed his position on the squad bench nearest the rear doors. The entourage soon pulled off the apron to resume the thirty-minute trip to Boston. The Norwood patrol car trailed behind until they reached the town limits and then broke off.

Other instances of makeshift patient evaluations prompted derogatory comments toward Norwood Hospital and its administration. Some labeled the facility as a "drive-thru" where the reckless treatment delivered was equivalent to picking up a Big Mac meal at the nearby McDonald's; some quipped that the service rendered at the ER "drive-thru" was faster than the restaurant.

With bullet holes still visible in the exterior walls of the hospital, others insisted the hospital policy decision was well-founded. "Patient safety is paramount," said a spokesman.

Some EMS personnel chose to bypass the Norwood stopgap altogether, risking a longer transport with prison inmates directly to the designated Boston hospital of the month. The added delay for a driveway assessment with ER staff, many felt, often proved unnecessary and burdensome.

Further embarrassment was endured by the decision makers at Norwood when Stephen Barrett, the administrator of Glover Hospital in the nearby town of Needham, was asked by *Daily Transcript* reporter Ed Copp if they would accept prison inmates. "We accept any patients," Barrett stressed.

# THIRTY-SIX—CHASSON'S RUN

While Norwood Hospital management proceeded legally to protect staff and patients by diverting Walpole and Norfolk prison inmates away from their facility, the search for Leroy and Kathleen Chasson was gaining little ground. They were gone, without a trace. Days into the search, it was found that the couple had effectively covered their tracks. The fugitives had all but vanished.

Frustrated authorities simply had nothing to go on. Every shred of evidence and each lead received by police led to a dead end. The Chassons' escape plan included a well-concealed, obscure hideout—if, in fact, they were staying in a singular location. According to a newspaper account, "State Police Trooper Joseph Flaherty said police are working on the theory that the convicted murderer Leroy Chasson, 33, and his 40-year-old wife, Kathleen, are no longer hiding in Massachusetts." Flaherty believed it was more likely the pair was moving about, traveling from one point to another to mask their trail and evade capture.

Seventy miles north of the Norwood Hospital, in a small, nondescript roadside motel, a dazzling ray of sunshine pierced a narrow gap in the heavy drapes, settling on the face of a sleeping Leroy Chasson. The brightness and warmth of the gleaming light hastened him from his slumber.

It was Tuesday, September 7, 1982, and less than twenty-four hours had passed since his brash escape from the custody of a trio of MCI-Walpole corrections officers tasked with guarding him while Norwood Hospital medical staff treated his abdominal stab wounds. As he buried his head deeper in the pillow, Leroy grinned widely. It was not lost on him that this was the first time in more than four years that he had slept on a real bed, with a real mattress, warm covers, and a woman at his side.

Rubbing sleep from his eyes, Leroy stifled a pronounced yawn. Freedom was certainly sweet and he had the woman sound asleep in the plush queen-sized bed to thank for it. Kathleen had risked her neck to spring him from a life in the slammer and he could never repay her except to love and cherish her, the promise he made when they exchanged vows at their prison wedding a year earlier.

Rising from the bed, he parted the curtains, allowing the sun's rays to spill fully into the sparsely furnished motel room. The television, volume muted, flickered in the background. Unlocking and raising the window several inches, a gust of chilly, fifty-degree air rushed through the opening. It was refreshing and he inhaled deeply.

Kathleen stirred, muttering something about sleeping longer. He glanced at the clock on the nightstand. It was just after eight. Despite a good night's sleep, they were both still exhausted. The escape from the hospital, the ensuing gunfight in the parking lot, the vehicle exchange at the supermarket, and a tense hour-long drive north with multiple sightings of patrol cars hunting them had taken a heavy physical, emotional, and mental toll.

Leroy examined the bandages affixed to his abdomen and forearm. The bleeding, he noted, had all but stopped. There were dime-sized spots of blood that had seeped through the squares of cotton gauze but not as much as the day before. Kathleen, with her years of medical experience, had done a remarkable job patching his wounds once they safely reached the motel.

He gazed out the window, taking in the nearby scenery of Seabrook, New Hampshire. Their motel was on a barren stretch of Route 1 so there wasn't much to see. A picturesque coastal town fifteen miles south of bustling Portsmouth, Seabrook was best known for its pristine Atlantic coastline and nuclear power plant, the second largest in New England behind Millstone in Connecticut. In 1977, far-reaching protests against the construction of the unpopular facility placed the little community of less than eight thousand people on the national map, and over time, resulted in fourteen hundred arrests. For Leroy and Kathleen Chasson, Seabrook would represent the first stop in a cross-country odyssey that wouldn't come to an end until they reached Colorado, eighteen months later.

Hearing Kathleen climb out of bed, Leroy sounded a hearty good morning. She mumbled a drowsy reply as she made her way to the bathroom. He began to slowly dress in her absence, donning some of the fresh clothing their friend had stashed in the second getaway car. He took great care not to disturb the bandages. Thankfully, it was cool enough on this early September morning to wear a long-sleeved shirt; it would effectively conceal the taped gauze. The couple planned to grab a quick breakfast in a nearby café and the bandages, if visible, would surely raise suspicions.

Kathleen soon emerged from the bathroom, freshly washed and brushed. She dressed hurriedly, stating that she was famished.

"There's a little place up the road," Leroy informed. "Walking distance."

During breakfast, the intrusiveness of the Seabrook locals became immediately apparent. The prolonged stares at the two strangers in their midst were unnerving. Conversation between the dozen or so patrons, boisterous when Leroy and Kathleen first strolled into the nook, had all but ceased. The room became perceptibly subdued. The Chassons ate their meals quickly.

"I don't think we'll stay in this town for long," Leroy whispered to his anxious wife. The last thing they needed, after all they had been through, was to encounter Seabrook's Barney Fife, seeking his moment in the limelight. Kathleen nodded in agreement.

The duo returned to the motel and gathered their meager belongings. Leroy paid the proprietor, an old-timer who did not seem to care who stayed in his rooms as long as the cash slapped on the counter was legal tender.

The Chassons were soon on the road, heading north along Route 1. Reaching the beach town of Hampton, they veered onto Route 27 and then 101 heading west, which was a secondary road. Just over an hour later, they arrived in the city of Manchester, New Hampshire. Leroy followed signs to the airport and parked in the long-term lot. He and Kathleen spent a few minutes wiping away fingerprints. He wasn't certain how long the car would be there—a day, a week, perhaps a month or more—but it didn't really matter. There was nothing incriminating to tie them to the now abandoned vehicle, which he assumed had been stolen by their helpful accomplice.

The couple collected their belongings and walked to the main concourse and a Greyhound bus terminal. Purchasing a pair of one-way tickets, they waited briefly until their designated bus arrived, adorned with the distinct racing greyhound dog stretched along the length of the vehicle. Smiling at his wife, Leroy pointed to the placard above the windshield. As they observed, the bus driver pulled a small lever, changing the destination from Manchester, New Hampshire, to Chicago, Illinois.

***

From the small-town coziness of Coastal Seabrook to the big city sprawl of Chicago, the hunted couple traveled from one to the other in a matter of eighteen hours on the Greyhound bus. There were a few brief stops along the way for snacks and restroom breaks. While the bus trip was uneventful and restful, Leroy would have preferred driving himself and having ready access to the transportation an automobile provided. But he knew keeping the stolen vehicle any longer would tempt fate.

Chasson soon discovered that the Elevated, or L as it was fondly known to commuting Chicagoans, was easy to navigate. After a quick lunch, the couple boarded a train bound for the South Side of Chicago. It was, by reputation, not the most desirable side of town, but Leroy knew the rents would be affordable.

The couple strolled for several random blocks and before long, came upon a "For Rent" sign in the window of a ten-story brick apartment building. Scribbling the phone number on the palm of his hand, Leroy tracked down a payphone, slid a few coins into the slot, and dialed.

"Yeah?" answered a gruff, gravelly voice at the other end.

"Good morning, sir," Leroy greeted politely. Then, for the first time since the escape, he summoned forth his new alias, which he would use for the foreseeable future. "My name is James Garrity. I'm interested in your vacant apartment on West 79th Street."

"Yeah, there's a two-room place above a storefront, across the street from the city bus terminal."

"That's the one," Chasson acknowledged as he glanced upward at the apartment described. "Can we have a look?"

"Be there in twenty."

The slumlord soon arrived, unlit cigar in mouth. He had squinty, nearly closed eyes, like movie star Clint Eastwood; although unlike the Western film actor, the man was short and plump. He shook Leroy's hand and said, "Good to meet 'cha, Jim and…"

"Kate...Kate Garrity," Kathleen offered after a pause and with a convincing smile. She realized their altered names would take some getting used to. Thankfully, their helpful accomplice back in Norwood had already provided identification and other false credentials, including fake driver's licenses.

"Okay, folks, follow me."

Leroy and Kathleen trailed their prospective landlord into the building, which had seen better days. There was a heap of old newspapers and supermarket flyers stacked in the foyer near the mailboxes and the carpeted floor was in desperate need of replacement. The landlord continued to gnaw on the cigar as he led them up a steep, narrow flight of creaky stairs to a second-floor apartment. Keying the lock, he pushed the door open to reveal a small flat with little more to offer than a living room, a bedroom, a kitchenette, and a closet-sized bathroom. It was musty and dusty and needed a serious scrubbing, much like the littered, graffiti-filled streets in the neighborhood. But the apartment came furnished and was a spacious paradise compared to Leroy's six-by-nine at Walpole State Prison. When rent was discussed, he found the two-hundred-dollar monthly figure fit right into their limited budget.

The cigar-chomping slumlord's squinty eyes grew wide as he watched his new tenant count out twenties for the first and last month's rent from a wad of cash in a white envelope. "I'll see you on the first of October for next month's rent," he said excitedly as he stuffed the bills in his shirt pocket and departed.

***

Several months passed in Chicago as the outlaws settled in. They kept to themselves and wiled away the hours watching television. Their money in short supply, Leroy found work as a line cook in a small mom-and-pop restaurant within walking distance of their apartment. Kathleen, meanwhile, supplemented their flagging income with occasional work in her line as a home health aide.

They spent free time traipsing about the sprawling lakefront metropolis and grew comfortable; so much so that they began to visit tourist haunts such as Navy Pier on Lake Michigan and Miracle Mile, Chicago's popular shopping hub. Unlike tiny Seabrook, New Hampshire, Chicago, the third largest US city with three million people, allowed the couple to blend in.

Leroy began to think their stay in the Windy City might become permanent. That was until the awful day when Kathleen was apprehended at Target attempting to steal a television. With their second-hand TV at home on its last leg and not enough money to buy a replacement, she visited the Target on a pre-Christmas day when it was crowded with holiday shoppers. With the television wedged in a carriage, she hurried toward the exit.

A hand gripped her upper arm as a voice yapped, "Ma'am, you need to come with me." Her captor was a smallish twenty-something and Kathleen thought about making a run for it, but she had used a taxi to reach the Target. There was no way out of this jam. And the store detective who continued to clutch her bicep – tightly, she recalled – had a crime-fighting partner—a tall, athletic man who didn't look like he would lose many foot races.

Leroy was summoned. Kathleen used a telephone in the store detective's office to call him at work. She was distraught. He hitched a ride from a coworker at the restaurant and made his way to the Target. During the trip, he weighed his options. Leaving Kathleen at the mercy of the hounds certainly was not one of them. Once he got inside the store, he could create a distraction and they could escape together. He regretted leaving his gun at home. He usually carried it for the "what if," and more so since the day when Leroy thought he and his wife were recognized in a coffee shop. But when he worked in the restaurant, he left the .45 in his apartment. He couldn't risk someone in the kitchen catching sight of it stuffed in his waistband.

Once reaching the store detective's office, Leroy was led to Kathleen. She was sitting quietly in a small room filled with assorted products—stolen goods, he assumed. A large cardboard-boxed television was resting on the floor adjacent to where Kathleen sat. Despite the dire circumstances, Leroy found it humorous that his wife thought she could make off with an item of that size.

Kathleen's eyes were bloodshot and puffy. She had obviously been crying. Leroy blamed himself. If he had just been more sparing with their money or found the means to make more, Kathleen wouldn't have felt the need to steal a television.

"Mr. Garrity," began the young woman who had apprehended his wife.

"Yes?" Leroy glanced around the room and noticed there were no Chicago Police on hand. *Were they still on the way?* Then his question was answered and it was good news.

"We tend to handle these things in-house," the store detective said. "We find that the police are far too busy to handle every shoplifting incident, especially at this time of year." As she explained, the woman moved her arms in an outward sweeping motion, indicating the products stacked up in every available space. Leroy nodded that he understood. "So, if you and Mrs. Garrity would agree to pay a nominal fine and sign a form promising not to enter this store again, I believe we can resolve this without involving the police."

"How much is the fine?" Chasson asked, bracing for the worst.

"One hundred."

Leroy nodded as he pulled cash out of his pants pocket. It was tightly wrapped in a rubber band. Thankfully, his boss at the restaurant had paid him his week's wages earlier that day. He peeled off five twenties and handed them over to the young woman. Kathleen signed the paperwork in front of her and the couple was soon on their way. As Leroy flagged down a taxi, a light snow began to fall. Glancing skyward at the spinning flakes, Leroy realized that he and Kathleen had dodged a bullet. A trip to a Chicago police precinct would have revealed their true identities and resulted in a prompt trip back to Massachusetts. Both he and his wife had come dangerously close to observing the Christmas holiday from the confines of a jail cell.

\*\*\*

With the two near misses behind them, the Chassons decided it was time to be on the move again. Chicago, despite Leroy's desire to make the Windy City their home, had become too risky. Kathleen's shoplifting episode aside, there were other signs indicating that it was in their best interest to find new digs. There was nothing concrete, of course. Just a sense that the authorities might be closing in. And perhaps it was a case of paranoia on his part but on a number of occasions, he suspected they had been recognized by random strangers.

Leroy frequently purchased a copy of the *Chicago Tribune,* which, like most newspapers across the country, had carried stories of the escape when it took place in September. But it was now late December and coverage of the two fugitives had long since dried up. The media had moved on to more pressing coverage. Leroy had visited a post office branch or two in his travels and FBI wanted posters were not to be found pinned to bulletin boards, at least not in the Chicago area. He discussed a move with

Kathleen over dinner. She wholeheartedly agreed. She was still in shock over her gut-wrenching narrow escape from the department store.

Unlike their rapid departure from Seabrook, the couple took several days to prepare for their next trip. Over time, Leroy and Kathleen had accumulated a few things for their barren apartment, mostly decorative trinkets. They had added several small appliances, such as a toaster and a coffeemaker, to make their lives on the run feel somewhat normal. The scant collection of personal belongings was still far too much to haul across the country on a Greyhound bus. Kathleen had noticed a few people, down-on-their-luck types, living in their building. On a piece of cardboard, she scribbled the words "Free—Take Me!" and placed it on a table in the shared lobby. She added the belongings they could not take along. Hours later, she checked the table and everything except for the handwritten sign was gone. It made her feel good that she could help someone less fortunate.

Several days later, under gray morning skies and a winter chill, Leroy and Kathleen boarded a bus bound for Seattle, Washington. It was the beginning of a year-long trek that included extended stops in the Pacific Northwest, Nevada, Kansas, and Colorado. The Chassons kept to themselves, steadfastly maintaining a low profile wherever they went and avoiding trouble. There were times, however, when trouble found them.

While checking into a small roadside motel in Bellevue, Washington, which was a medium-sized suburb east of Seattle, Kathleen was accosted by a pair of twenty-something Native American vagrants who wandered off the street. The two men were obviously intoxicated and badly in need of a bath, and set upon her without invitation.

Leroy had stepped into the motel office to arrange for a room while Kathleen strolled around the parking lot, stretching her bus-weary legs. The two men approached her and even though they were speaking broken English, their intent was obvious. They were seeking to rob her and have a little fun at her expense. They were grabbing at her maliciously. The motel attendant alerted Leroy.

"Isn't that your friend out there?" he asked, pointing toward Kathleen as he traded room keys for the fifty dollars Leroy placed on the countertop.

Leroy turned and saw his wife being cornered by a pair of strangers; they were laughing and jabbing fingers at her. She pleaded with them to leave her alone and was clearly on the verge of tears. Leroy bolted from the motel office and hurried in Kathleen's direction. His hands balled in white-knuckled fists and face reddened with murderous fury, he launched an attack. Leveling the first man with a solid blow that shattered his nose, Leroy went for the other. This man, seemingly drunker than his defeated companion, took a flailing swing at the attacker. The response was merciless as an incensed Leroy shoved the man against a parked car and began to pound his face to a pulp. Blood poured from the man's nose and mouth as he tumbled to the asphalt below. He cowered in a fetal position, whimpering as he tried in vain to fend off the continued beating. Leroy turned to Kathleen, who was trembling violently.

As he soothed her, a Bellevue patrol car turned into the lot, tires chirping as the driver brought it to an abrupt stop. Two police officers, their faces bathed in the flashing blue light from atop their vehicle, emerged and cautiously approached the scene. Both were gripping their holstered service weapons.

"What's going on here?" one of the cops insisted as he glanced at the two battered men lying prone on the ground.

"These dirtballs were harassing my wife," Leroy answered in a remarkably calm, even tone. There was no mistaking that he was the perpetrator in the assault. His hands were covered in the blood of the two injured Native American men.

The officer glanced at Kathleen and said, "Are you all right, ma'am?"

She nodded in response.

"Okay," he said. "Just stay put for a minute while I speak with the motel clerk." He headed for the office while his partner remained with the Chassons and the two casualties of Leroy's wrath. Both were moaning in pain. Returning to the group, the Bellevue police officer began, "All right, Mr....."

"Garrity... James Garrity."

"All right, Mr. Garrity," the lawman continued. "It seems your story is in order. The motel clerk corroborated what you had to say. Are you staying here tonight?" Leroy dangled the room key as proof. "All right, if we have any further questions, we know where to find you. In the meantime, we'll take this *trash* down to the station."

Leroy smiled at the cop's description of the Native Americans. The officer didn't try to conceal his grin. He obviously approved of the beating Leroy had dished out.

***

Leroy Chasson was briefly jailed in Seattle following a bar fight in which a patron was stabbed. Once again, police failed to scrutinize their detainee. Instead, he was released from custody after the man he allegedly stabbed, who was on parole, refused to testify.

The Chassons lingered in the Seattle region until the winter season ended. Leroy once again took work in a small café while Kathleen found a well-paying job as a nursing assistant in a local home for the aged. The couple discussed their living arrangements at length and decided against renting an apartment. Leroy had proven adept at negotiating affordable long-term rates in a succession of out-of-the-way motels. It wasn't the most comfortable lodging but made the most sense. Kathleen agreed with her husband that an apartment would only complicate matters when it came time to move on.

In mid-April 1983, the Massachusetts fugitives put the Pacific Northwest in the rearview mirror of yet another Greyhound bus, this time making their way south to Kansas. Again, because of a probable short-term stay, they checked into a series of no-name motels situated around the perimeter of Kansas City, staying only a few days at a time in each. By the end of a summer in the Dust Bowl, so named because of the historic Midwest droughts of the thirties, the Chassons were on the move again, traveling west to Nevada. Leroy and Kathleen didn't have the money to live it up in Las Vegas but that did not prevent the couple from enjoying the sights and sounds of Sin City with brief visits to the casinos and occasional strolls along the Strip.

As September rolled around, the wanted pair marked the one-year anniversary of Leroy's escape from Walpole State Prison by way of Norwood Hospital. Two months later, as the Christmas holiday neared, the Chassons boarded yet another Greyhound for what they hoped would be their final bus ride, destined for the Rocky Mountain State of Colorado.

Leroy and Kathleen first settled in the quaint community of Manitou Springs, situated at the base of Pikes Peak and minutes northwest of Colorado Springs. For the first time since they left Chicago, the fugitives decided to rent a small apartment. Leroy found a suitable residence, furnished and move-in ready, near the business district. Without access to a vehicle, the Chassons had little choice but to live within walking distance of provisions.

While crisscrossing the states of Kansas and Nevada, Leroy was able to accumulate a tidy cash reserve, stashing away some of his pay working in assorted restaurants as a dishwasher and line cook. To supplement his income, he also took odd jobs as a handyman and house painter, harkening back to his days as a youth. Kathleen easily found work within the nursing profession and was able to contribute to the fund. The money was sufficient enough to cover rent costs, as well as a few necessities for their apartment.

Kathleen enjoyed the opportunity to visit with her children. The brood had settled in Colorado Springs, six miles from Manitou Springs.

The MacDonald children had been living with their father, Daniel, for a number of years after their parents divorced. But according to an anonymous source, their lives in the South Shore community of Weymouth, Massachusetts, were miserable. Their father had remarried and their stepmother treated his children poorly. The eldest sibling, Michael, had reached adulthood and was serving in the US Army at Fort Carson in Colorado Springs. Galvanized by the strife in the lives of his younger brothers and sisters, Michael took charge, petitioning for and winning custody of the MacDonald children. All five eventually traveled to Colorado to live in his home under his guardianship. It was a much more favorable situation for all involved.

Kathleen, while delighted at the prospect of having her children nearby, took great care to limit her visits. She was, after all, still on the lam with her husband Leroy. She feared if the authorities discovered her refuge, the younger children might be declared wards of the state and face foster care. Kathleen was aware that Michael had worked extremely hard to provide a stable home for his sisters and brothers, and she did not want him to answer charges of harboring fugitives if the police managed to track down Leroy.

Over time, as their nest egg grew, Leroy and Kathleen Chasson, aka James and Kate Garrity, decided to move to a nicer, more comfortable apartment in the city of Denver. They had long since chosen to make Colorado their permanent home. The city of Colorado Springs was pleasant enough, but Leroy Chasson took a dangerous misstep, drinking far too much at a local watering hole one night and getting into an altercation with another patron. The police were summoned and he was nearly charged with being drunk and disorderly. But much like his assault of the Native Americans in Seattle, the Colorado Springs Police let him off the hook with a stern warning. He was now known to the police, however, and would not get a second chance, so a move made the most sense.

After a brief search, the couple took an apartment on East Tenth Street in the Capitol Area of downtown Denver, just blocks from the state capitol building. Leroy continued hiring himself out as a handyman and, over time, became quite proficient in carpentry. Kathleen, meanwhile, was in high demand as a home health aide and never lacked an assignment. Work was plentiful. The Massachusetts fugitives settled in and before long, day-to-day life in Denver became a welcome routine.

Meanwhile, the search for the pair continued unabated. The FBI, while persistent, was unable to pick up a trail. Leroy and Kathleen had done a remarkable job meandering across the country and leaving few traces. The FBI needed a break in the case and, in 1988, six years after Chasson's escape from Norwood Hospital, they got one.

# THIRTY-SEVEN—AMERICA'S MOST-WANTED

July 27, 1981, was a typically hot and humid mid-summer day in Hollywood, Florida, a popular beachfront community wedged between Miami Beach and Fort Lauderdale. While throngs of tourists flocked to the Atlantic beaches, the boardwalk, and the pounding surf, scores of residents were known to frequent area air-conditioned shopping malls and department stores to escape the oppressive South Florida heat.

That Monday afternoon, Revé Drew Walsh and her six-year-old son Adam visited the Sears Department store in the Hollywood Mall, today known as the Hollywood Hills Plaza. While she paid a visit to the lamp department, little Adam joined a group of older boys who were playing video games nearby on the store's display televisions. When store security asked the rambunctious boys to leave, Adam went outside with them without his mother's knowledge. As the youths dispersed, pedaling away on their bikes, the youngster was left alone in a deserted alleyway.

Two weeks later, on August 10, the severed head of Adam Walsh was found by a motorist in a drainage ditch alongside the Florida Turnpike near Vero Beach, one hundred and thirty miles north of Hollywood.

Investigators later determined that the boy had been abducted by Ottis Toole, a suspected serial killer, and driven north on the Florida Turnpike toward the kidnapper's Jacksonville home. When Adam grew unruly in the car, Toole punched him in the face and then permanently silenced the boy, strangling him to death. For reasons unknown, the sick-minded Toole took a machete to the boy, decapitating him. According to investigators, Adam Walsh's body was never found. Toole eventually confessed to the killing (twice), as well as five additional Florida murders, but later recanted (also twice). The prosecution's case against him fell apart because a number of police agencies in the mix allegedly misplaced key evidence, including the perpetrator's bloodstained vehicle and the machete. Toole, who was eventually convicted of six murders, died of liver failure at the age of forty-nine in 1996, while behind bars in a state prison in Starke, Florida.

In the aftermath of their son's tragic death, John and Revé Walsh set out on a personal crusade that ultimately led to an offer from the Twentieth Century Fox Television Network to host a new investigative true crime show, called *America's Most Wanted*. 1988 was an ideal time to launch such a series. Television viewers had an insatiable appetite for the crime genre. And John Walsh, who had a flair for the dramatic, was the perfect host for a show of this nature.

At the outset, each installment would feature an FBI's Top Ten Most Wanted criminal, complete with photographs, description, a detailed reenactment of the crime committed and a catchy toll-free phone number: 1-800-CRIME-TV. *America's Most Wanted* viewers, upon recognizing a perpetrator, were urged by Walsh to call the number and share their tips, which were then referred to the FBI or the corresponding police agency. New findings were regularly televised, as well as case-closed episodes heralding *AMW* apprehensions. The Fox Network took immense pride in a twenty-four-year run with Walsh at the helm. The show, in no small part, contributed to more than twelve hundred confirmed captures. It has been revived in January 2024 with a second season in April 2025, featuring John Walsh back as host alongside his son, Callahan.

Soon after the premiere broadcast on February 7, 1988, the *America's Most Wanted* producers decided to feature the elusive Massachusetts offenders Leroy and Kathleen Chasson in an upcoming episode. The couple had been at large for six years when producers began to piece together the installment.

During the spring of 1988, *AMW* representatives appeared at the administrative headquarters of Norfolk-Bristol Ambulance, located in a one-story cinderblock building on East Vernon Street, Norwood. The company's offices and adjacent garage were two blocks from the hospital from which the Chassons launched their notorious escape.

*AMW* producers were soundly rebuked, however, turned away by Norfolk-Bristol office workers. At the time of the visit, the owner of the rapidly-growing ambulance firm, Robert Zammito Sr., was facing intense scrutiny from the *Boston Globe* spotlight team, an investigative journalist unit founded in 1970. The *Globe* spotlight team was best known for uncovering the Catholic Archdiocese of Boston child sex abuse scandal.

Zammito Sr. was embroiled in an investigation of workers accused of defrauding the city of Boston with false disability claims. A former Boston firefighter, he was alleged to be collecting funds illegally after sustaining a permanent back injury while throwing a smoldering mattress from a window. The entrepreneur invested in an ambulance startup and was doing well financially when the investigation began. It was clearly a witch hunt by the city of Boston and Zammito Sr. was eventually cleared of any wrongdoing. But in the midst of the probe, paranoia in the office and at his Foxboro, Massachusetts, home was rampant. Norfolk-Bristol employees were prohibited from speaking with visitors. *AMW* producers arrived to find segments of cardboard taped to windows. There was fear that *Boston Globe* photographers were perched on the rooftop of a residential home opposite the company's offices in hopes of snapping a picture of Zammito Sr. climbing into his pricey cherry-red Corvette.

The *America's Most Wanted* representatives presented credentials and a detailed explanation for their visit and were eventually granted permission to meet with company leadership. EMT Daniel Greene was on hand completing ambulance trip sheets when he overheard a conversation that caught his attention. The producers were talking about Leroy Chasson and were interested in filming a reenactment of his escape for their TV show. They needed to hire an ambulance and an EMT crew to participate in the taping at Norwood Hospital and, subsequently, Walpole State Prison. Norfolk-Bristol would be generously compensated.

"Hey, Dan," said Bruce Valade, the longtime office manager. "You missed out the first time around, here's your chance." Valade was referring to Labor Day weekend 1982, when Greene chose to visit Montreal, Canada, with his girlfriend. He swapped the holiday work assignment with colleague Bobby Zammito Jr., the company owner's son.

Greene vividly recalled his exchange with Bobby Jr. when he reported for work on the Tuesday morning following the Chassons' escape. Entering the office that September morning, Bobby met Greene near a shelving unit where he was replenishing a metallic clipboard with paperwork for the day ahead.

Reaching out, Bobby seized his partner's throat and hissed, "I am never working for you again." Of course, the scene was all in jest because the assailant, who was known for his pleasant disposition, was grinning as he slightly tightened his grip, which he released after just a few seconds.

"What is it, Bobby?" Greene asked. "What happened?"

The tall, lanky EMT with a thick mop of sandy brown hair said, "It was because of you and your little trip to

Canada that I had a gun held on me. I could have been killed!"

Greene soon learned of the inmate's breakout and how Bobby, Paul Kilroy, and several others were held at gunpoint in the Norwood Hospital Code Room while convicted killer Leroy Chasson and his wife took flight. Of course, Zammito Jr. held no grudge against his coworker and friend. It was little more than a coincidence that he accepted the shift swap from Greene that put him in harm's way.

Six years later, as the *AMW* producers worked out the details with Norfolk-Bristol management, Valade urged Greene to accept the detail.

"No, thanks," he said. "I'd rather not be associated with the likes of this guy Chasson."

"Suit yourself," Valade said with a slight shake of his head. "I think you're going to regret it."

Greene did, in fact, regret his decision. As it turned out, the Fox Network mailed royalty payments in the amount of two hundred and fifty dollars for each of the two appearances, the initial adaptation and the subsequent follow-up episode that was televised at a later date. The extra money would have come in handy for Greene, who was married with a three-year-old daughter at home and living off EMT wages, which were paltry.

Valade, responsible for scheduling, arranged for a pair of part-time employees to report for the filming, which producers requested the next day. He sent out the information for the detail and, before long, part-timers Ann Healy and Jane Pratt checked in to accept the assignment. According to Healy, an attractive middle-aged woman who made her living teaching emergency medical services at Norwood Hospital, it did not matter that both stand-in staff members were women while the personnel on duty when the actual event took place were male. The *AMW* folks were fine with the discrepancy. The attention was on the criminal act and not the gender of the actors tasked with reenactment.

Viewers of the television show were unlikely to pay much attention to the supporting cast.

The Chasson segment aired on June 11, 1988, in a 7 p.m. time slot. Ironically, on many networks, the broadcast was wedged between a pair of popular television crime shows, *MacGyver*, which depicted a character known for elaborate escapes, and *Murder, She Wrote*, a series in which actress Angela Lansbury, playing the role of Jessica Fletcher, hunted down wanted killers.

Viewer's tips and potential sightings of Leroy and Kathleen began reaching the toll-free number almost immediately. The FBI dispatched agents to inquire about the more compelling leads but turned up little. Most were dead ends. A few police encounters related to the segment featuring Leroy Chasson proved outright embarrassing.

Soon after a repeat broadcast in July 1989, for instance, a Bremerton, Washington, man was arrested at gunpoint because of his resemblance to the fugitive. As he drove about the waterfront city of forty-five thousand, sixty miles west of Seattle, Al Clark was in good spirits. With his fiancée, Virginia, at his side, he was driving around in his yellow van, polishing off a number of errands in preparation for their wedding, which was set to take place the very next day. His cheerful mood, however, was crushed moments after he waved in greeting to Bremerton Officer Rainey Woods, who was a long-time acquaintance.

Earlier that day, a viewer of *America's Most Wanted* telephoned the tip line, where he was referred to Bremerton Police Captain Joe Hatfield (yes, his real name). Officers canvassed Clark's neighborhood, and a business manager was shown the eight-by-ten mugshot of Leroy Chasson. He said that Clark frequented the store and agreed that he looked "extremely similar" to the man in the photo.

On orders from Hatfield, Officer Woods initiated a traffic stop of Clark on the Warren Avenue Bridge and waited for backup. Hatfield soon arrived with a substantial portion of the Bremerton Police Department, all pointing guns at the stunned motorist. In a standard "felony stop," the police brusquely pulled him from his vehicle but he wasn't taken into custody. Suddenly realizing the error of their ways, the red-faced police holstered their firearms and muttered apologies. Al Clark was not Leroy Chasson, despite the resemblance. While he was of similar height and weight, the wrongly accused Clark was only thirty-three while Chasson was forty—seven years his senior.

"I don't look anything like that guy," a perturbed Clark told Creg Darby, staff reporter from the *Bremerton Kitsap Sun*, "and I've never been to Massachusetts."

The couple went ahead with their nuptials the next day as planned, but Clark harbored a great deal of resentment toward the Bremerton Police for the foul up. A spokesman from Fox Broadcasting attempted to defend *America's Most Wanted*. Phil Gonzalez, Fox publicist, told reporters that forty-nine fugitives were in custody as a direct result of the television show, which had been on the air for eighteen months, and only twice during that span was there an "error" in suspect identification.

"Sure, they're getting a lot [of] bad guys," a victimized Clark said to reporters, "but there's other people suffering for their mistakes."

\*\*\*

Fourteen hundred miles southeast of Bremerton, Washington, in a tidy apartment in downtown Denver, a couple sat upon their plush couch, preparing to enjoy a late dinner. They had just arrived home from work and were settling in to watch a few shows before calling it a night. Leroy turned on the television and waited patiently to see what broadcast was next. What they saw as the TV came in view was unnerving. In stunned silence, their mouths agape in shock, Leroy and

Kathleen Chasson watched as a well-groomed man profiled for his audience the subjects of that night's installment of *America's Most Wanted*.

"Good evening, I'm John Walsh," said the host, his sleeves rolled up, his tie loosened, and a deadly serious look on his face. "Welcome to another edition of *America's Most Wanted*."

The Chassons watched with rapt attention as Walsh previewed the episode, describing Leroy Chasson, the convicted killer who escaped from Massachusetts with help from his wife, who was armed and disguised as a nurse.

Leroy and Kathleen stared blankly at each other for a moment and then turned their attention back to the TV, which had gone to commercial. Neither said a word. There was nothing to say. Despite the warmth of the Denver July night filtering through the open windows of their apartment, there was suddenly a distinct chill in the air. Leroy shuddered. As he stared at the television, his dinner growing cold on the plate on his lap, he reached the stark realization that their days of freedom might be numbered.

As it turned out, however, the disturbing *America's Most Wanted* broadcast changed little in the lives of the couple. They waited for the fateful knock on the door—or worse, the front door to come crashing down as storm troopers forced their way into the apartment. Days turned to weeks, weeks to months, but the anticipated arrival of law enforcement did not materialize. Perhaps his likeness on the TV broadcast was not recognized. Over the years, he had slightly altered his looks, lost the Fu Manchu mustache, and trimmed his hair. Maybe… he and his wife were just plain lucky. They had, after all, sidestepped arrest during several encounters with police as they fled across the country. It often seemed that Leroy and Kathleen possessed a perpetual "get out of jail free" card. Whether it was shoplifting in Chicago or an assault and battery in Seattle, the duo walked away from each transgression unscathed. They were Teflon criminals.

Whatever the reasons behind the lack of a police raid on their lives, Leroy was able to breathe a sigh of relief as time passed and he and Kathleen continued to remain free from the bite of handcuffs.

Another year would uneventfully pass before that would change.

# THIRTY-EIGHT—FUGITIVES FOUND

Outdoors, Denver was baking in temperatures nearing ninety degrees, quite unseasonable for a late September day in the Western city of nearly half a million residents. But the inhabitants of this pleasant "mile high" city knew that the lingering summer-like conditions were fleeting, indeed. Two weeks earlier, a telltale sign of things to come had blanketed the region with several inches of snow. The magnificent Rocky Mountains, in full view from about any vantage point in Denver, remained snow-covered. It was another indication of winter's imminent approach.

As the television blared in the adjacent living room, James Garrity, aka Leroy Chasson, rummaged through the refrigerator in search of a sandwich he knew was buried somewhere amid the assorted leftovers crowding the shelving. As midday approached, he was seeking a quick bite to fend off encroaching hunger. He knew his wife Kathleen had prepared the snack before heading off to work earlier that morning. As he searched for and found a ham-and-cheese tightly wrapped in cellophane, along with a cold beer chaser, Leroy had no idea that he was about to indulge in his last meal.

\*\*\*

Denver FBI Special Agent in Charge Robert Pence and his crew were scattered over a one-block segment of East Tenth Avenue in downtown Denver. The agents were concealed from sight, tucked into the alleyways and foyers of nearby apartment buildings lining the quiet residential street. Each of the highly trained lawmen remained at full alert, prepared to engage the fugitive if the need arose. This grew increasingly more difficult as time ticked toward midday. The unseasonably hot conditions made the stakeout too much to bear.

Pence moved about the tension-filled scene, chatting with his men like a coach prepping athletes for the big game. But this was no game. There was no question in any of their minds that their suspect, a convicted murderer who had escaped from custody under a hail of gunfire seven years earlier, was armed and dangerous.

Agent Pence was acting on a tip received through the popular true crime television program, *America's Most Wanted*. One of the show's earliest broadcasts in July 1988 had featured Massachusetts prison escapee Leroy Chasson, but the telecast failed to yield useful results. Most of the calls to the toll-free number turned up empty leads. Thirteen months later, in August 1989, the network decided to air the episode a second time with a few added details. Unlike a year earlier, serviceable intelligence began to surface. While callers to the *AMW* tipline were entirely anonymous, the FBI gathered that the tipsters were Denver neighbors, some of whom Chasson had befriended over the years. Once the location of the fugitive was narrowed to an East Tenth Avenue apartment building, Pence was tasked with the arrest.

When asked, SAC Pence admitted that he did not immediately contact either federal marshals or the Denver Police Department about the operation. He was confident in his men. He felt the FBI could collar Chasson without additional resources from other agencies. He did, however, take the time to reach out to Massachusetts authorities who had received a number of the *America's Most Wanted* calls directly. "After receiving the tip, we placed a phone call to the Massachusetts people," recalled Pence, who joined the FBI in 1960 as a probationary agent and steadily climbed the ranks over the next three decades, ultimately reaching the top job in the Denver Field Office. "They provided guidance and an additional description of the subject."

The stakeout dragged on for hours without results. Strategically positioned observers armed with binoculars reported movement inside the apartment but the subject was obscured from view and the agents were unable to make a positive identification. Pence, realizing he might be facing a long night on East Tenth Avenue, decided to grab a dinner break at his home, which was a short drive from downtown. He wasn't there for long, however. He was just settling in when the house phone rang. Rushing to answer, he lifted the receiver on the first ring.

"I think we have him," the FBI agent on the other end excitedly declared. "We're going to arrest him."

Hearing that, Pence bolted for his car, flipped on the lights and siren, and began to race back to the scene. His heart pounded in his chest as he drove.

The Denver SAC would later learn what took place on East Tenth Avenue soon after he departed for home. In his absence, Pence's agents brainstormed and produced a scheme to get closer to the targeted apartment. One of the undercover G-men, a seasoned distance runner, retreated to his car and changed into his "jogging suit," as Pence described it. He then began to jog along the roadway. As he approached Chasson's apartment, the agent had an unexpected brush with their quarry.

"The subject, who was shirtless, came out of his apartment," Pence recalled years later. "He was friendly and actually greeted our agent."

That jolting close encounter was enough to authenticate the subject's identity. James Garrity, according to the jogging FBI man was, in fact, Leroy Chasson.

The fugitive did not linger outside. He ducked back into his apartment. There was a sense among the observers that their subject had "made" them, to coin popular law enforcement lingo. There was conjecture that Chasson had seen something through his apartment windows that raised his suspicions, and he stepped outside to get a better look but quickly retreated.

After a few tense moments, the wanted fugitive showed himself again. Earlier, he had been shirtless, his chest bare. This time, agents noted Chasson was wearing a long-sleeved t-shirt. At first, the lawmen failed to understand the purpose behind the change of clothing. It was uncomfortably hot. Why put on a heavier shirt with sleeves? The reasoning soon came to light.

As the undercover men observed, their antsy subject paused, his head twisting nervously left and right, first glancing to the east along East Tenth Avenue, and then to the west, toward the distant snow-covered Rockies. His motions were jittery. The G-men began to slowly emerge from concealment, each drawing a firearm from holsters as they took tentative but purposeful steps toward Chasson. Without word or warning, Leroy Chasson reached beneath his shirt, yanking a .45 automatic from the waistband of his trousers. It was later determined that it was the same gun used by his wife Kathleen seven years earlier to help in the escape from the custody of several Massachusetts corrections officers.

As the FBI agents closed in, Leroy began firing at them, swinging his arm wildly back-and-forth. He sprayed bullets in a haphazard, random pattern, not aiming at any man in particular. One of the agents sustained a superficial bullet wound to the hand but there were no other reported injuries to law enforcement in the hostilities. Propelled by pure adrenaline, agents advanced without pause, returning the fugitive's fire. A torrent of searing projectiles slammed into surrounding buildings, scattering shards of concrete. Nearby apartment windows were shattered by stray rounds. Other slugs found their deadly mark, however; Chasson was riddled with bullets, struck twice in the upper torso as well as several times in his extremities. He began hemorrhaging from each of the wounds. His life's blood gushed with each contraction of his gradually slowing heart. For little more than a minute, he lingered on the verge of death.

The forty-one-year-old convicted murderer met his end, collapsing to the scalding sidewalk with a sickening thud. A contingent of sweating FBI agents encircled their prey, guns pointed, guardedly observing as Leroy Joseph Chasson drew his life's final breath.

As the gunfire concluded, a number of neighbors began to emerge from the relative safety of their apartments. Many affirmed that they had plunged headlong to the floor when the shooting commenced. Jon Genovese, who lived across the street from Chasson, said to reporters, "This is not a normal neighborhood happening on a Friday afternoon."

The Chassons' landlord, John Sternberg, described Leroy as a model tenant who always paid his rent on time. "He was a really charming guy."

According to police accounts, resident Louise Easty happened to be jogging along East Tenth Avenue, enjoying the unseasonable warm weather like many other Denver inhabitants. She was a firsthand witness to the gunfight. Taking cover flush against the side of a sun-warmed building, she tentatively peered at Chasson, who was on the sidewalk, bleeding profusely. His pallid face was frozen in a painful grimace, sweat still glistening on his forehead. "Two agents had the guy down, with guns pointed at his head," she told the Denver Police. "They looked at me and shouted for me to call an ambulance."

# THIRTY-NINE—
# KATHLEEN'S FRIEND

Leroy Chasson was already dead by the time Bob Pence reached the Capitol Hill shooting scene. The FBI Special Agent in Charge slowly approached the corpse, which was awkwardly posed in a thick pool of congealing blood.

The agents who were involved answered questions from Pence, filling him in on the details of the fatality. There was little to share, however. They approached the subject, as they explained, hoping to make an arrest, and Chasson suddenly began firing at them. Lethal force was their only option. It was clearly a justified shooting.

In 2022, amid the Covid pandemic, SAC Pence wrote and published a biography entitled, *My Non-Political FBI: From Hoover to a Violent America*. In one of his chapters, Pence described the events of that day, September 29, 1989, in downtown Denver.

WE SECURED A FEDERAL FUGITIVE WARRANT AND BEGAN TO CHECK OUT LEADS PROVIDED BY DENVER CALLERS. AN SA (SPECIAL AGENT) DRESSED AS A CASUAL JOGGER MOVED THROUGH THE SUSPECTED NEIGHBORHOOD AND ENCOUNTERED THE FUGITIVE IN A BRIEF CONVERSATION, MAKING A POSITIVE IDENTIFICATION. CHASSON THEN RETURNED TO HIS APARTMENT AND CAME BACK OUTSIDE SHORTLY THEREAFTER, WEARING A CHANGED LONG SLEEVE shirt. As the arrest team of SAs closed in, he pulled a handgun from under his shirt and began firing, forcing the SAs to return fire. It goes without saying that, in my experience, SAs always planned and spared no efforts to affect arrests without resorting to firearms. Regrettably, in this case they had no alternative.

When the gunfire ceased, a nearby homeowner summoned the Denver Police. A small army of officers soon arrived and sealed off the scene. The coroner appeared and after photographs were taken, the body was unceremoniously zipped into a black vinyl body bag. Hastily moved to the rear compartment of the coroner's van, the corpse was carted off to the Denver General Hospital, where Chasson was officially pronounced dead.

Under the direction of the FBI, the police began scurrying about, collecting evidence. They conducted a thorough search of Chasson's apartment and his belongings, rifling through bureau drawers, closets, and storage bins. In the postscript of the escape and the Chasson couple's seven-year cross-country run, the FBI agents believed they might recover items that could establish improved methods in tracking escaped prisoners.

In the meantime, word of Chasson's demise began to trickle back to the Bay State. Leroy's former girlfriend, Linell Travers, learned of his death while watching a television news broadcast. After getting over the initial shock, she realized it was time to come clean with her son Derek, now a teenager.

"Derek, he was not your dad," she divulged abruptly to the fourteen-year-old, who was dealing with a range of emotions upon hearing that Leroy Chasson, the man he believed was his father, had been gunned down on the streets of Denver.

"Why are you telling me this now?" Derek asked. "The man is gone."

Linell, who in her youth was a slender, attractive brunette, enlisted the boy's godmother Patricia Santos to help convince him. He did not believe what he was being told.

"Your mother is not wrong," Santos stressed. "She was lying to you all those years to protect you. And to protect herself."

Later, as an adult, Derek Travers was better equipped to grasp the reasoning behind his mother's actions. "She always feared that he would just show up one day, grab me from school, and take off," he said.

There was a time, Derek learned, when Leroy questioned his mother about whether the little boy was his child. Linell fearfully explained that Derek had far more of her traits than his. Leroy seemed content with that explanation, she said.

"I've seen photos of me and him together, when I was a toddler," Derek shared, who is today a Plaistow, New Hampshire, firefighter and married with a grown son of his own. "If I'm not mistaken, Leroy was incarcerated when I was born. My mother took me to visit him, and in the pictures of us, he was wearing prison blues."

While some of her friends from the seventies managed to lead productive lives, Linell was unable to break free from the grip of addictive drugs and a two-pack-per-day cigarette habit. She contracted throat cancer while suffering from uncontrolled diabetes. Confined to a nursing home in her early fifties, Linell soon passed away at the Newton-Wellesley Hospital.

"When you do drugs for forty years, it catches up with you," said Derek. Later in life, he was able to determine the identity of his biological father via the DNA subscription service, 23andMe. While he discovered the man was deceased, Derek did have the opportunity to meet blood relatives at their homes in New York City and kindle relationships.

As for law enforcement notifications, Curtis Wood, the former captain of the Massachusetts Department of Correction Fugitive Squad, was alerted almost immediately of Chasson's demise by the FBI. "Our agency had been on his trail since the very beginning," recalled Wood, who also served as security cabinet secretary and chief information officer for former Massachusetts Governor Charlie Baker. "We never let up in our search for him," the longtime lawman told *Boston Globe* Staff Reporter Peter Canellos.

Wood and his fugitive squad, which was launched as a result of the Chasson escape, investigated more than three thousand leads. At times, Wood assigned two full-time men to the case. When word of Leroy Chasson's death reached Wood, there was a sense of relief.

"When they called me, it was a feeling of elation—that the case was over," Wood told Canellos. "We don't like to see anyone killed, but we figured that he'd shoot it out. We were always prepared for that."

Over a recent lunch, the retired Wood explained what became of Leroy's widow, Kathleen. She had been at work with an elderly patient as the FBI closed in on her husband. Learning of Leroy's death from a television broadcast, she made her way to Denver Police headquarters and surrendered. Kathleen was jailed in Denver awaiting extradition to Massachusetts.

According to Wood, Bob McGuinness, a representative of the Massachusetts Department of Correction, was dispatched to Colorado to retrieve Kathleen. She was released into his custody. The Denver Police gave the pair a lift to the Stapleton International Airport, where they caught a flight to Boston. Kathleen's trial was brief. She was found guilty of aiding an escape, as well as being charged with the Bartley-Fox Gun Law, which was a Massachusetts amendment passed in 1974 calling for a mandatory one-year sentence for an individual illegally carrying a gun—wielding the .45-caliber handgun in the Norwood Hospital ER automatically added a year to Kathleen Chasson's time behind bars.

Two weeks before her forty-seventh birthday, Kathleen Chasson was incarcerated at MCI-Framingham, an all-women's prison in a medium-sized community midway between the cities of Boston and Worcester.

Opened in 1877, Framingham State Prison was the site of a misguided experiment conducted by Massachusetts correction officials. To reduce same-sex relationships, common in a prison environment, administrators launched a pilot program in 1973, jailing men and women together at Framingham so that their environment and lifestyle were more in line with that outside of prison walls. The pilot program was a resounding failure for obvious reasons, and by 1980, Framingham had resumed its women-only platform.

Kathleen Chasson, her sentence shortened by good behavior coupled with chronic prison overcrowding in Massachusetts penitentiaries, was paroled in 1992 after serving three years. She soon made her way to California and briefly settled in Fort Ord, which was a former military base on the Pacific Coast near Monterey. While there, Kathleen struck up a correspondence with Patrick O'Shea, a cop killer serving life at MCI-Norfolk. Coincidence, perhaps, but Kathleen had a penchant for murderers possessing a knack for prison escape.

By most accounts, Patrick John O'Shea was a dangerous man. As a convicted cop killer, the portrayal is well-deserved. But the unscrupulous O'Shea, in his day, was also a prominent bank robber and escape artist; two labels that adequately described the long-time criminal then, today an eighty-four-year-old who remains behind bars.

It was a crisp Wednesday morning, December 10, 1980, when Milford, Massachusetts Police Sergeant Walter F.

Conley pinned on his badge and strapped on his gun belt for the last time. Conley, sixty-one and nearing retirement, reported to the Old Colony Bank on Route 140 in downtown Milford to escort an employee. In a tragic twist of fate, the detail had not originally been assigned to Conley but rather a colleague who was detained and unable to report. At the last minute, Conley agreed to fill in. He was a generous, helpful man, loyal to his family and coworkers alike.

"Watch your back, be careful, and be safe, and make sure you get home at night to be with your family" was something Sergeant Conley would fervently advise, wrote *Milford Daily News* reporter Danielle Ameden, who spoke with Milford Officer Frank Minichiello during a 2007 memorial. "He was very fair, very honorable. He was by the book."

On the fateful December day, the Milford Old Colony Bank had requested an officer to accompany an employee from their branch to the Milford Savings Bank, which was across the street. The bank teller, Michael Hogarth, was entrusted with a branch-to-branch money transfer. Hogarth carried a small canvas pouch which, according to reports in the aftermath, contained little more than a small amount of rolled coin. What should have been a simple task soon became a living nightmare for Sergeant Conley.

Suddenly, a blue Chevrolet station wagon with two male occupants sped into the Milford Savings Bank parking lot, blocking the path of a startled Conley and Hogarth. Their forward progress interrupted, the police officer and the bank employee came to a stop.

Driving the vehicle was twenty-seven-year-old John Currie. Patrick O'Shea, thirty-nine at the time, rode in the passenger seat. Currie rolled down the window and O'Shea leaned across. He began shouting at Conley, demanding the money-filled satchel. He had previously cased the two banks and found the cross-street transfers to be commonplace.

O'Shea believed—mistakenly, in this instance—that the bank teller was ferrying a substantial sum of money.

"Hand over the bag!" the menacing thief demanded.

Conley said nothing in response but instinctively reached for his holstered firearm, a .38-caliber revolver. Currie extended his arm from the car, pointing a 9mm handgun at the officer. O'Shea followed suit, shoving the barrel of a long gun through the opening of the same driver's side window. Both men began firing. Conley never had a chance. Shot in the abdomen, he stumbled and fell to the asphalt, bleeding from a wound that would prove fatal. In a final heroic act, Sergeant Conley was able to shove Hogarth out of harm's way as searing lead whizzed by.

Ballistics later revealed that Moose, as he was affectionately known to police colleagues, was killed by bullets fired from O'Shea's M14 rifle.

Forty years later, when asked to describe what took place, Patrick O'Shea insisted that he and Currie did not start shooting without hesitation, as officials claimed.

"I spoke to the police officer," he wrote in a letter describing the incident. "I told him that nobody needed to get hurt. All he had to do was hand over the bag of money and he could walk away, unharmed."

There was a brief pause, according to the bank robber, but then Conley slowly shook his head and reached for his service weapon.

O'Shea and Currie fled the scene, driving thirty minutes to a Framingham, Massachusetts, motel where they had been staying prior to the Milford hold-up. That evening, the wanted men left the motel and made their way westbound on the Massachusetts Turnpike. They had a brief discussion and agreed that it would be best to flee to California, several days' drive. It was merely several hours, however, when they were apprehended by troopers on the New York State Thruway, armed with an APB distributed by Massachusetts authorities describing their vehicle. The two men were arrested without incident and later indicted in the college town of Utica, New York.

Both Patrick O'Shea, originally from Waltham, Massachusetts, and John Currie, from Middleboro, Massachusetts, were charged with and convicted of Sergeant Conley's murder. The killer and accomplice were soon incarcerated, facing life sentences. But O'Shea, true to his reputation, did not remain behind bars for long and absconded from several jails only to be captured and returned each time.

***

Despite presumptions on the part of several well-informed MCI-Walpole correction officers and others with knowledge of the case who felt the lifer might have played a significant role in Leroy Chasson's escape, Patrick J. O'Shea denied involvement in the plot.

Oddly enough, the lifelong criminal wasn't directly asked the question but nonetheless, provided an answer. "I never knew Leroy but Kathleen did tell me that he was aware of my escapes," O'Shea claimed in a 2021 letter. "Leroy was quite a person. They don't make them like him anymore."

O'Shea went on to question the methods of the FBI agents in downtown Denver. "The FBI did not have to end it as they did in Colorado," he insisted. "But then, that's what they do when they are scared of someone. I know that to be true from personal experience."

He also seemed very fond of Leroy's wife, Kathleen. "In letters we shared, Kathleen opened up and we became friends," O'Shea said. "Her unconditional love for Leroy was a testimony of her very being. She often told me that she had, at first, suffered great difficulty after Leroy was shot and killed by the FBI. But when she said, 'til death do us part,' she meant it one hundred percent. She was a remarkable woman of great personal strength."

# EPILOGUE

Hours after the fatal ambush of wanted fugitive Leroy Chasson, which took place in the late afternoon, a small army of reporters descended on the quiet residential neighborhood just blocks from the Denver State Capitol. There was no lack of East Tenth Avenue residents willing to share their opinions. Neighbors told the FBI and reporters that "there was no reason to suspect the two were fugitives from Massachusetts."

"Chasson's neighbors all said he was very charming," recalled SAC Robert Pence, who today travels a professional lecturer's circuit, speaking to law enforcement agencies across the country. "They agreed that he seemed to have a good relationship with his wife Kathleen."

The couple would regularly hike on nearby Rocky Mountains trails and enjoy picnic lunches in several Denver parks, most within walking distance of their home. An *Associated Press* account quoted one neighbor as saying, "They made painful decisions about whether to root for their hometown New England Patriots or the Denver Broncos of their adopted home of seven years."

"He seemed to be somebody you could trust," said neighbor Doug Honnold when interviewed by reporters from the *Denver Gazette Telegraph*. He said of Leroy: "He liked to talk about the weather and his garden."

Others spoke highly of the Chassons as grandparents. "Two small grandchildren often visited and stayed for a week or two at a time," recalled observant neighbors.

Jailhouse officials granted permission to reporters seeking comments from Kathleen, who sat behind bars in the city jail restlessly awaiting extradition back to Massachusetts. "It wasn't going to last," she told reporters several days after the death of her husband. According to the widow, Leroy would repeatedly make statements to that effect.

Kathleen Chasson passed away on September 1, 2017, at the age of seventy-five in her Maine home. Over the years following her release from MCI-Framingham, a number of her children moved East, settling in Maine and New Hampshire. She lived out her final years in peace, surrounded by family.

One of the more memorable comments she shared with Denver Police and reporters after the fatal shooting of her husband, Leroy, was something she claimed he would frequently repeat over their years together on the run. "I'll never go back to jail," he would say. "They'll never take me alive."

If nothing else, Leroy Chasson was true to his word.

*For More News About Daniel Zimmerman, Signup For Our Newsletter:*

**http://wbp.bz/newsletter**

*Word-of-mouth is critical to an author's long-term success. If you appreciated this book please leave a review on the Amazon sales page:*

**http://wbp.bz/chassonsrunreviews**

## ALSO AVAILABLE FROM WILDBLUE PRESS AND DANIEL ZIMMERMAN

http://wbp.bz/sitda

*"The fascinating story of the 1963 deaths of Boston mobster Rocco Balliro's girlfriend and her son in a police shootout . . . a real page-turner."*—**Dennis N. Griffin, bestselling author of** *The Rise and Fall of a "Casino" Mobster*

www.ingramcontent.com/pod-product-compliance
Lightning Source LLC
Chambersburg PA
CBHW070320010526
44107CB00004B/370